Here's Ireland

overleaf: Near Gortahork, Co. Donegal

BRYAN MACMAHON

Here's Ireland

E. P. DUTTON & CO., INC.
New York   1971

6/1972
C. R. Allen

To
Maurice Hayes of Downpatrick
and
Richard E. Dodd of Georgia

good friends who went with me on this journey

First published in the U.S.A. 1971 by E. P. Dutton & Co., Inc.
Copyright © 1971 by Bryan MacMahon
All rights reserved
First Edition
Printed in Great Britain

Library of Congress Catalog Card Number: 72-156264

SBN 0-525-124004

Contents

List of Illustrations

Acknowledgments

The Author and Publishers would like to thank the following for permission to reproduce the illustrations appearing in this book.

Bord Fáilte Éireann 3, 5; Jim Bennett 2, 4, 12, 14–16, 18, 19, 21, 22; Noel Habgood FRPS *frontispiece*, 6, 17, 23; A. F. Kersting 20; W. Suschitzky 7–11, 13.

Introduction

I saw the man come up the companionway of the ocean liner at Cobh. He was dressed in a vivid red dressing-gown.

His eyes were bleary.

'Wha' country is this?' someone asked him.

'Ireland—a stagnant country.' The speaker's lips writhed about the words.

The comment made me thoughtful.

Stagnant? Retrograde? What then is the norm by which one judges? Individual happiness? Prosperity? Mental enlightenment? Permissiveness? Educational fulfilment? Economic sufficiency? A sense of congruency with one's surroundings, with one's neighbours, with the story of one's country? A sense of satisfaction with one's work? A goal achieved?

The comment forced me to attempt to assess my country in a new light.

I know Ireland too well, perhaps, for one who hopes to write about it objectively. The Irish invariably suffer from nostalgic asphyxiation. I am no exception. The small island pulls.

Sometimes it even pulls the stranger. I met an American on the Irish roads. He was a wealthy man who liked to put his hands in his pockets and loiter through the land.

'Where do you go?' I asked him. 'Killarney? Tramore? Bundoran?'

'Nadd in County Cork, Rosegreen in County Tipperary, Modeligo in County Waterford and Gweedore in County Donegal.'

'What do you find in these places?'

'Human beings!' he said and went his way whistling.

The Ireland I offer is bound to be subjective. I'm not quite sure whether you will see Ireland through the eyes of MacMahon or MacMahon through the eyes of Ireland. In turn I may be prejudiced, wilful, discursive, amiable and cantankerous. I may even tell stories as I go.

But by and large, I'm an optimist. I see only sunshine and forget the rain. *After reading MacMahon's stories,* Frank O'Connor once wrote in an anthology foreword, *I was left with the delighted impression of sunshine in a land where it is always raining.*

Julius Caesar encountered the Celtic Gauls in Middle Europe. He wrote two remarkable comments on them: *The Celts,* he said in effect, *are forever running around the country looking for news. And they are mortally afraid of their druids.*

These comments seem incongruously true even to the present day.

The Celts possibly came originally out of the territory that lies between the Caspian and Black Seas. History records them as being settled at the source of the Danube: they sacked both Delphi and Rome—the aborigine in me likes to recall their tugging the beards of Roman Senators.

The substratum of Lower Middle Europe is basically Celtic: overthrown by the Romans, the memory of this Celtic empire now survives only in the minor epiphany of an archaeologist's find. The Celts had druids who sacrificed in oak groves and bards who made poetry. They also possessed a knowledge of iron and enamelling.

Their instinctive cry was: 'Westward to a land that is destined to be our home.'

From Spain, perhaps, they leapfrogged into Ireland, where, chiefly because of their knowledge of iron, they overcame the original inhabitants; thereafter their language prevailed, as also did their wondertales and their wild grace-noted music, a type of music which, like that of the Chinese, was not based on 'the tyranny of the tempered scale'.

Patrick brought them Christianity: this belief seemed accurately to fit their mood and idiom. From 500 A.D. to 800 A.D. Ireland knew a Golden Age. Wandering monks from the Island of Saints and

Scholars relighted the quenched lamps of Europe: at home they established 'universities' such as those of Clonmacnoise and Lismore —institutions numbering their undergraduates by the thousand.

From the year 800 A.D., when they sacked the monastery on Skelligs Rock off the Kerry coast, the Danes harried the island. Growing still bolder, they later settled in Ireland. In 1014, BrianBorú of Clare, then High King of Ireland, defeated the Danes at Clontarf— the area is now a Dublin suburb. Thereafter the Danes mated with the Irish, so that the Black Foreigners and the Fair Foreigners were deliciously lost in the arms of Irishwomen. Irish names like Setright (Sitric) and McAuliffe (MacOlaf) still proclaim an ancient mating.

Comparative peace reigned in Ireland until 1169, when a row over a goodlooking woman (this and/or a convenient Papal Bull of English Pope Adrian) brought into Ireland the Dane-descended Normans, who, in 1066, had invaded England from Normandy.

For a time the ill-equipped Irish kerne in his grey shirt and trews battled with the mailed and mounted Normans who had the option of retreating to their castles of stone. As the years passed the Normans intermarried with the Irish chieftainry and, growing more Irish than the Irish themselves, came to resent the later arrival of further English planter-adventurers.

In effect, the Famines of 1847-48 halved the Irish population of 10 millions and sent hundreds of thousands scurrying to America in coffin ships. Guerilla warfare originating in an idealistic rebellion of 1916, conceived and born almost in verse (Yeats: 'A terrible beauty is born'), culminated in 1921 in a measure of freedom being granted to 26 Irish counties, leaving six northern counties still flying the Union Jack.

A civil war followed, the issue being largely whether or not to accept this partial freedom: 50 years later the embers of this conflict are now being slowly stamped out. There still exists a strong opposition to seeing Ireland dismembered.

That's the story to date. And to be candid, a bloody litany it is. But it is also the story of the single self-governing remnant of the once-powerful Celtic Empire.

Its ancestral language is still intact. Led by the Gaelic League there has been an idealistic movement towards Revival. There's even a Book Club in Irish. Almost everyone in the country has had, at a minimum, eight or nine years instruction in the language. Through perversity some Irish adopt a patronising attitude towards 'the patois of the peasants'. 'What good is Irish?' is their cry.

The English language offers us Irish entry to the cultural resources not merely of England but, in translation, to those of very many nations with identities similar to ours.

But the Irish language enshrines the beliefs, hopes, despairs, benedictions, maledictions and valedictions of our people. The phalarope becomes extinct . . . humanity is the poorer. By the loss of one species of plant the world is diminished. By how much more would the world be poorer by the death of the indigenous Irish tongue? What I call this world aspect of the Irish language is rarely stressed.

Heigho! Nowadays the frame of reference tends to be touristic.

Even as I write, Ireland is changing character. Much as I love the rich quiet past I'd be a damn fool to try to stop the runaway horse of change.

Even the apparently monolithic Irish Catholic Church is changing the accent on certain aspects of its teaching. At the other end of the scale, the old Irish pub is evolving.

But, if we are not prudent, plastic storks, parasols in a largely mythical sunlight, mock jalousies, pseudo-carriage lamps, hotels like shoe-boxes with holes poked in their faces, bandstands, caravan parks and crazy-golf courses will take the place of God's good grass. Some evangelist should go through Ireland and preach the gospel of minimal intrusion.

On Telefís Éireann the worthwhile indigenous wars with the cheap imported. The fortunes of the beer and oil wars ebb and flow; there are mergers, and flags are moved on a map. Age-old customs become folksy and barren as mules; cement is slammed on an old stone courthouse and the country goes festival crazy.

And there still lingers the Irish reluctance to mate.

Some years ago a scholarly American priest, Father John O'Brien of Notre Dame University, said, in effect, to Ireland's writers:

2 Dublin at night. Westmoreland Street and College Green meeting at the gates of Trinity College

'What's wrong with you people anyway? Don't you want to marry and have children? Are you Irish like the lemmings who rush into the sea and drown themselves? Writers of Ireland, tell me why?'

We told the good man. With our telling began emancipation of utterance. A lot of pious people bellyached. Time passed. Now that the wheel has turned full circle we who wrote are in grave danger of being canonized.

Ireland. The Irish. Pigs, priests, potatoes, piety, porter.

A traditional image once established, tends to die hard.

One day there was a knock at my door. The representative of a North American broadcasting company entered; a normal-looking man complete with a be-jeaned wife. He told me that he had come to Ireland to record two interviews—one with a matchmaker, the other with a leprechaun.

The *ch* of leprechaun he pronounced softly as in 'chair'.

I laughed outright. The man and his wife stared at me.

'A matchmaker?' I said aloud. 'Yes, we could possibly find you something approximating to one. But the lep....'

'The lepre*ch*aun. I appreciate the difficulties. But I'm told *you* can get it for me.'

His wife charm-whinnied. I looked from one to the other. The man's eyes began to smoulder. What is one to do in a case like this except play the small town game of 'Sending the Fool Farther'?

A travelling showman kept a midget who sat on a pint glass.

Once, when the booth was empty, the little fellow told me: 'In a village in South Cork, late one night, after the show had closed, I went for a stroll in the fields. I sat on a log smoking my pipe and looking up at the moon. Then I heard a rustle behind me; I saw a country chap and his girl standing courting against a tree. I was caught by the throat by two hands like steel. "Your pot of gold, leprechaun!" the hoarse voice said.'

'I kicked, bit, shouted, swore and spat. I began to see stars. Only that the boss came up I was a goner.'

3 Decorated stone, Newgrange, Co. Meath

The Irish. Paddy and his pigs. 'The top o' the mornin' an' begorrah to you, surr. . . . *Erin go brágh.*'

I spent over 30 years collecting the speechmoulds of the Irish country people. I recorded some remarkable concatenations of words but never once did I hear anyone say: 'The top o' the mornin',' or 'Yer honour'. I add that I was 35 years of age before I saw a shillelagh.

Grotesquely simian, the faces of the Irish. And yet people like Yeats, Joyce, O'Casey, Shaw, Synge and Beckett simply do not square with the piggy-bank face and the clay pipe in the caubeen.

The real Irish way of life was almost lost in a battle at Kinsale in Cork in 1602. The Spanish under Don Juan del Aquila who had come to help the Irish—and themselves—were in the town, the English ringed it round, while the Northern Irish chieftains, O'Neill and O'Donnell, after an epic march through snow, surrounded these in turn. A Brian McMahon got drunk, was captured by the English, bragged and blabbed. The battle went against the Irish.

As a result of this defeat the traditional chiefs of Ireland assembled at Rathmullen in Donegal in 1608 and set sail for the Continent. There, they were received as princes but the dolorous Irish love of home proved a cancer in their breasts. 'Some day we'll see a bright day in Ireland', they shouted in their cups.

And yet, when a schoolmaster angrily cleans a blackboard, words or phrases are sometimes left behind. So it was with the Irish language: it lived on in Kerry, Cork, Clare, Galway, Mayo, Donegal and Waterford—*Gaeltachta* (Irish-speaking areas) lying largely on the western seaboard.

With the consent of all political parties, the independent Irish State decided to restore this language.

Previous to this, men like Douglas Hyde of the Gaelic League had traipsed the Irish roads gathering the fragments that remained. 'Bicycle men', or itinerant teachers, like Fionán McColum and Tomas Ó Donnchú of Kerry or Tomás Conbá of Limerick carried the message of revival to the towns and villages. On a parallel course the Gaelic Athletic Association revived national pride in the old games.

Out of this flux was born the pride that led to the 1916 Insurrection and the growth of the Abbey Theatre. Irish is now taught in all Irish schools: every person under 50 understands it. Do they speak it? The heart says: This is the ancestral language: do not dare to let it die. The head says: What use is it?

Is Ireland, 'the Pope's Green Isle' as the Americans call it, a priest-ridden island?

Through the period of the Penal Laws the faith of the proscribed priest—the price on his head was the same as that of a wolf—and the sometimes inchoate nationalistic fervour of the patriot were complementary: the common enemy was Protestant England.

With Catholic Emancipation in 1829 the official outlook of the Catholic hierarchy shied away from the patriotic, which at times appeared tinged with the egalitarian doctrines of the French Revolution. This despite the fact that priests had, in Wexford, led the rising in 1798.

A notable dichotomy between priest and patriot occurred in the 1860s when the Fenians were church-condemned. One bishop declared: 'Hell is not hot enough nor eternity long enough to hold the Fenians.'

With the signing of the Treaty with Britain in 1921 something noteworthy occurred: it was as if someone—or everyone—decided that the vacuum left by the uprooting of gigmanity should be filled by the Catholic clergy. Subsequently, the moral line which, possibly, had its origin in the teaching of Jansenistic priests from France appointed to the faculty of Ireland's National Seminary at Maynooth, was drawn inhumanly tight.

This is a time in the life of the Catholic Church in Ireland on which I do not like to dwell. What should have been an hour of glorious Christian experiment was a time of mediocrity. It has passed. Relations between priest and people have never been better. The current danger is that neo-humanists will reduce, largely by sly ridicule, the role of the Irish priest to that occupied by the ineffective English clergyman of the picture postcard.

A few points of possible friction remain. For example, the

machinations of such semi-secret you-scratch-me-I'll-scratch-you Catholic organizations as The Knights of St Columbanus have engendered mistrust among thoughtful Catholics.

But above all the Irish priest has now to work his passage; no longer can he depend upon facile condemnation. The priest participates in the drama movement: he is in charge of the dance halls his predecessor condemned. As a result his prestige stands high, fair and free. But is he the less a priest for all this?

And what of your writers? Your Censorship Board? What of the men of genius—those whose weapons were 'exile, silence and cunning'?

Some of the decisions of the Censorship Board have been ludicrous. On a local level I have seen a small town censor remove a novel from the library shelves because of the occurrence of the word *demi-monde*. On their part the priests have maintained that they were laity-ridden: a play called *Is the Priest at Home?* has been written on this theme.

Yet it is true that some of our finest writers have been reduced to acid as a result of their work being branded as 'in its general tendency indecent'.

Again a great measure of commonsense now prevails.

If balance is to be preserved other comments need to be made: some of our writers are addicted to self-flagellation as a motive power for writing. And again, no one is naïve enough to believe that publishers of pornography do not exist.

What else is there to talk about in Ireland?

The Book of Kells, sunsets, evening in the grounds of Blarney Castle, Willie Yeats, Grafton Street, Dublin on a Saturday morning, the Cross of Cong, a hurling final in Thurles down in Tipperary, the little Kerry cow and the new industrial estate at Shannon Airport, sea trout, hydro-electric development, a ballad called 'The Rocks of Bawn', the black wine of the country which is known as Guinness (Beamish and Murphy also deserve mention!), the stone rooms of Aran, the Host in the monstrance raised over worshippers, tweed,

tweed and more tweed, an old parish priest beloved for his eccentric wisdom, the ubiquitous Aran gansey worn by the amateur ballad-singers, beaches frontiered by clamorous breakers, the thock of a golf ball, the thrust and parry of words, the smell of peat smoke, heel ball, and burning horse hooves in the little towns, the engine-throb of Irish-owned jets, the medieval banquets at Bunratty Castle, old-as-time Gallarus Oratory in Kerry and the loyal walls of Derry-O, the torques in the National Museum vouching for an ancient sense of craftsmanship, the stories of Frank O'Connor, an old woman seated under a hedgerow telling her rosary, King Salmon and the mad bounce of the individual people one meets.

And there is always the sense of the other world which is just around the metaphysical corner.

Depending on what you wish to see, Ireland has many faces.

Historical Ireland, geographical Ireland, teenage Ireland, Ireland-in exile, Irish-Ireland, vanished Ireland, religious Ireland, literary Ireland, sporting and athletic Ireland, urban (or industrial) Ireland, rural (or agricultural) Ireland, divided Ireland, festival Ireland, sober Ireland, tipsy Ireland, television Ireland . . . they're all there. We shall see their faces as we go round the land.

CHAPTER ONE

Dublin

As I went round Old Dublin City

From artifacts found in the Dublin area it has been established that in the age of prehistory a huddle of people lived at the mouth of the Liffey.

The Greek geographer, Ptolemy, in 140 A.D., marks the place, calling it Eblana. The Danes were there in the 9th century, brazenly setting up a primitive ship-fort, to be followed by the Anglo-Normans. For the English the city was, for centuries, the capital of an enclave or Pale; later Dublin knew a soupçon of Jews, a dash of Huguenots, and finally the Irish tribesmen who exultantly poured down from the Wicklow hills to recover what they had always claimed as their own.

The city should properly be called *Dubh-linn*, or, as the Norse had it, *Dyflin*, which literally means Blackpool: cumbersomely enough, in modern Irish it is called *Baile Átha Cliath* which means The Town of the Ford of the Hurdles, a name derived from the feat of Conor MacNessa, an Ulster king, who, finding the river swollen as he returned from a foray into the South, had a crude bridge of hurdles made so as to cross the flood.

What is now tranquil Mount Street has probably seen human sacrifice offered to the Danish god, Thor (of Thursday fame); Leixlip (Salmon's Leap), Howth (Head) and Skerries are pure Norse names, as indeed are Wicklow and Waterford.

It is a cliché but nonetheless true, to say that Dublin is a city of ghosts: the ghost of the poet, James Clarence Mangan, dying in degradation in Cuffe Street, the ghost of Buck Whaley betting his fellow bucks—you can see the gaunt ruins of their Hellfire Club on the slope of a mountain south of the city—that he would travel to

Jerusalem and play handball against the walls of the Temple, the ghost of Lord Edward Fitzgerald wrestling for his life with Major Sirr in Thomas Street, the ghost of Dean Swift balanced between genius and insanity and the ghost of Zozimus, a Dublin balladsinger addicted to grandiosities in verse.

There is also the modern ghost of William B. Yeats whose footsteps I, as a young man, shadowed in Dublin of the late 1920's, and the spirit of Maud Gonne MacBride, the beautiful woman beloved of the same poet, to whom I listened each Sunday speaking at street-corner meetings where she preached uncompromising republicanism. On all sides in Dublin are Georgian streets and squares that seem more suited to blue darkness, sedan chairs and the torches of link-boys than to the open sunlight.

Grafton Street on Saturday morning is a pleasant place of perambulation. Fully at ease with the world, I strolled down it, humming to myself:

> *As I went round old Dublin City*
> *As the sun began to set*
> *Who should I spy but the Spanish Lady*
> *Catching a moth in a golden net?*

Still humming I turned into Duke Street, where begins the area in which one hunts for souvenirs—tweed ties, Aran ganseys and crioses or woven belts, whimsical wooden statues of the saints according to Fergus O'Farrell and pottery of various designs.

Hanging from the front of Davy Byrne's pub in 21 Duke Street,— the place is mentioned in James Joyce's masterpiece—were baskets with trailing geraniums; on the side door entrance was written the word 'Ulysses'. American tourists took turns to stand beside the doorway to take one another's pictures.

On an impulse I decided to become a tourist for the nonce.

So I hurried down the Quays to *An Busárus*, headquarters of Irish bus-dom, a building in modern design, and there queued up in odd anticipation.

As the bus moved off, the guide-conductor told of the burning of the Custom House in 1921, of nearby Liberty Hall and of James Connolly the Labour Leader ('We serve neither King nor Kaiser but Ireland.'), who, as a result of the courts-martial following the Rising of 1916, was shot dead seated in a chair because his gangrened legs could not bear him up.

We passed close to the spacious New Abbey Theatre—opened in 1966. Founded in 1904 in what had once been a morgue, the original Abbey building saw a great flowering of genius as exemplified by such names as Yeats, O'Casey, Synge and Lady Gregory. The old Abbey building was destroyed by fire in 1951.

Turning into O'Connell Street the guide prattled of Daniel O'Connell, the uncrowned 'King of the Beggars' who, in 1829 had won Catholic Emancipation for the Catholic Irish.

Daniel O'Connell of Derrynane in Kerry, for whom Dublin's principal street is named, is one of Ireland's great folk heroes. Popular legend has endowed him with the potency of a stallion, the mind of Machiavelli, and the soul of a saint. Were it not for the first and second attributes he would long since have been called Blessed. A whimsical ballad I once ran to earth was entitled: *Daniel O'Connell Makes Children by Steam!* To my mild surprise this ballad bore no reference to Dan's virility.

It opens with an old countrywoman milking her cow by the roadside. A jolly tinker comes along.

'Have you heard what Daniel O'Connell is up to now?' he asks the old woman. 'No!', says the old lady, ceasing her milking. 'It's the talk of Ireland,' said the tinker. 'Dan has invented a machine that can make children by steam! Woman's reign is over!'

The old woman grows vituperative. 'I'm an old woman,' she says, 'but if I was put to it, even now, I'd make better children than Dan with his infernal machine.'

While I had been recalling King Dan the guide told of Thomas

Moore, born in Aungier Street and son of Kerryman John Moore, the parlour-poet par excellence, who with Robert Emmet was drummed out of Trinity College at the behest of Black Jack Fitzgibbon, the provost, for suspected sedition. In College Green we halted ('Half a bowshot from the College, half the world from sense and knowledge') and entered Trinity College. Dutifully climbing the stairs we entered the great library to view the Book of Kells, the work of ancient Irish scribes and reckoned the most beautiful book in the world.

Cut in stone outside the Kildare Street Club in Dawson Street were monkeys playing billiards; salvias blazed in front of the Mansion House, the residence of the Lord Mayor. In the Round Room beside it an International Folk Festival was in full swing: outside the human pack was being shuffled—an Irish dancer was in conversation with what appeared to be a Basque.

At the north east corner of St Stephen's Green— an oasis of flowers in the city centre—stands a gateway embodying modern Delaney statuary that indicates its vitality by the discussion that ebbs and flows on its merits or demerits. There flashed past the little Huguenot Cemetery close to the Shelbourne Hotel, many churches – one of Perpetual Adoration—and later we swung, first south, then west past Wesley College where George Bernard Shaw went to school, and University Church where fashionable weddings still take place. Circling again towards the east we came presently to the centre of residential Georgian Dublin. Here the passengers gave a united 'Oh!' of astonishment.

This was occasioned by what at first sight appeared to be the intrusion of the American embassy building into an area of Georgian quietude. The building, functionally aesthetic, is bewildering at first: yet I am convinced that it is aesthetically of a piece with its surroundings.

'Ladies and Gentlemen! This is a picture of the great stallion, Arctic Prince, standing at Brownstown Stud.' (That word 'standing' never fails to intrigue me by its rural delicacy.)

'And this, my friends, is the huge drum from which the lucky tickets are drawn. The draw takes place under the supervision of the police! And the entire profits go to the erection and maintenance of Irish hospitals.'

We were at the headquarters of the Irish Hospitals' Sweepstakes at Ballsbridge.

The attendants gave each one of us a drinking glass with the lucky sign of the Zodiac on it—this presumably to toast one's luck if one's ticket drew a winner and one of the £50,000 units this connoted.

The ladyguide laughed; a visitor, thinking she was actually in an hospital, had asked where the patients were. The guide had difficulty explaining that this was the site of a national raffle. History, dealing as it does with the past tense, lends itself much better to exactitudes.

The Normans came to Ireland in 1169. They made Dublin their chief city. Henry II presented himself there in 1172 to ensure that his lords did not become unduly unmindful of their sovereign master and formally placed the city under the protection of the people of Bristol. For centuries Irish clans such as the O'Tooles and O'Byrnes glared down out of the Wicklow hills and watched the walled city take shape.

Now and again the raiding Irish slaughtered the citizens disporting themselves on the meads without the walls. As a result of this the citizens paid 'protection money' to the Irish chieftains.

Meanwhile the Normans had fanned out through the island. Once entrenched, the great Anglo-Norman families struggled among themselves for supremacy. For many centuries the fortunes of Ireland were conditioned by the struggle for power between the Geraldines (Fitzgeralds) of Kildare and the Butlers of Kilkenny.

In the south transept of St Patrick's Cathedral may be seen a door with a hole in it: through this opening, representatives of these families once shook hands in fleeting reconciliation. A short time before, they went within an ace of butchering each other in

the Cathedral proper, when, during a meeting of the rivals, some
bored archers began to take potshots at a mock target in the ceiling:
the thud of the arrows striking home into the timber had caused
the cry of treachery to be raised.

Presently the old rivals were again at each other's throats. The
Geraldines were impetuous, the Butlers cautious and canny. The
Geraldines were beloved of the mere Irish with whose leading families
they had intermarried. But the rashness of the Fitzgeralds proved
their downfall.

They almost fell when they threw in their lot with a charlatan
called Lambert Simnel whom they had crowned King of England in
Christ Church in 1487 but they came a complete cropper when
their dandy, the beloved Silken Thomas, believing the false rumour,
spread possibly by the Butlers, that his father had been hanged in
London, rode at the head of a host of horsemen into Dublin and
flung his father's Sword of State on the great table of St Mary's
Abbey (off the present Capel Street) and declared himself a foe of
the English Crown. All this to the crazy accompaniment of the
Geraldine bard playing on the harp.

For this the Fitzgeralds paid dearly: gunpowder was first used in
Ireland on the Geraldine Castle at Maynooth, the Kildare town which
is now the seat of the National Seminary, and Tom of the Silken
Clothes and his five uncles were hanged as a warning to all such
rebels.

In the crypt, the oldest part of Christ Church, we gazed on a
strange sight: a mummified cat and rat who in their age-old chase
had scampered into the organ pipes and were there imprisoned.
Their bodies were found after a considerable number of years.

Crudely constructed, the crypt ran under the whole cathedral and
gave weird perspectives evocative of old Dublin. The Cathedral had as
its first founder King Sitric, the Danish King of Dublin who became
a Christian; it was later rebuilt by Strongbow, Earl of Pembroke,
spearhead of the Norman invasion of Ireland, whose age-polished
sarcophagus is in the aisle above. Beside the tomb lies the fore-
shortened statue of his wife Aoife.

Passing Dublin Castle, once the seat of English power in Ireland,

and as such, a name calculated to strike terror into Irish hearts, I was reminded that Dublin City saw James II of England, the sham hope of the Irish Catholic cause, arrive within its gates after his disastrous defeat at the Battle of the Boyne, approximately 30 miles away. This was July, 1690.

William of Orange, aided by the Blue Dutch Guards, French Huguenots and various German and Danish regiments, had triumphed; thus the Battle of the Boyne, ostensibly a struggle between Catholics and Protestants, although the Pope is alleged to have sent congratulations to the Williamite victor, is still celebrated in Northern Ireland on the 'Twalth o' July' by the beating of Lambeg drums, the carrying of pictorial banners, and the daubing of 'No Pope' on cowhouses.

James the Worthless had an earthen nickname among the Irish which most derogatorily follows all Irish Jameses to this day: *Séamus a' Chaca* he was called: the Latin word *caecus* offers the clue to its faecal connotation. 'The Irish ran away!' he whined to a lady he met at the gates of Dublin Castle. The lady bowed low. 'Your Majesty won the race', she said.

But if the memory of James was execrated, highly revered in Ireland was that of his son Charles, later carried into Scotland from France in the slave brig of Irishman Antoine Walsh. Charles Stuart was sung of secretly and sweetly by Gaelic poets who knew him as 'The Merchant's Son' and 'The Blackbird'. Most romantic indeed, but for the Irish it was wasted effort.

The next century saw the Protestant Ascendancy secure a measure of independence and Dublin's development as a city of architectural beauty. This was the time when Dean Swift—he had two brilliant women on his hands, Vanessa and Stella, in one of the most perplexing and delighting love-intrigues ever—reigned in St Patrick's Cathedral where he was idolized even by the poor of Dublin. The atmosphere of Marsh's Library off Kevin Street with its wall-chained books is still redolent of this age when social elegances were the norm. Then came the rising of 1798 with its brilliant but impractical leaders.

Two years later, William Pitt intimidated the local parliament into voting itself into full union with England. The year 1800 marks a turning point in Irish history.

But by an odd turn of fortune, Dublin, subsequent to the Act of Union, from being the capital of an English enclosure became for the first time in its history an Irish city.

The Famine did not carry disastrous implications for an urban community; nevertheless Dublin was thronged with the destitute on their way to England.

Towards the end of the nineteenth century, the patriotic meteor was Charles Stewart Parnell, a Protestant of the landlord class who all but won Home Rule for Ireland, but whose brilliance, consequent on his liaison with Mrs Kitty O'Shea, dimmed in bitterness.

Dying at Bournemouth of, it could almost be said, a broken heart, he left behind him an acutely divided land. Some of his followers remained loyal to the ivy leaf of the Chief known to the ballad-singers as 'The Blackbird of Avondale'. This sense of bitter loyalty is powerfully conveyed in James Joyce's story *Ivy Day in the Committee Room*.

The beginning of the present century saw the rise of the Separatist Party, *Sinn Féin* (pronounced Shin Fayne which means 'Ourselves Alone'). The severity of the quelling of the poetically-conceived Easter Rising of 1916 swung an apathetic Ireland into the *Sinn Féin* camp with the result that the party won an unqualified victory in the 1918 General Election.

There followed in the first and second years of the 20s what are euphemistically called 'the Troubles', a guerilla war between the Irish and the British, on which a considerable body of literature exists. This culminated in the Anglo-Irish Treaty of 1921 and the Civil War that followed.

Subsequent developments, one leading to the enactment of *Bunreach na hÉireann* (Constitution of Ireland) in 1937, another to the Republic of Ireland Act in 1948, are mainly constitutional.

CHAPTER TWO

Ring Around The City-O

'Sons of the Gael, men of the Pale,
The long-watched day is breaking . . .'

A semi-circle swung within a 50-mile radius of Dublin touches
Dundalk in County Louth at its most northerly point, Enniscorthy
in County Wexford at its most souterly point, and bears, on its
western periphery, the semi-midland towns of Mullingar, Tullamore
and Portlaoise.

The area thus enclosed embraces much of the old Pale together
with the counties of East Leinster.

From Dublin city the roads strike into this hinterland like spokes.
The half-moon of terrain thus enclosed is largely level and fertile:
the exception is the area immediately south of Dublin, the heather-
clad granite slopes of the Wicklow mountains, a district historically
serviceable to outlaws and intransigents.

Ever since as a kilt-clad boy of seven, my habiliments kept together with massive safety-pins and mock Tara brooches, I won as
a prize for speaking Irish at a Feis, a book called *The Humours of
Shanawalla*, a series of rollicking incidents told by one Patrick Archer
of north County Dublin, that area has exercised an unusual fascina-
tion for me.

To me, as a child, places like Malahide, Swords, Rush, Lusk,
Skerries and indeed the territory of Fingal as a whole, were quite
familiar. Until comparatively recent times, this, an essentially
garden area for Dublin City, was relatively unspoiled.

Beyond Baldoyle Racecourse (Joyce mentions 'the hippic run-
fields of breezy Baldoyle') one looks out on the comparatively tranquil

Irish Sea, with Ireland's Eye, an attractive little island, sitting staunchly on the steady waters. At golfic Portmarnock there is the usual to and fro of a minor seaside resort: the two-mile beach is close enough to the city to make its presence valuable to the citizens.

In 1949 the University of Yale acquired the Boswell Papers found in Malahide Castle (the late Lord Talbot de Malahide was a direct descendant of Boswell); the papers, now being published, shed a clear light on the life and times of Boswell—and of Johnson. Ireland's greatest landscape painter, Nathaniel Hone, is also associated with this area.

Further to the North is Swords (*Sord Cholm Chille* signifies the Well of Saint Columcille) once an important ecclesiastical and military centre. Its undoubted attraction for me was diminished by the presence of an ill-sited advertisement. Averting my eyes, I passed on to Balbriggan so well-known as a centre of the hosiery manufacture that items of men's hosiery and indeed undergarments in general, were once referred to as balbriggans—with a small b.

If Irish history may be said to have a sound, it is certainly the clack of a Franciscan sandal.

The Four Masters, those great medieval chroniclers of Irish history, were the spiritual descendants of the Poor Man of Assisi.

There is scarcely a county in Ireland that is not indebted to the men in brown who nowadays are concerned with poverty of spirit.

Walking the halls of Gormanston College, three miles northwest of Balbriggan and once the seat of the Preston family, noting the carved fireplaces, climbing the great staircases and entering the well-appointed classrooms, I rejoiced that an education foundation based squarely on the native had prospered. As it was summer the din of schoolboys was not in evidence.

I entered the Language Laboratory where Father Cormac Ó Huallacháin, o.f.m., and his fellow helpers have done a superb job in setting the teaching of the Irish language on scientific foundations.

Later, I found the door leading to the college swimming pool guarded by an old and resolute nun.

'No! No!' she said, showing her palms in horror. Baffled, I retired. With the length of a corridor between us, the holy woman and I glared at one another.

Along came a sweet young nun, her reticule bulging with towel and bathing costume. 'Ah!' she said, taking in the situation, 'We nuns travel out each day from the city to attend the Summer Course here at Gormanston. We are allowed the exclusive use of the pool for the hour. It's cordoned off!'

'And guarded!' I said.

My ears ringing with a tale of Gormanston foxes lamenting the dead, I peeped rather shudderingly into the mysterious aisle of yews in the castle grounds and then drove off.

Drogheda is a churchy, busy town rendered anthill-like by the sight of cement buckets swinging in a never-ending chain from the higher ground nearby. In 1649, Cromwell butchered many of its citizens; the descendants of the survivors are today more numerous than ever. The town has the thirteenth century barbican of St Lawrence's Gate, one of the ten original gates of the walled city. The embalmed head of Blessed Oliver Plunkett, Archbishop of Armagh, hanged, drawn and quartered at Tyburn, is here revered.

The navigable mouth of the River Boyne meets the sea five miles to the east at the salmon fishery at Mornington.

At Oldridge, four miles west of Drogheda, on July 1st 1690, a battle took place which proved fatal to the kingship of James II. Here, on opposite sides of the river, James, backed by the Irish, and King William of Orange, rival contenders for the Crown of England, drew up their battle-lines.

Previous to the fight the Irish were jubilant at their wounding of William as he rode reconnoitring, so that later King Billy went into battle with his arm in a sling.

William's General Schomberg, with a force of French Huguenots, Dutch Guards and Enniskillens led a crossing of the Boyne River at Oldbridge but was himself slain as also was Bishop Walker of

Derry. Danes and Germans forced a further passage and encamped on marshy ground on the Irish side of the river.

Harassed by an attack on the wing the Irish finally fell back on Duleek. They fought well as they retreated but eventually were roundly trounced. Thirty-six thousand on the English side overbore 25,000 on the Irish side. The memory of this battle, now firmly polarized as a Protestant victory over Catholics is still most violently alive.

Six miles west-north-west of Drogheda is Monasterboice, the site of an ancient monastic settlement: it boasts a round tower, an ancient Muireadach's Cross and interesting grave-slabs.

Five miles almost due west of Drogheda are the ruins of Mellifont Abbey, the first Cistercian House in Ireland, its first abbot having been trained at Clairvaux by the great St Bernard himself.

At Mellifont, in 1172, Henry II received the submission of O'Neill and the Northern chieftains.

In this area also, Dervorgilla, wife of O'Rourke of Brefni, the runaway wife responsible for bringing the Normans to Ireland, spent her last years in the sackcloth of penance. She was buried in the Abbey in 1193. Here also in 1592, Red Hugh O'Donnell, escapee from Dublin Castle, found sanctuary. Quite close to the original Abbey, the Cistercian monks in 1939, after a hiatus of 400 years, demonstrated once more the vitality of history by founding New Mellifont on part of the original abbey lands.

The area also has remarkable associations stretching back into the pre-Christian period.

Newgrange Tumulus, or *Brugh na Bóinne* (Boyne Palace), a burial place associated with Aongus, a pagan divinity, stands on a river strand of the Boyne five miles from Drogheda and twelve from Tara. Excavations in this area, particularly in the tumulus of Knowth, are still in progress; the fuller story of Ireland's Bronze Age (2,000 to 200 B.C.) as indicated by this burial district, gives promise of providing intense excitement even for the average observer.

I ran my fingers over the spirals and whorls on the stone at the entrance to the Newgrange mound; then with a mounting sense of atavistic terror, I moved along the narrow passage of the tumulus, touching stones incised with zigzags and spirals. At last I reached the central chamber.

There I saw the flat stone which some archaeological authorities believe was once a sacrificial altar: it took little imagination to picture a bound, naked man spreadeagled on this slab with the knife of a pagan priest uplifted above him. Ornamented stones, a broken sarcophagus and slabs with lively patterns of religious or historical significance were also to be seen.

Newgrange mound was originally 55 feet high and a little short of 300 feet in diameter. Now covered with clay, grasses and overgrowth, at one time the bare quartz stones of its exterior must have sparkled in the sunshine to evoke in the minds of our forefathers of prehistory vague thoughts of the land 'beyond beyond'.

Through the green pastures of County Meath I raced through Navan until at last I came to the ancient capital of Ireland—Tara.

My first impression of Tara proved prosaic: a boy at a hut extracted a small toll, then resumed his kicking of a red ball. Over the green pastures I strode until I came to the edge of an impressive ridge. A truly royal vista spread below me.

Tara was once the very core of Ireland. In legend, tale, poetry and song, the variegated story of the Irish people is bound up with this noble ridge where long since the halls of wood and clay have melted into the grass. The origins of Tara are lost in the arabesque of fairy lore associated with the mythical Tuatha-Dé-Danaan.

Hard on the heels of the Tuatha-Dé-Danaan came the Milesians: tales of the Milesian kings still survive. Here it was that Conall Cearnach found two men playing football with the skull of his comrade Cúchulainn. Here, too, were held the great triennial assemblies at *Samhain* or November, a custom that persisted for many centuries.

In the 3rd century A.D. we find King Cormac Mac Airt directing the chroniclers of Tara to set down the sagas and legends of the Irish people and ordering his poets to enshrine the more dramatic

4 Carlingford, Co. Louth. The town as seen through the arch of the Tholsel House

of the then current events in verse that would endure as long as man walked the earth.

Legend also tells that at Tara there once stood a huge copper cauldron in which the carcases of 12 cattle and 12 pigs could be cooked simultaneously—perhaps this was the origin of Irish stew! Conn of the Hundred Battles and Niall of the Nine Hostages are the thunderous names of two of its later kings.

Today a shoddy statue of St Patrick fails even remotely to convey the fanaticism inherent in Tara's Christian associations.

For fanatic Patrick undoubtedly was: legend tells us that it was in Tara that King Laoire grew furious at the sight of the first Christian paschal fire blazing on the Hill of Slane to the north east—how dared anyone kindle a blaze before the royal fire was lighted on this pagan sacrificial day! Here also Patricius Calpurnus is believed to have crouched to pluck the shamrock so as to illustrate the mystery of the Trinity.

Below us the silver Boyne played hide and seek in the foliage; if legend is not a fluent liar, Fionn Mac Cumhaill had caught the Salmon of Knowledge in the river and, placing his thumb on a blister on the cooking fish, had ever after only to suck his thumb to gain wisdom.

In more modern times there are rich literary memories in kingly Meath.

Slane, in its turn, recalled Ledwidge, the gentle poet of the Boyne who sang of the blackbird of the leafy river as being 'half of him passion, half conceit'. A short time before he was killed in the First World War, Ledwidge lamented the execution of Thomas MacDonagh, one of the leaders of the 1916 Rising, in lines that bear internal assonance reminiscent of traditional Gaelic poetry.

> *He shall not hear the bittern cry*
> *In the wild sky where he is lain*
> *Nor voices of the sweeter birds*
> *Above the wailing of the rain....*

Today the literary associations are still in evidence; close to Bective Bridge in her farm by a reaping-hook of the Boyne, Mary

5 The Hurling Final, Croke Park, Dublin

Lavin, one of the best short story writers of our time, continues to write so masterfully that in years to come literary pilgrims will again and again journey hither to recall her name.

Dundalk, a walled-in fortress of the Pale and originally a de Verdon stronghold, was the starting place of many an English foray into the northern territory held by the O'Neills and O'Donnells. The town is a half-way house between Dublin and Belfast; standing in what is called 'The Gap of the North', it is named for a prehistoric fort in the neighbourhood.

The city is associated with the legendary hero Cúchulainn (The Hound of Culann) who earned the nickname (his earlier name was Setanta) from a boyhood incident when he killed a fierce mastiff that guarded the stronghold of Culann the Smith; in contrition the lad agreed to take the hound's place until another watchdog had been trained to guard the fortress.

In Dundalk I recalled the quiet spirit of St Brigid who was believed to have been born in Faughart, a few miles to the north; this area was also the scene of the battle in which Edward Bruce of Scotland met his death in 1318. Here the body of Bruce lies buried.

Brigid, the nun-saint, is more readily associated with Kildare where she established a nunnery. She is often referred to as 'Mary of the Irish'. On the eve of her festival, February 1st, her cross of rushes is still made in many thatched cottages of the western seaboard. The cross reputedly had its origin when Brigid had a golden cross stolen from her: she later plaited rushes to form a cross that would be quite as devotional as that made of gold and yet would be unworthy of the attentions of a thief. Today this cross is one of the symbols of Irish television.

Carrickmacross in the County of Monaghan, famous for its lace, is almost due west of Dundalk. Innishkeen is halfway between the two places.

Paddy Kavanagh the poet hailed from Innishkeen: though his poetry is as spare as the stony fields of Monaghan, it glitters with a mica of beauty. His 'A Soul for Sale' (*My soul was an old horse,*

offered for sale in twenty fairs . . .) and 'The Great Hunger' a poetic
study of the futureless, featureless life of an introverted country
bachelor are most worthy examples of his best work.

Let me tell you where I first met Paddy.

Macmillan of London threw a party for their writers: I was there
as a young man. I spoke with Rebecca West and learned that she
was descended from the Blennerhassets of Kerry. Frank O'Connor
was there too; he made a striking figure striding down St Martin's
Street with his green tweed overcoat hanging cloak-like from his
shoulders. The learned Monk Gibbon I also spied—what a fine job of
work he did in rescuing from oblivion *Thy Tears Might Cease*, the
single novel of that sensitive soul, Michael Farrell, whose pioneer
work in reviving popular interest in amateur drama in Ireland
deserves to be well remembered.

At the party I met Paddy Kavanagh.

'Where are the Sitwells?' Paddy boomed in my direction as the
great room in St Martin's Street throbbed with the chatter of English
literary eminences. I moved in his wake as he surged through the
room. We found the Sitwells grouped in a circle. 'You're worth
meeting!' Paddy said in a resonant voice that made everyone turn.

As if by magic the circle opened and Paddy and I were admitted
into its hallowed space. Someone tugged at Paddy's jacket. He
rounded on the tugger: 'For Christ's sake,' he roared, 'Don't
introduces me to nonentities!'

Swinging south again I reached into Ceannanus Mór (Kells), once
a famous ecclesiastical centre, to which the Columban monks of
Iona repaired early in the 9th century after having been expelled
by the Vikings from their holy isle. In Ceannanus Mór in the latter
part of the 8th century, the monks indited what is indisputably
the most precious possession of the Irish people—the Book of Kells.

It is not surprising that the Kells area is replete with tangible
evidence of the early Christian story of Ireland.

St Columba's House, a stone-roofed structure offers an example
of cylindrical vaulting: it recalls another example of similar
Hiberno-Romanesque architecture—St Kevin's Kitchen in Glendalough, County Wicklow. The Round Tower also is a perfect example

of those early Norse-raid shelters. Among the embellished and sculptured crosses extant, the Market Cross standing in mid-town is outstanding.

This cross shared a grisly affinity with a certain giant called Yeoman Hepenstall, inasmuch as, in the rebellion of 1798, cross and yeoman both were used as a gallows!

Hepenstall placed a noose round the neck of his victim; with a prodigious effort he then swung the rebel over his shoulder where the unfortunate man kicked out his life. Many an Irishman in search of freedom also kicked out his life swinging by the neck from the arms of the Market Cross of Kells. But then, we are inclined to forget that a cross was originally an instrument of execution.

Still in County Meath, An Uaimh (pronounced Un Oo-ivh) or Navan, famous for its carpets and furniture, turns its back on the rivers Boyne and Blackwater which join beside the town, thus denying the traveller a single riverside vista on which to regale his eyes.

Sited at the hub of delightful country, the town was originally granted to de Lacey, who in turn granted it together with Ardbraccan, to Nangle or de Angulo. Saints revered in the An Uaimh district include St Cassan, the wonderworker of Donaghmore, St Breacan, St Ultan of historic Ardbreccan, the patron of children and, of course, St Brigid.

Athlumney Castle was fired by its owner so that it shouldn't offer even a night's shelter to William of Orange. This area must not be left without noting Donaghpatrick between Navan and Kells, site of an ancient patrician church, and Teltown, a palace site in an inchland of the Blackwater river where in prehistoric days funeral games were held in a cemetery, a custom which evokes classical echoes.

At these games the High King of Tara presided; in modern times these games have been revived under the name of the Tailteann Games.

Teltown with its contests in wrestling, swimming—and up to the early nineteenth century chariot-racing—for many years possessed an amorous and humorous survival of its possibly pre-Gaelic assembly.

Here the marriageable girls arranged themselves on one side of a long wall and the nubile boys on the other. On a given signal a girl thrust her arm through an aperture in the rock face: if the projecting arm was admired by a boy he took its owner in an espousal that approximated to marriage. Selection went on until all the available lovers were paired off.

If the marriage did not prove a success the couple returned a year and a day later to the nearby height of Ráth Dubh. The girl faced north, the boy south and, *signo dato*, they stalked away from one another into a dissolution of the marriage bond.

'A year and a day, like a Teltown marriage!' is an old saying in the County Meath.

The fertile plains of Meath must always have drawn towards them the eyes of the land-greedy.

Indelible is the apposite word to describe the variety of shafted castles and noble ruins, that, wholly unexpectedly, met my eyes as I approached the stalwart town of Trim.

Single castle walls stood upright on a landscape of noble proportions lighted by the mirror of the Boyne.

In mid-Trim King John's Castle stood striking and impressive, its turrets soaring to a height of over 70 feet, and its outer wall little short of 500 yards in length. A moat, to which the waters of the Boyne were admitted when exigency compelled, rendered the place almost impregnable. Although the castle founded in 1173 by Hugh de Lacey carries King John's name he did nothing to merit having it named for him except to sleep for a single night under its grey turrets.

Once burned by its constable as King Roderic O'Conor, the last High King of Ireland, approached, the castle was rebuilt to house several parliaments, to serve as a prison cell for Henry of Lancaster —afterwards Henry IV of England – and for a period even to house a mint!

The Duke of Wellington lived here in his youth. 'Since you were born in Ireland, you are, of course, an Irishman?' one importunate questioner asked the victor of Waterloo, to receive the answer which is still anathema to the Irish people: 'If one is born in a stable, is one a horse?'

There are precious few horses on the Bog of Allen, a region that stretches wild and desolate across Offaly and North Kildare and constitutes a wedge inserted between the green fields of Meath and the crisp plains of Kildare.

Giant machines grumble over the bogland to produce milled peat designed to meet the special needs of British gasworks and foundries, shiny mahogany-hued briquettes to brighten Irish hearths, moss peat for gardening purposes, and fuel to generate some of the electricity on which Ireland depends so much as a source of power.

Villages such as Kilcormac in County Offaly house *Bord na Móna* (Turf Board) employees. When the boglands of Ireland are completely exhausted, it is hoped to use the 'cutaway land' for reafforestation.

Once the seat of the Moores, Earls of Drogheda, to whom Mellifont Abbey was granted in 1566, Moore Abbey in Monasterevan in County Kildare was later the residence of Count John McCormack, the Irish tenor, and is now a house where the Sisters of Charity treat epilepsy and kindred ailments.

Sipping a cup of tea in a corner of the great library and looking at the whimsical head of a rag donkey I had been given as a souvenir of my visit, I glanced around to find that the nun, who a moment previously had been standing at my elbow, had disappeared. It was as if the enormous calfbound, gilt-lettered tomes on the walls had swallowed her.

And this is exactly what had happened! As I continued to gape, a section of the bookcase behind me swivelled soundlessly open and my nun-host reappeared bearing a plate of hot, buttered scones.

So rich was the Kildare area in Franciscan, Augustinian and Carmelite monasteries and so coveted by recurrent forces of disorder that from the Danish invasion until the dissolution of the monasteries, the story of this area is stippled with gore.

As I have already indicated, the greatest of all Irish nuns is associated with Kildare (*Cill Dara*, The Church of the Oak Tree). Towards the end of the 5th century, St Brigid, 'Mary of the Irish', founded in Kildare a religious community in which nuns kept the sacred fire of St Brigid burning for almost a thousand years.

The ancient monastery of St Brigid was a double one, that is to say, half the foundation was reserved for nuns and the other half for monks. A great painted screen extending from the centre aisle of the church ensured the minimum of male-female distraction during divine service. One conjectures at the didactic nature of the paintings on this screen. The fires of Hell? Lot's wife? The woman taken in adultery?

The Curragh of Kildare constitutes 5,000 acres of cropped grassland in an area as yet unenclosed. The Curragh Sweeps Derby is one of the richest races in the world. When the summer sun has set, bleating sheep rove off the commonage to lie on the warm tarmac of the roadway.

In the pubs of Kildare town, knowledgeable tipsters whisper from their mouth corners. Patriotic songs are sung about the arrival of aid from France in 1798: *And where will they have their camp?/Says the Shan Van Vocht./On the Curragh of Kildare/And the boys will all be there/With their pikes in good repair/Says the Shan Van Vocht*, the speaker in the song being The Poor Old Woman, or Ireland, looking to France for aid. Hereabouts too is Donnelly's Hollow where prize-fighter, Dan Donnelly, in the year of the Battle of Waterloo, beat his English opponent, Cooper.

In mid-Kildare town a fingerpost indicated a Japanese garden laid out in the demesne now associated with the National Stud.

I reached this arboreal depiction of man's peregrination through life on a day when it rained as if in prelude for the Deluge. Streams ran where streams never ran before. Trees dolorously dripped. I skittled through a watery life, a watery birth, a watery prime and finally reached a watery grave, whence at last I emerged deeply depressed.

I was far more fortunate at a later date when, following a finger-post, I reached the Grand Canal Fiesta held each year in late July at Robertstown a village 'geographically coy' about 28 miles from Dublin and almost ten miles due north of Droichead Nua. At Robertstown I spent a delightful Georgian afternoon in the rejuvenated Grand Canal Hotel in the company of period-costumed beauties on whom candelight shed its benediction.

Three miles to the south-east of Naas is Punchestown, a racecourse beloved of those addicted to steeplechasing—an Irish invention this since it had its origin in County Cork where the squires most ferociously rode their horses in cross-country free-for-all scrambles from one village steeple to another.

I rubbed my eyes at the sight of the new Dominican church in the town of Athy on the banks of the River Barrow, for the building had many quite remarkable features of architecture and appointment.

To restore my perspective I walked up and down on the river-bank with a venerable Dominican priest who had seen missionary service in many parts of the earth.

We talked about the Mote of Ardscull, four miles to the north-east, close to which in 1316, Edward Bruce of Scotland had defeated an English army, of the Quaker Settlement at Ballintore, with its neighbouring panelled High Cross of Moone (I kept meeting German tourists obsessed with High Crosses) and of the Rath of Mullaghmast, scene of a massacre of the Irish by the English in 1577. Nor did we fail to mention the splendid-in-decay ruined castle atop the Rock of Dunamase, four miles to the east of Portlaoise town in the County of Laois and set right in the heart of O'Moore territory. The castle was sited on the foundations of an ancient earthen fort which the Vikings had sacked as remotely in time as 844. This fortress Diarmuid of the Foreigners gave as dowry to his daughter, Aoife, on the occasion of her marriage to Strongbow.

Possession of Dunamase Rock shuttled back and forth with the ebb and flow of war and counter-war; from Anglo-Norman to mere Irish it sped thence to Parliamentarian, to the Catholic Confederates and finally to the Cromwellians who destroyed it in 1650.

Carlow of the sugar-beet factory, and of the curved weir in the River Barrow, has a history similar to that of other towns in this area. The 1798 Insurgents of South Leinster tried to capture the place but were repulsed with over 400 dead.

At Ballaghmoon to its north-east, Munster's king-bishop, Cormac Mac Cuilleanáin, died fighting in battle; his subjects, disagreeing about the place of burial, placed the royal corpse on a wagon drawn by seven oxen, and allowing the beasts to move where they wished, the oxen finally stopped at Colbinstown, in County Kildare, where, in the burial ground of Cillín Chormaic, the king was buried. Legend places the exact site of the grave beneath the imprint of the paw of a hound who, at the time of the interment, had leaped down from a nearby hill.

It would be unjust to leave Carlow without some mention of the Mount Browne Dolmen in Ballykernan, a couple of miles east of Carlow town, which is reputed to be the finest dolmen in Ireland, its capstone alone weighing more than 100 tons.

Entering Shillelagh in the southwest nook of County Wicklow I recalled a remarkable wanderer I once knew.

Every man who takes to the roads invariably has one gift or obsession: with Thomas it was memory.

I spent a memorable night at Puck Fair in County Kerry asking him questions. 'On what day was Kevin O'Higgins shot?' 'What was the voting in favour of the acceptance of the Anglo-Irish Treaty?' 'Name the man or men who went over Niagara Falls in a barrel?'

Thomas's eyes glittered above his black beard as, to the accompaniment of a high cackle of glee, he answered each question accurately. Shillelagh he claimed as his birthplace; passing through the town for which the Irish cudgel is named, I smiled in belated respect for the scholarship of one of its sons.

I retired to bed with the music of streams in my ears; in Avoca at morning I saw the tree beneath which Tom Moore composed *The Meeting of the Waters*. I was tempted to go prospecting for placer gold in the Avoca and Aughrim Rivers in the hope of discovering the motherlode which must exist somewhere in the Wicklow Hills.

Picture-pretty Glendalough (Glen of the Two Lakes) with mountains beetling about it and plumes of turf-smoke uprising, was surely made to the order of a prosaic professional photographer.

Here, among the mountains, St Kevin the Hermit made his dwelling place in the 6th century. He had his 'bed' in a cave 30 feet above the lake; he also had a temptress called Kathleen who figures in balladry of a mild bawdiness.

The road has always been a tamer of intransigence. And the old Military Road now under my tyres was laid down to subjugate the tribes of Wicklow, where, for centuries, the forest shade enabled them to play merry hell with the English of the Pale.

The O'Byrnes of Valley Glenmalure gave ready asylum to Red Hugh O'Donnell, the northern chieftain after his escape from Dublin Castle at Christmas 1592; this same glen was the lair of Michael O'Dwyer, the Wicklow Lion, who later died in exile in Australia.

Birches galore in the hills, bolls of bogcotton wagging their episcopal heads, the TV mast of Glencree showing stark against the evening light, erratic glimpses of the Irish Sea, and a sense of terrifying peace pervading the little cemetery where (relics of sea- and dog-fights) serried solid crosses German war-dead lie— then it was the Sugar Loaf Mountain and a series of rounded hills to the west, with, in the east, the town of Bray, a seaside resort brummagem in its season but redeemed by its headland and the cultural efforts of its nobler citizens. At Pine Forest and Sally Gap, a scant 11 miles from the city centre, I paused at dusk on a summer evening.

Below, framed in pine branches, lights blazed in what has but comparatively recently become an Irish city. Howth Head was a rosary of illumination across the bay. The granite boulders beside me sparkled in the dying light. Enormous beech trees sung of by Synge towered above me. Somewhere—not far away—there was an obelisk.

Descending from the hills, a squadron of ghostly roisterers, saints, rebels, conquerors, and dead airmen accompanied me into the genteel Dublin suburbs of Rathfarnham and Rathmines.

CHAPTER THREE

Wexford, Waterford, South Kilkenny

'...and old Wexford is won,
And the Barrow to-morrow we cross!'

The word 'husbandry' comes readily to mind in any description of the south-east corner of Ireland, an area embracing the counties of Wexford and Waterford with South Kilkenny thrown in for good measure.

The delighting Wexford countryside is perhaps a shade too tamed for an eye accustomed to the savage dimensions of the western seaboard, but it is still admirable in its eastern context.

Between the counties of Wexford and Waterford, the sister rivers, Barrow, Nore, and Suir, now conjoined, enter the sea in estuarine pride. Not far from the point of confluence, on the Wexford side, lies the sea-coast village of Bannow where, in 1169, the Normans first landed in Ireland.

One finds Wexford town still branded with the aftermath of the 1798 revolt.

If there are statues they represent pikemen who so valiantly rose; if a band comes marching downstreet, it's odds-on it's playing *The Boys of Wexford or Kelly of Killanne*; if a voice is raised in erratic porter melody, it's probable that the ballad lauds the priest-rebel 'Father Murphy of the County Wexford' who 'swept o'er the land like a mighty wave', and if a *seanchaí* is in yarning form, he'll likely tell of the rebel duckshooting lads from the dunes who filled their satchels with grain and chewed it in lieu of battle commissariat. After the engagements the dead bodies of the 'Croppies' were cursorily buried, and lo! with the passing years the satchel seams split underground, the corpse-manured grain sprouted, and up came

43

the wheat blades as closely bound as *fasces* of Roman old. Thus were the secret burial places poetically marked and revolt given a new impetus.

Once in a crowded public house on a western peninsula I heard Séamus Heaney, the Belfast poet, recite his poem on this phenomenon; the recital moved rough and ready drinkers almost to tears.

And it is in Wexford County too, or more accurately in the baronies of Bargy and Forth, that an ancient dialect for long survived probably deriving from the original language of the Anglo-Norman settlement.

In Gorey (of '98 fame) I sat on a seat in midroad and chatted with an old man who showed surprising alternations of mood.

'This is a dead ould place', he said, glumly looking down at the dust. A second later he raised his face to the sky and added brightly, "Tis only lately this town is picking up—we've a foundry up the road.' Again with his head on his bosom: 'The shopkeepers has us fleeced: butter is threepence a pound cheaper in Arklow.' Then, head uptilted: 'There's fine businessmen around here, I tell you.'

But wherever one goes in Wexford County there are still echoes of insurrection. The name Tubberneering on a roadside memorial-cross reads like a trumpet blast of revolt. The slab on the cross erected at Clough vaunts 'the memory of three priests, Fathers John Murphy, Michael Murphy and Philip Roche, who defeated the English on 4th June, 1798.'

Ferns, a peaceful village on the road to Enniscorthy gave its name to an ancient diocese; it has had a chequered monastic history and was once the residence of Diarmuid of the Foreigners.

On the roadway some miles north of Ferns I met an old labouring man who, dressed in out-of-fashion black, looked somehow like a down-at-heel schoolmaster. 'I have done jail!' he told me abruptly. 'Where?' I asked. 'In Wandsworth and Frongoch—for the liberation of my country,' he said, drawing himself up proudly. 'Wormwood Scrubbs, too,' he added by way of afterthought, 'as a protest against landlordism and its attendant evils.'

The old man looked around at the golden fields of grain. 'My father was evicted out of 300 acres of land; that left me a wandering labourer. Is it any wonder I'd be mad?'

I looked after him as he marched proudly away.

Enniscorthy sits above the pleasant tidal Slaney; in retrospect I think that its steep streets must fall (or rise?) at an angle of 45°. The surrounding countryside is plumed with trees.

The slender spires of the town—St Aidan's Gothic-Revival Cathedral is Pugin-designed—were offset by the tent of a visiting circus, this in turn was backed by straggling Vinegar Hill, site of the last stand by the ill-armed insurgents against 20,000 troops under Generals Lake and Johnston.

Vinegar Hill, viewed even to the accompaniment of circus music, is a bitter name on Irish lips: here, as the rebellion moved to its end, the insurgents slaughtered cattle, roasted sides of beef spitted on their pikes until at last, with no means of disposing of the offal, the hillside stank to heaven. Father John Murphy the leader, was captured, placed on the rack and his body burned.

Narrow-streeted Wexford, once a Norse settlement, was still Danish in 1169 when it was the first town occupied by Strongbow. It was later granted to the Anglo-Normans, Fitzstephen and Fitzgerald; today it is famous for its all-embracing Festival of the Arts centred largely on the 18th century theatre in McSweeney Street. Of this Festival I have delightful memories!

Wexford town has been the scene of two ferocious massacres: one by Cromwell, the other (in '98) for which, for a change, we Irish must cry *Nostra culpa*! The Bull Ring, where bulls and human beings were baited and slaughtered, is of interest to the seeker of the macabre, while Oscar Wilde's memorably quaint and brilliantly endowed mother—her pen-name was 'Speranza'—was born in the old rectory in South Main Street. Henry II did penance here in a local priory in 1172 for the crime of having murdered Thomas Á Becket. A statue to Wexford-born Commodore Barry, Father of the American Navy, stands on the Quays.

In New Ross itself, where bearded and imposing Andy Minahan, some time chairman of the local council, rises to peaks of protocol on occasion involving the dignity of his township, I read on a finger-post 'Dunganstown 4½ miles'.

Straightaway I was off to the south-west in search of the original Kennedy homestead whence Patrick Kennedy, great-grand-father of U.S. President John F. Kennedy left for America, the family possibly being under suspicion by the English since it had played a valorous part in the Wexford uprising.

The road narrowed as I went, with hedges constricting my passage until presently I drove through a green tunnel illuminated from above by light that had sieved through silken leaves. J.F.K. himself, when his father was U.S. Ambassador to Britain, and again when he himself was U.S. President, had slowly travelled this road to find the particular outcrop of Irish rock whence his forbears were hewn.

The drowsy lane continued to switchback while on either side thorn trees stood on tiptoe to seek the upper air. Nearing the Kennedy house I came round a bend to find myself bonnet to bonnet with a Rolls Royce! An eager-faced, elegant young woman, obviously an American visitor, sat at the wheel; a pale grey scarf covered her hair and brow.

As a flock of sheep came baa-ing out of nowhere the woman and I were momentarily alone and face to face in an ocean of fleeces. She smiled pleasantly at our predicament.

The snarl disentangled, I emerged into the open space where the Kennedy homestead sat. Green-roofed, with trim cattle byres and rounded gate piers, a cloud of white dust rising from the nearby paddock where a lime-spreader was at work, the house was marked by a shingle which read: 'The Kennedy Homestead.'

The yard gate opened; what we Irish call a 'fine-looking' woman came out. As Josie Ryan tilted her head the likeness to the dead American president was startling. 'You get used to it,' she said quietly, with reference to the cars that arrived every day. Josie's sister, Mary Anne, it was who represented the family at the funeral in Arlington of her kinsman.

Kinswoman Mrs Kirwan, third cousin to John F., sat on a chair in the cemented yard, her face upturned to the evening sun. As another car bearing visitors arrived she barely batted an eye-lid. *Is fearr an timreas ná an t-uaigneas!* I said consoling her with the Irish proverb which states that fuss is better than loneliness. She chided me by saying: 'We don't mind people coming. They wish to show respect.'

A white-headed boy swung on a gate, red-hot poker blooms were vivid torches beside the gables, a man wearing a black huntsman's peaked cap went riding past the gate—one had the impression that despite the spotlight of international attention focussed on this spot these people are still as natural as the river Barrow that flows below their home.

The nearby south Kilkenny countryside has an air all its own: I am now thinking of towns like Graiguenamanagh, Thomastown, Callan, Castlecomer and even Piltown to the south. Somehow, despite the years, the district has managed to retain a certain Norman quality difficult to define.

Around the foot of Mount Brandon, which looks down on historic Graiguenamanagh, each barley field seemed the perfect barley field. And the whole subtly suggested the beer that the metamorphosed barley would yet become.

This consideration set me thinking of the Kilkenny Beer Festival, for in Kilkenny (The Marble) City, history, beer and literature characterize the once proud capital of the pre-Norman kingdom of Ossory.

In its day Kilkenny city saw many parliaments: the infamous Statute of Kilkenny, passed in 1368, tried in vain to prevent the Anglo-Normans from intermarrying with the mere or pure Irish and laid down the severest penalties for any breach thereof. But the edict was rendered ludicrous by the wise but sly women who, by bringing their Norman lords to heel—and to bed—merged the two races.

Kilkenny also saw a Confederation of the old Irish and the Anglo-Irish; it was once virtually a capital of Ireland to which a Papal

Nuncio in 1645 hied himself with treasure and arms. But the Confederation split into two conflicting camps; its brilliant military leader, Owen Roe O'Neill, died so suddenly as to warrant a charge of poisoning. This melancholy occasion is recalled with bitterness by the Irish poet who began his denunciation with the lines:

Did they dare, did they dare to slay Owen Roe O'Neill?
Yes, they slew with poison him they feared to meet with steel.

St Canice's Cathedral, believed to occupy the site of the 6th-century church of St Canice, has many interesting architectural features. A finely preserved round tower stands close to its walls. The Dominican church embodies some elements of the first Dominican Black Abbey originally built in 1225. Also of note are the Rothe House, the home of Bishop Rothe at the time of the Confederation, and Kyteler's Inn, Kilkenny's oldest building, once owned by Dame Kyteler who, in 1324, survived the major charge of witchcraft and the apparently minor charge of poisoning her four consecutive husbands, to have her maid, Petronilla, convicted in her stead and burned as a witch.

In High Street stands the Tholsel, also called the Town Hall, with its odd clock-tower and Arcade. And honourable mention must be made of the thirteenth-century Kilkenny Castle, chief seat of the Butlers, on its eminence above the river Nore.

Today the city of Kilkenny is concerning itself with offering Ireland firm leadership in industrial design.

Castlecomer of the collieries, called, 'Comer' in affectionate diminutive, lies in the centre of the south-Leinster anthracite fields. Alas! Three hundred years of coal mining in Castlecomer now seems to have ended.

Here and there on farmland are out-crops of coal which I once saw farmers dig out, pile in the haggards and mix with water and yellow or blue clay. Well-shod horses then trod down the mess until it resembled wet cement. Finally a labourer squatted at the edge of the pile making by hand egg-sized ovoids called 'bums' which, when dried hard, made superb fuel.

6 Round Tower at Glendalough, Co. Wicklow

In Callan, a historic town where in 1407, fell 800 of the O'Carroll clan with their poetry-loving chief at the hands of O'Carroll's brother-in-law, Butler, 4th Earle of Ormonde, I thought of Humphrey O'Sullivan (1780-1837) the Kerry-born schoolmaster, who set down in his diary the simple events of the Callan day, a record which brings the town of that time to whimsical life a century and a half later. But O'Sullivan's memory fades beside that of Callan-born Brother Rice, founder of the Irish Christian Brothers.

First raised to God's glory in 1180, Jerpoint Cistercian Abbey beside lovely once-walled Thomastown continued its monastic reign until its suppression in 1540.

I spent a pleasant afternoon rambling under its effigies. Raucous rocks cawed above the heads of workmen most prudently disentangling carved stones from heaps of rubble and clay.

This is a countryside beloved of Kilkenny novelists Francis McManus and Patrick Purcell, and to some extent of Tipperary's Charles Kickham of yesterday and Patrick Brady (*The Big Sycamore*) of today. In the novels of these men the names of fishing villages like Mooncoin and Knocktopher are as beloved as time-polished beads.

It is impossible to speak of the city of Waterford, on the broad-breasted Suir, without making some mention of Waterford glass, an industry once dead but latterly revived with conspicuous success.

Once a Danish settlement (*Vethrafjorthr*) of the early 10th century, Waterford for centuries held the Irish at bay. Even when the Danish Remnant had become Christian they insisted on forming their own distinctive type of diocese.

When the Anglo-Normans took the town in 1170, Strongbow, their leader, gave his invasion the gloss of indigenous rectitude by marrying Aoife, daughter of MacMurrough, King of Leinster, while the city streets 'sluiced with blood'.

In 1171 Henry II passed through the narrow Waterford streets scurrying to ensure that his knights did not set up a separate kingdom—or republic! Century after century saw the city remain firmly united with the English crown: as proof of its loyalty it resolutely spurned two impostor kings from its gates. Although in 1649 the redoubtable Cromwell besieged it in vain, it fell to Ireton, his son-in-law, the following year.

In the latter middle ages Waterford produced a host of brilliant scholars and theologians. Not the least gifted of its sons were 'Meagher of the Sword' who, exiled from Ireland largely because of an inflammatory speech in favour of physical force, became governor of Montana, and theologian-leaders like Fathers Luke Wadding of Salamanca and Hearn of Louvain, this last-named known as 'the saviour of the Flemish language'.

Due south of Waterford City is Tramore (The Great Beach) a foremost east-coast seaside resort. It is also well-known for its Metal Man standing on one of three white pillars—navigational landmarks on Great Newton Head.

On the western shore of Waterford Harbour, two miles south of Passage East (the views from the hills beside this village are superb), the odd place-name Geneva recalls to memory the abortive idealistic attempt of 1782 to found here an intellectual city based on the silversmiths, goldsmiths, watchmakers and scholars from Geneva in Switzerland.

Dunmore East is the Harbour of Silver Darlings. As the seasonal herring shoals approach the south-east coast of Ireland the activity at its little pier sometimes boils over into quarrels that have to do with the purchasing and marketing of herring. Continental buyers are there a-plenty and the word 'cran' is common coinage.

With particular affection I recall dallying on the coast road from Tramore to Dungarvan at a wee place called Clonea, a minor resort favoured by the few. Dungarvan town, the story tells was saved from Cromwellian bombardment by a roguish woman emerging from its gates, tongue-in-cheek, to drink the health of the Lord Protector himself.

But for me, Dungarvan, and indeed Waterford county itself, will forever signify a Gaeltacht called *An Rinn*, or Ring, which has miraculously survived, complete with its stamp of Irish identity, until the present day.

Tribute must be paid to a physically-huge scholar named Hough—

he was known as *An Fear Mór* (the Big Man)—who, for his labours in Ring Irish College is affectionately remembered by thousands of his ex-pupils.

From Helvick Head there are heart-warming views of the distant Comeraghs across the span of Dungarvan harbour. To the south-west is Ardmore, until recently an Irish-speaking area with its pleasant beach and sand dunes.

The local saint, Declan, founded a monastery here in the 7th century; still in an excellent state of preservation is its 99-foot-high round tower, its oratory of Saint Declan and its ruined Cathedral.

Lismore is superbly situated at the foot of the Knockmealdown mountains and on the banks of the scenic Blackwater: the town somehow I associate with drowsiness and physical relaxation.

Lismore once had a double monastery founded by St Carthach and for centuries it maintained firm monastic connections with Wales. In the high noon of its greatness the place bragged 20 churches.

Today, oddly enough, it brags by the name-dropping of Fred Astaire whose sister, Adele Astaire, married Lord Charles Cavendish and lived for some years in the comparatively modern but magnificently impressive Castle.

Between Carthach and the Astaires there is the normal Irish litany of pillage and bloodshed, ecclesiastical eminence and semi-eclipse, with adventurers like Myler MacGrath, Walter Raleigh and Richard Boyle, Earl of Cork, as vivid protagonists.

A special word of grudged admiration goes to that swaggering adventurer, Richard Boyle, 'who arrived out of England with a pair of velvet breeches and £23. 3s. in his purse' and who ended his days owning enormous tracts of Munster land, with three of his sons ennobled and his daughters married into Ireland's most eminent families. As a final piece of impertinence he adopted as his motto 'God's providence is our inheritance'; the words are still cut in stone above the gateway of Lismore Castle.

Still in monastic mood which is quite impossible to evade in this area, let me take you east a few miles to wooded and scenically endowed Cappoquin and thence northwards along the mountain road to Mount Melleray Cistercian Abbey, an 1832 foundation by Irish monks expelled from France, which occupies a foremost place in Irish affection and anecdote.

Long before the advent of Alcoholics Anonymous the monks of this monastery had done a great amount of positive good in caring for those addicted to *uisce beatha* (whiskey).

But this is but the shy elbow in the ribs. The reality of the foundation and its later development contain the elements of a saga.

The Trappist Abbey lies on the flank of what was once a barren mountain; leasing a tract of dour land from Sir Richard Keane ('from today till tomorrow' so the story goes, which in reality means forever) the monks were initially aided by the populations of nearby towns turning out in traditional Irish *meitheal*, or working party, to give them a helping hand.

Now the wilderness blooms. There is a thriving community with a secondary school attached. The guest-house, as in the Middle Ages, offers hospitality to rich and poor alike without charge for food or accommodation, although quite rightly, it is usual on departing to leave a small donation.

Here the white-clad fathers live out their lives of strict discipline in silence, in abstinence, in labour and in early morning watches spent in psalm and prayer.

I stood high in a choir-loft watching the monks file towards the altar. Their chanting transported me in imagination across the face of the world: I stood again amid the snows of Iowa and looked up at the façade of New Melleray, an offshoot of this parent monastery in the Knockmealdown Mountains.

As pilgrims continued to arrive, I tiptoed out of the abbey church. I rode north to 'The Vee'—a unique pass over the hills and for an unconscionable period of time looked northwards over the great panorama of south Tipperary.

CHAPTER FOUR

Cork and Kerry

'o'er the ferry—spell me "that" without a k'

Cork and Kerry, the two picturesque counties forming the torn toecap of Ireland, are husband and wife. Between the populations of these two counties there exists a type of love-hate conjugal relationship.

Cork, the largest county in Ireland, dominates the marriage by sheer force of personality! Kerry makes up for any deficiency(?) by craft and subterfuge.

Cork has its breeches polished from swinging over shop-counters; Kerry has its elbows patched from studying at the head of the kitchen table.

Cork is easily the most friendly of Irish cities: shop assistants, waitresses, railway porters, bus conductors, many of them hailing from the rocky west-Cork area, are still vitally interested in you as a human being.

They'll claim kinship with you through your grandmother, express amazement at the fate of your cousin in New York, or sympathize with you on the demise of your alcoholic uncle in Camden Town.

Kerrymen, like freemasons, are forever making cryptic signs to each other.

Their (our) enemies declare that (we) Cork—and Kerryfolk are too damn cunning by half. Which indeed they (we) are!

Crossing the broad estuary of the River Blackwater from Waterford county into Cork and entering the New-Englandish town of Youghal (pronounced Yawhl) with its attractive Clock Gate, one remotely expects, à la New England, to see ladies in black perched on the widows' walks of the seaport houses awaiting in sorrow the return of whaling ships.

The image of the whaling boat is not inapposite since it was in Youghal that the film *Moby Dick* was made.

In Youghal I like to visit an artistic shrine by sculptor Séamus Murphy; cut from a marmalade-coloured stone it cheers the spirit after the depressing memory of the cohort of pseudo-Gallic grottoes, sick relics of a Marian year, which, many of them simply upended bathtubs in concrete, their insides daubed with blue distemper, disfigure our countryside.

From its foundation by the Anglo-Normans in the thirteenth century, the town of Youghal was part of the span of land granted to Sir Walter Raleigh at the Plantation of Munster.

A pleasant but lying tradition asserts that it was here Raleigh planted the first potato, that homely tuber which because of its failure, occasioned the Famine of 1846-'47, thus affecting the history of the world.

An equally lying tale tells of a somnolent Raleigh smoking Ireland's first pipe of tobacco in the town and being 'quenched by a servant maid who, thinking he was on fire, poured water on his head'.

The real Raleigh emerges, bloody sword in hand, on the red sands below Fort del Oro on Smerwick Harbour in Kerry, where in 1580, 600 Italian, French and Irish soldiers were butchered out of hand.

The year 1602 saw Youghal in the possession of the ubiquitous Earl of Cork, Richard Boyle; subsequently the town became a bastion of English defence.

South-west by the shore road to Ballymacoda and the fishing village of Ballycotton, then due west to view the oil refinery at Whitegate, thence to Cloyne where the greatest hurler the national game has ever seen, Christy Ring, was born.

In his prime, Christy played this most exciting (and to the neophyte, most dangerous) game with a panache that took all Ireland by storm.

But, Christy Ring apart. Cloyne has roots going deep into the soil of Irish history. Here in the 7th century Saint Colman, its patron saint, a poet in Latin and Irish, founded a monastery of which the 100-feet-high round tower still stands.

The roster of Cloyne's bishops, Catholic and Protestant, affords interesting sidelights on Irish history. Dean Swift's mysterious lady friend, Vanessa, bequeathed money to Bishop Berkeley of Cloyne, who utilized it for the foundation of a University in Bermuda. Both this area and nearby Midleton have links with the Fitzgeralds, Knights of Kerry.

At Carrigtuohill I headed for Cobh (pronounced Cove); presently between tall, terraced walls above the sea I saw below me the spread of Cork Harbour. A tender had just arrived from a liner anchored in the bay: I clung to the railings to view the homecoming of etiolated exiles who had given the lust of their lives to the United States.

Shouts of 'I see her!' rose on the air, to be followed by furious wavings from those embarking from the tender.

I found Cobh a town of tears and laughter: a town of greeting and farewell, a place of consolatory proverbs and heartbreak ('There's hope from the ocean but none from the grave'). All summer glitter and bright plumage, its porters worked like demons. Looking into the weary faces of the disembarking passengers I thought of their last febrile night on board; spying the first lights of Ireland every manjack of them recites the sentimental poem beginning: *T'anam chun Dia, but there it is, the dawn on the hills of Ireland.* . . .

Spike Island in Cork Harbour was the traditional place of incarceration for Irish rebels. John Mitchel of Newry (his *Jail Journal* is considered a masterpiece of jail literature) prior to his transportation to Botany Bay, heard his cell door clang open on this island and turned to see gentle Edward Walsh, the garrison school-master and poet, bidding a sad farewell to the erudite rebel.

Cork City I love! The friendly throng of people on its streets. The goldfish on Shandon Steeple. The mullet nosing in the River Lee. The red roofs of Gurraneabraher.

In the draper's shop I buy sports trousers: 'Arrah, man, send it back to us if you don't like it!' the assistant says. In the restaurant the waitress says to a child: 'I'll paper a few vienna rolls for your breakfast.' Lovely, friendly, rebellious Cork. Its industrious citizens make gin, motorcars, stout and hosiery.

In the 6th or 7th century St Finbarr here founded a monastery which figured in medieval vision literature. St Fin Barre's Protestant Cathedral may well occupy the original site of Finbarr's foundation.

For centuries Cork City was a skin pulled asunder by three dog packs, Norman, Danish and native Irish. It earned the name of 'Rebel Cork' because of the stubborn manner in which its citizens held fast to the abstract idea of freedom.

I go to Watercourse Road to see my friend, sculptor Séamus Murphy, a man whose work, inexplicably, was not commissioned for the rosary of new churches which encircles the city.

Séamus wrote '*Stone Mad*' a whimsical revelation of the minds and labours of the old 'stonies' or journeymen stone-masons with whom he spent his youth.

A great artist and great human being, Séamus has a wonderfully puckish face. He is sincere, diligent, integral, brave and humorous. As he tapped away, using a mallet made from the female crabtree, Séamus and I talked about Father Prout who made the doggerel song about Shandon bells. People in stone ringed us round; Michael Collins, Saint Patrick (now in St Patrick's College, Maynooth), the Virgin Mary, and a group of stone children with heads most winsome.

We talked, too, of Daniel Corkery, that seminal writer whose work, deriving from Gogol, Turgenev, Chekov, and Maupassant, fertilized the minds of his pupils, Frank O'Connor and Sean Ó Faoláin.

I had always been a spiritual pupil of Corkery so I went to visit him a short time before he died: he lived in a high bungalow above the sea near Fountainstown, outside Cork.

Old but still vital as he then was, he had many a shrewd phrase that pulled one up short. His *The Hidden Ireland* indicated the wealth of poetry concealed among the ordinary Irish-speaking country people. His collections of short stories *A Munster Twilight* and *The Threshold of Quiet* are landmarks in Anglo-Irish literature.

If it be true that all the short story writers in the world have emerged from Gogol's *Overcoat*, we who write out the indigenous resources in Ireland owe a great debt of thanks to Corkery, and through Corkery to O'Connor and Ó Faoláin.

I stood stripe-faced in the sunlight under the awnings of 'Pana' or Patrick Street, Cork's main thoroughfare.

Day-dreaming I heard the cheers that in 1495 greeted Perkin Warbeck, pretender to the throne of England, I saw Cromwell and John Churchill, Duke of Marlborough, stride down the cobbled thoroughfare, and yet again I heard the tread of Sarsfield and his Jacobite army of 1691 marching to embark for France. I also heard the anguished cries of the soldiers' wives, their fingers slashed from the gunwales as they tried to clamber aboard the boats and follow their men to the continent.

I also recalled Cork as it was in 1920, its streets aflame (afterwards, the Auxiliary Forces of the British Crown ironically tied burnt corks to their jackets) with one of its Lord Mayors assassinated and the other dying after 74 days of hunger strike in Brixton Prison.

We sat on a seat under the quayside trees, an erect well-groomed man and myself. It was an afternoon in mid-summer.

He wore a suit of grey Donegal check tweed, a wine-coloured tie with blue spots, a soft hat and well-shined black shoes. His face was thin, as was his body. His eyes were hazel.

Judging by the manner in which he carefully placed a cigarette in a cigarette-holder—the minor affectation of one in the public eye—he could have been a retired surgeon or a retired stockbroker. Anything but the man he was.

For this was Tom Barry, one of Ireland's great guerrilla fighters. And a man who is a legend in his own day.

In the eyes of the afternoon strollers, I read recognition and respect.

Forthright and aloof, Tom Barry can be abrupt with those he suspects of twisting his words. He can also be frank with those to whom he takes a chemical liking.

I found it difficult to identify this man with the man who had fought duel after duel in the streets of west Cork towns. Only an occasional tensing of his features showed the granitic nature of his character.

Somewhat in the nature of a descent from the sublime to the affectionately ridiculous, I suddenly remembered the Blarney Stone.

Once, in the United States, I was interviewed by a newspaper correspondent in connection with a St Patrick's Day feature in a local newspaper.

'Have you ever kissed the Blarney Stone?' the sweet-voiced reporter asked. 'Yes!' I replied. 'Have *you*?' she asked, my wife who smiled and shook her head.

Picture my reaction when, on the feast of our national apostle, the interview contained the following item in leaded type: MacMAHON STATES THAT HE HAS OFTEN KISSED THE BLARNEY STONE, BUT NOT HIS WIFE.

Blarney Castle is a bare five miles to the north-west of the city. Here, as every manjack in creation knows, high in the MacCarthy castle, with splendid views from the parapet, is embedded a stone which, when kissed, gives the embracer the gift of eloquence!

I climbed the stairway to the battlements. Two men sat above a stone recess through the barred base of which one could see the foliage below.

One by one the tourists, mostly women, lay on their backs, while the guardians of the stone having first modestly ensured that the ladies' skirts did not fly above their ears, cajoled them to inch ever downwards, their lips puckered in anticipation of the precious kiss. Some of the visitors screamed and protested; yet they insisted on going through the ordeal.

In the end I tried it myself—for the second time in my life; the menacing upside-down appearance of the puny trees far below as one gropes to kiss that infernal rock is not readily forgotten.

This custom probably had its origin in Queen Elizabeth I's comment on Chieftain MacCarthy's continued postponement of the hour of his surrender: 'I'm tired of all this blarney', her Majesty is alleged to have said as her patience wore threadbare.

Three main roads from Cork City, all moving westward or south westward, open up the territory that is west Cork.

The Cork City-Macroom road along the Lee valley leads eventually to Killarney; the Cork City-Bandon-Dunmanway road leads to Bantry, and the Cork City-Kinsale-Clonakilty-Skibbereen coastal road also finds its destination at the head of Bantry Bay.

North of this rather arbitrary road network is sited the prosperous area of north Cork with its fine towns like Mallow, Kanturk, Rathluirc, Mitchelstown and Fermoy.

Mallow, the chief town of this northern area and site of a major sugar-beet factory, was once a spa where Anglo-Irish bucks disported themselves, thus earning for the place a reputation for riotous behaviour as perpetuated by the song, 'The Rakes of Mallow'.

With the turn of the nineteenth century, Mallow redeemed itself in full measure and gave Ireland three men who, each in his own fashion, left his stamp on the Irish people.

The balladry of Thomas Davis, leader of the Young Ireland move-ment and founder of *The Nation* newspaper, as recited weekly in the forges of the land, roused its hearers to a high pitch of patriotic fervour. As a novelist, Mallow-born Canon Sheehan and sometimes parish priest of Doneraile was well above his hour, but due to the traditional literary fetters imposed by the priesthood he wrote well below his undoubted talent. William O'Brien, also a Nationalist leader on the political field, wrote with incisiveness and had a Euro-pean outlook on Irish affairs.

Anthony Trollope and Mrs Henry Wood also lived in Mallow. At Bowenscourt (near Kildorrery) stood the home of the writer Elizaabeth Bowen, the novelist and short-story writer.

Kanturk, a prosperous town noted for the manufacture of hosiery, was once the seat of the MacCarthys of Duhallow with whom jealous English settlers continually bickered.

Castle Magner, five miles away, recalls the presence of mind of Richard Magner who, in 1649, when his loyalty to England was in doubt, hastened to Clonmel to present himself to Cromwell. The dubious Cromwell gave him a letter addressed to Colonel Phaire, Governor of Cork, ordering that the bearer be executed at once. On his way back Magner opened, read and resealed the message and cunningly asked his arch-enemy, the Cromwellian governor of Mallow, to deliver it to Phaire. This that most gullible man did with the result that Phaire, somewhat mystified, had the governor executed on the spot.

Kilcolman Castle outside Doneraile was once the residence of the poet Edmund Spenser. For his notorious views on how to treat the native Irish he was ostracized, even by his own stratum of ascendancy society. An ironic quirk of history ensured that one of his descendants was exiled to Connaught 'as a papist'.

In Newmarket I shinnied over a cemetery wall to stand above the grave of Sarah Curran, daughter of the celebrated advocate John Philpot Curran and sweetheart of the executed patriot Robert Emmet.

As I stood there I seemed to hear the strains of Thomas Moore's song *She is Far from the Land* which has to do with sundered lovers; irony again intruded, for Sarah later married an English officer. For which conjunction I for one, cannot place a featherweight of censure on her pretty head.

The only woman Freemason in the world, born Mary Barry and later wife of the first Viscount Doneraile, is also buried in this grave-yard. She hid herself in a grandfather clock in a hall wherein a meeting of Freemasons was being held and so learned their secrets. Discovered, she was sworn into the order so as to keep her mouth buttoned up.

Ráthluirc, otherwise Charleville, and named for Charles II, as well as being, like Mitchelstown, a well-known cheese-manufacturing town, has lively associations with things cultural, its annual drama festival being a well-known event in mid-Munster. The literary background of Ráthluirc possibly derives from 'The Court of Poetry' once held locally under the auspices of Seán Clárach Mac Domhnaill (1691-1754), a Gaelic poet.

In neighbouring Buttevant (from the Anglo-French *boutevant*, a defensive rampart), centre of a de Barry area, is held each year the famous Cahirmeè Horse Fair.

It was at this fair that Napoleon's famous horse, Marengo, was bought, probably from a member of the O'Connor family from north Kerry.

Mitchelstown, a cheesemaking centre, is a well laid-out town with sombre echoes of the Land League struggle still resounding in its spacious square. The so-called Michelstown Caves, near Ballyporeen in County Tipperary, are certain to attract the curious as well as those interested in speleology.

Led by a comely torch-bearer I descended 30 rungs of a ladder until I reached the mouth of a long passage; feeling slightly claustrophobic I decided against going further and so missed the wonders of the East Chamber in the Desmond Cave wherein the Earl of Desmond once hid, and the marvels of the New Cave, with its mile and a half labyrinth of passages and its array of stalactites and stalagmites.

And so to picturesque Fermoy, situated like Mallow on the lovely Blackwater River. Fermoy owes its existence to a Scotsman called John Anderson; in the middle ages it was the site of a twelfth century abbey, once Benedictine and later Cistercian, all traces of which have disappeared.

Anderson cajoled the British government into erecting a barracks in the growing township; thus Fermoy became one of the great bastions of British occupation in Ireland, being capable of housing a garrison of 3,000 soldiers.

Consequent upon the withdrawal of British forces from Ireland following the Anglo-Irish Treaty in 1921 and the inevitable economic upheaval this entailed, Fermoy had to do a great deal of rethinking on new economic lines. And to its credit it did—and survived.

After such a forced march through north Cork, refreshment, even vicariously consumed, is in order, so let us consider the little village of Killavullan between Fermoy and Mallow where originated the Hennessy family, the original distillers of brandy!

By the most northerly of the three roads I have already mentioned, after a journey of 23 miles due west from Cork City, with a choice of two sub-roads for good measure, both poised on the edge of a valley drowned in the dammed-up waters of a hydro-electric development scheme, one arrives at Macroom.

Once a MacCarthy seat, Macroom finally fell into Cromwellian hands; in 1654 no less a person than Cromwell himself bestowed the castle and manor of Macroom on Admiral Sir William Penn, father of William Penn of Pennsylvania.

On the road to the west may be tempted to visit Kilcrea 'Abbey' not far from Ovens, a Franciscan friary dating from 1584, where lies buried an ex-officer of the Hungarian Army, Art O'Leary of Raleigh, Macroom, slain by the English as an outlaw in 1773.

His memory is perpetuated by the famous *Caoineadh Airt Uí Laoire* or *Traditional Lament for Art O'Leary*, composed by his widow, Black Eileen O'Connell of Derrynane, Co. Kerry and aunt of The Liberator, Daniel O'Connell. From this area also hailed Canon O'Leary, a well-known writer in Irish.

West of Macroom the road winds through the Derrynasaggart mountains amid which lies the Irish-speaking district of Bally-makeera, Ballyvourney and Coolea.

Bardic schools were a feature of ancient Ireland; young bards served a long apprenticeship to storytelling, playing on the harp, recitation, genealogy and history.

The sophomore poets were confined by day to rooms 'deaf to sound and blind to light'; at evening they emerged into a candlelit chamber to read their compositions in the presence of critical poet-masters.

One frosty night some years ago with the stars like steel splinters, on receipt of a summons to the last of the bardic schools, a friend and I stumbled into Irish-speaking Coolea.

We found a young man lighting a paraffin heater in the local hall: presently the hall was crowded. A man called *An Suibhneach Meann* took the chair; the pronunciamento, calling the bards to order, was read and soon the school was in full session.

Poet after poet, mostly farmers, shopkeepers, and labourers, stood up to declaim in different parts of the hall; each poetic effort was greeted with applause.

Afterwards we had tea and barmbrack. The old man who made the Irish song *An Poc ar Buile* ('The Crazy Billygoat') was then alive and gave a splendid rendering of his spirited song.

Nor shall I readily forget a visit, or pilgrimage, to the Whitsun Patteran at Ballyvourney village, also in the centre of this Irish-Ireland area. Held at Whitsun, and called locally 'The Fitchin'—it is as medieval a survival as is to be found in Ireland.

In the village of Ballymakeera itself, providing a secular side to the ceremonies, there were all sorts of games and swingboats; chalk Christs, china dogs and Infants of Prague were offered as prizes for success on the wheel of fortune.

To a thirteenth century wooden statue of St Gobnait (Abby is the local corruption of the name) woollen thread or ribbon is applied and thereafter used for curative purposes.

The ruined medieval church called *Tempall Ghobnatan* is the scene of rounds of pilgrimage; it also possesses a mask-fragment in stone called The Black Robber named for a mason who stole the tools of one of his fellow-masons and was, as punishment, execrated forever in stone. Over one of the church windows is what appears to be a Sheila-na-gig (*Sighle na gCíoch* or Sheila of the Breasts), a pagan fertility image.

Presiding over all is a delightful statue of St Gobnait by Séamus Murphy; the saint is dressed in a hooded cloak and stands on a beehive with which legend associates her.

'What do you think of her?' I asked in Irish of an old woman fervently praying for the intercession of her saint. This with reference to the statue.

The old woman gaped upwards.

'At first,' she said, 'we didn't like her at all—she was so like ourselves. Now we're crazy about her—and that's a God's true fact!'

Bandon, an angling centre, the last of its old women still dressed in the Bandon or Macroom cloaks, sits on the 'middle road' through west-Cork.

Bandon town was founded by Boyle, Earl of Cork. He banged out the native clans and, planting the place with English Protestant settlers, raped the timber and mineral resources of the countryside.

A letter of his boasted that 'no popish recusant or unconforming novelist was admitted to live in the town'. It was alleged also that over one of the gates was inscribed an anti-papist inscription; the mere Irish retaliated with 'Bandon, where even the pigs are Protestant'. But these vituperative days are long forgotten and the town is now most ecumenically neighbourly and prosperous.

In the Dunmanway area, if you happen to encounter a couple of hundred men walking the roads on a Sunday or holiday afternoon, take good care lest a mighty bowl of iron descend upon your skull!

As one who tried vainly to learn the game of bowling from a Dunmanway giant let me murmur that this is no game for weaklings. But it's worthwhile standing for a spell to watch a skilful practitioner 'loft' the bowl (the word rhymes with 'howl') over an awkward corner and, by putting a spin on the bowl, force the fallen sphere to run along the tarmacadam crown of the roadway.

Returned again to the hub that is Cork City and now travelling southward along the coast line, I was at once taken by the ridges of rolling land, enlivened by gilt quadrangles of ripe wheat set in a countryside that was well-treed in its hollows and where the rivers are clear-flowing.

To my left was the coast road through Monkstown with its ferry to Rushbrooke and the castle which a woman is said to have erected for the sum of fourpence. To my left too, was Carrigaline with its well-known pottery. Had I visited Carrigaline, I would have hummed Denny Lane's well-known song *Carrigdown* with its reference to the Owenabwee River which meets the sea at the town. Likely as not I would also have recalled Sir Francis Drake taking refuge from the Spaniards in Drake's Pool in 1587.

As it was, I headed for Kinsale, a name that tolls like a bell of doom in the ears of students of Irish history.

The Anglo-Normans, de Cogan and de Courcey, were granted this area as swordland; later they adopted Gaelic ways and names. De Courcey, Baron of Kinsale, won the right to have his head covered in the presence of royalty—this because he had acted as the champion of King John of England against the champion of Philip of France in a dispute concerning the Duchy of Normandy.

History records that when the French champion looked on de Courcey's terrifying countenance he clapped spurs to his horse and never cried halt until he arrived in Spain.

In 1601, a Spanish fleet, under Don Juan Del Aquila and with 3,814 infantry on board, landed at Kinsale, seized the de Courcey castle and held out against an encircling force of English under Lord Mountjoy and Sir George Carew. 'We hold Kinsale for Christ and the King of Spain', was the slogan of the Spaniards.

To relieve the Spanish force the Northern Irish chieftains, O'Donnell and O'Neill, made a forced march of over 300 miles in the depth of an unusually harsh winter:

> *O'er many a river bridged with ice*
> *Through many a vale with snowflakes dumb*
> *Past quaking fen and precipice*
> *The Princes of the North have come . . .*

Reaching Kinsale, they in their turn surrounded the besieging English, who, plagued by hunger and disease, were soon in distress. Some of the Irish leaders urged that an attack be mounted at once; others counselled a policy of caution. Eventually it was decided to attack at dawn on Christmas Eve.

After floundering all night through bogland in foul weather, the Irish forces, the Spaniards having previously failed to attack from the inside as agreed upon, found themselves confronted by the comparatively prepared English army and were utterly defeated.

Thus it was that the old Irish order was struck a deadly blow.

It was in Kinsale in 1689 that James II landed in a vain effort to recover Ireland. From Kinsale he sailed after the Battle of the Boyne.

Nowadays, a new Kinsale, known chiefly as a sea-angling and sailing centre, is emerging. It is a place begonia-bright and fashionable. People stroll past a hotel annexe, its newly painted wrought-iron front reminding one of New Orleans. On the pierhead beside its newest hotel, a blue shark, its mouth drawn sidelong by the weight of its body hanging from a hook, its navy blue back paling in the first sloe-bloom of decay, hangs crucified against the sky.

Across the causeway below Kinsale town and southwest I go, bound for Clonakilty and Skibbereen, thence north-west in the direction of Bantry. Good green grass grows right down to the edge of the sea; greenery is backed by a plentitude of barley fields.

On a height near Ballinspittle above the Estuary of the Bandon river, my only comrade a scarecrow in a brilliant red jersey, I stayed to look back upon hill behind hill, stretching eastward into a haze.

For vying colours I possessed the purple of the loose-strife, the red purple of the fuchsia, the red of the heather and the orange red of seaweed that edged the shore.

Presently I arrived at Timoleague and viewed the piled ruin of a Franciscan Friary, pleasantly sited on the water's edge.

Founded by Donal Glas MacCarthy in 1312, on its disestablishment it experienced the normal—or abnormal—vicissitude of ruin. Its monks subsequently crept out of the woods to repair their broken house and resume the traffic in smuggled wine from Spain. The local tale has it that Timoleague Abbey had a thousand barrels in its vaults when it was burned.

Remembered too in an Irish poem is the generosity of the monks to the poor and leprous – these latter were accommodated for mass in a lazaretto or leper-squint looking sidelong on the altar.

At Courtmacsherry at evening the houses of the village shone along the western curve of the bay. Giant beeches grew at water's edge. The ebbing tide hissed over clean gravel. The lights came on in the village and made a horseshoe of illumination about the water.

In the porch of the hotel was displayed a poem praising the beauties of the locality: later I found the poet Willie Fitzgerald of Ovens and his wife Nan. As the night was still young we chatted: Nan Fitzgerald told me that her uncle was with Scott and Tom Crean of Annascaul, Kerry, on the Scott Expedition to the South Pole.

'When my uncle was on the Expedition,' she said, 'my mother, his sister, sent him a postcard depicting a girl playing a harp. The card bore the legend "The Harp that Once Through Tara's Halls".'

'Only a few years ago Australians who visited the Scott hut at the South Pole found the postcard nailed to the door and returned it to our family. It was still legible.'

Rare books, a pair of superbly designed chairs and a wardrobe dated 1746—these were some of the appointments of the room in which I slept in Courtmacsherry.

The following morning I searched for the Coolim cliffs.

When at last I found them, they were quite undramatic—shafts of rock descending to the sea at an angle of 70 degrees. However, the sight of the Old Head of Kinsale in the distance compensated for my disappointment.

Pleasant places like Barry's Cove and Dunwhirley moved past me, fawn clay cliffs pink-stained with sandstone hung above me and aubretia lighted the road edge with Saint Anthony's Fire as I moved towards Clonakilty.

A bakery-smelling, resilient town Clonakilty most certainly is. Finding the tide of emigration sapping its resources, 'Clon' decided to do something about it.

Through the open doorway of the Carbery tweed factory, housed in the old station building, I saw coloured tweeds enliven the looms. As I stood gaping a man spoke to me in Irish.

'I met you in the west Kerry at Brugh na Gráige,' he said, 'I was there learning Irish with Father Tadhg.' Father Tadhg Murphy of Carrignavar in Cork is as kindly a man as ever drew a surplice over his head—he has conveyed to hundreds of young men his own glowing affection for the ancestral language.

In Woodfield, a few miles from Clonakilty town, was born Michael Collins, whose guiding brain established a native secret service that helped to break British power in Ireland.

I remember, as a boy, seeing him on his last journey to the south during the Civil War—a journey that was to end in his tragic death at Béal na mBláth in West Cork. It is said that as a child Collins had seen a poor family evicted from a cabin and had vowed that he would help build an Ireland where such things could never again happen.

Along an unappetising estuary to Inchadoney Strand, a huge sand bar athwart the mouth of Clonakilty Bay. There lie twin beaches with a spit of high land between them, the whole backed by a hill of bracken. Spread-eagled on the grass, my belly to the sun, I thought that someone should tell West Cork even in mangled metaphor that the rape of virgin coastline will eventually strangle the touristic goose that lays the golden eggs!

An inevitable causeway to cross, afterwards it was southwest towards Galley Head where a lighthouse once made history with the clear quality of its light. Near Dunmore I looked back and saw Inchadoney Strand from a novel and admirable angle. For an hour I loitered in sundrenched Duneen Bay. Only a few lobster fishermen vouched that the place held the pulse of life. I was deliberately dawdling, for I knew that three delightful beaches lay ahead of me: Red Strand, Long Strand—otherwise called Castlefreke Warren— and Inch Strand. So I had to choose. And it was for the Long Strand that I settled.

The dry sand beneath my footsoles was blisteringly hot; it also twinkled with the silver of tiny dead fish. I lazed on the mile-long beach with scarcely a hundred people upon it. I examined the rocks that protruded from the beach and found them almost of purest slate.

I drove along the tattered avenue and entered the comparatively modern but ruined castle of Lord Carbery. The walls and ceilings still retained their original paintwork though the floors showed gaping holes. By a spiral staircase I climbed to a turret, thence I moved on to a flat roof, and spent some time looking south-west over landscape and seascape.

Hard by Rosscarbery of the Hundred Isles, the sun, obscured for a time, came blindingly out. I left the car, and standing beside a fence, cocked an ear in an effort to hear one of the great traditional sounds of Ireland—*Tonn Chlíodhna*—goddess Clíodhna's wave.

I heard only the lark in the clear air, and, later still, the far-away sibilant rumour of the sea.

Rosscarbery was once a place of monastic importance. In the 6th century St Fachtna had a monastery here; the place subsequently gave its name to the diocese of Ross. The little town perched above the sea looked somnolent enough as I swung around in the square. Yet, here was born that 'unconquered and unconquerable' Fenian leader, O'Donovan Rossa. Descending a steep hill I turned left and went off with the vague idea of searching for a lost copper lode above Glandore.

The minerals of West Cork are no illusion, even though the broken walls of derelict mining buildings stark on the horizon, infer otherwise.

But lovely Glandore had forgotten its days of copper glory. As I entered it at evening, the mackerel raced noisily in the tiny harbour that is canopied with trees. Anglers were standing on the twilit shore, their silver lures flashing above the shimmer of the fish.

'You should have been here a few weeks ago', an old man told me. 'The boys simply slaughtered them.'

As he spoke a hooked mackerel described an arc through mid-air and thumped the wall beside my head.

As the light faded I recalled that I had an appointment with a coven of druids. The sun was setting as I reached the ridge of Drombeg, a few miles to the east. I found the circle of stones possessed of a sense of mute power.

In the obtuse angle made by two western hills, the upended boulders cast intimidating shadows. Some of the stones were over seven feet high: the western outlier, which resembled a crude altar, was much smaller and flatter than its fellows.

As I loitered, I found the cupped valleys below the site became a vast temple, where, as the fire of the sun faded, thousands of devotees could be imagined looking westward to the diurnal death-throes of their god.

The outer stones inclined inwards to the centre flag-stone, beneath which in 1957, in a shattered urn, the ashes of a young man or woman had been discovered. In 1958 the base of a stone hut, together with roasting oven, water pit and an ingenious but crude method of drawing water, were also discovered.

I went my way singing the praises of the lecturer from University College Cork who had undertaken the work of unearthing this minor wonder.

Beneath the pierlights of Union Hall on the other side of Glandore Harbour stood an old fisherman. So intent was he on watching the bobbing lights that indicated the trawlers' return, that he answered my every query with a softly sung: 'I couldn't-tell-'ou!'

I tried him with the day of the week, the time of the day, almost the month of the year—but all I could get out of his mouth was 'I couldn't-tell-'ou!'

I thought that this mysterious watcher would have puzzled even Jonathan Swift. For it was to this peaceful peninsula of Myross that Swift came to write; later still, the place knew a merry roystering Gaelic poet called Seán Ó Coileáin who made Jacobite songs.

With the crack of day I hurried to Lepp ('Beyond the lepp, beyond the law')—if you are well-bred you may call the place O'Donovan's Leap—to see a painting of O'Donovan himself on his white horse prancing on the wall of an inn.

On a fuchsia-hemmed roadside I found a souvenir store set on a cliffside of pure slate: there I paused to buy my third copy of *The Mentor Book of Irish Poetry* with its wonderful mixture of the banal and the splendid. Standing at the doorway of the store I read for the twentieth time Paddy MacDonagh's poem 'The Widow of Drynam' and for the hundredth time Bertie Rodgers' poem called 'The Net'.

The bay below me was a platter of pewter. Above me the mountain peaks were touched with the faint bloom of ripe sloes.

There are people, who by warmth of personality impress themselves on a world, a nation or a town. One of these was Mary Ann of Castletownshend. I recall her some years ago when I first visited this slightly English-of-the-English village with its peeled orange-coloured eucalyptus trees that abide in the memory.

Down a steep hill I drove past walls of slate rock, that by optical illusion, appeared off the horizontal, all the while counselling myself not to crash against the sacred walled-in twin trees that stand in mid-road at the hill foot. And there to the right, in her neat little pub, Mary Anne Hayes presided.

Even though Mary Anne no longer reigns over her tavern, the impress of her character still lives on in Castletownshend.

I squatted on the pier. Bearded yachtsmen came and went. A blasted boatman careless with oil filled a rock pool with rainbows: children groped for minnows among the stones of a nearby stream. I hied myself to Skibbereen.

Here two MacEgan bishops met violent ends. One was hanged, the other was killed in battle. It was also, the centre of an area appallingly hit in the Famine of 1846-7.

Lough Hyne (or Ine), four miles to the South-west of Skibbereen is half lake, half sea-inlet.

The entrance from the sea to the blind alley of the lough is wide enough for a boat to enter; the filling and ebbing of the tides, being unable to synchronize their functions occasion a difference in the water-level within and without the lough. The result is, at high tide, a crazy pattern of beautiful but uncertain water.

Looking down on the little pier of Baltimore I munched a slab of cheddar cheese and drained a bottle of milk. From a rock above the pier abutted the ruins of the O'Driscoll Castle of Dunashad.

A motor boat, loaded with lads and lassies all singing gaily, moved out for Clear Island—or it could be nearby Sherkin with its stretch of silver strands. Clear Island, dedicated to St Kieran, is rich in ruin and legend. This island is Irish-speaking and had its Gaelic College officially opened by President Éamon de Valera, who, one fine day, descended on the islanders (as a *deus ex machina*) from a helicopter.

And south of Clear Island is the Fastnet Rock lighthouse, one of the loneliest light stations in Europe.

As I munched my cheese, my thoughts turned to pirates from Algiers.

These had descended on Baltimore one dark night in 1631 and carried off 200 of its inhabitants. The place had had a previous nightmare experience in 1537, when in retaliation for the seizing of a cargo of Spanish wine, the citizens of Waterford dispatched a vengeful fleet to sack the town.

Ever onward! An old man bearing a forkful of hay moved past me on the road-edge. A few swing boats and a shooting gallery crouched beneath the backdrop of the viaduct beside Ballydehob. The long ridges of Mount Gabriel (1,339 feet) swung into view as I thrust west into the heart of O'Mahony territory.

Beside Schull (*Scoil Mhuire* or Virgin Mary School) were pleasure boats aplenty; there too were trawlers with impressive catches of crayfish and lobster.

By this time I was travel-sticky; more than anything else I longed for a swim from a clean beach. But to find it, I had to travel almost to the Mizen itself, the most southerly point of Ireland.

Presently, I discovered that the complex of beaches about Barley Cove had already been discovered! A line of cars stretched along the road-edges. Beaches, cliffs, dunes, causeways, coves,—these have already been the subject of representations by *An Taisce* (National Trust) a body rightly apprehensive regarding coastal development. A number of chalets, overlooking the westerly cove above the Lake of Swans, have been the focal point of apprehension.

The Mizen itself proved to be a series of savage cliffs below a lighthouse, ending in a spine of sawtoothed rocks that reached out, *diminuendo*, into the sea.

Leaving Three Castle Head to the west I romped over the back of the first of the five great peninsulas of south-west Ireland. Day waned as I sped through Drishane and Durrus.

Kilcrohane! Let me find it on the map. Here it is. There I once spent some time a-lobstering. Every day with two local fishermen I went out in a boat from a little pier. Across Dunmanus Bay, I could see seals sunning themselves on a rock. A seal once followed the boat, his old man's moustache rendering him semi-human.

One day, the pots shot, one of the fishermen unrolled an oil-cloth parcel and showed me his store of books. For an hour we chatted on the literature of the world. At last we grew hungry, and returning to the pier scooped a cache of crab claws out of the embers of a smoking turf fire, and cracking them with a stone, laced them with slices of soda bread, and drank tea so strongly brewed that a mouse could walk across its face.

The crossing of the backbone of Seefin Peninsula, on the way from Kilcrohane to Bantry offers the wanderer one of the steepest, and certainly one of the most magnificent, mountain passes in Ireland—Goat's Path it is aptly named.

Rolling over the crest there is the reward of a memorable view of Bantry Bay, with the wraith-like Caha mountains pencilled on the next peninsula.

As I rode down into Bantry, with mackerel hissing in the sea below me, I saw a caravan approaching and recognized John Wilson, the balladsinger, who for many years had been the singing king of the Irish roads.

John told me that he had gone to live in England, where a job on railroads served to tide him over the slacker periods of the year. He had returned to Ireland at the start of the summer to go singing and rambling again.

'I must soon stay in England altogether', he said, not without sadness. 'There's only fifteen years of voice in the best chanter on the Irish roads.'

Inland from Bantry the terrain is brutally attractive while the sea-edge is fringed with orange seaweed above which are perched fine houses sheltering amid wind-pruned beaches.

Bantry and its open quays were chock-a-block with visitors. Presently I found myself in a parlour conversing with an Indian-born girl who had married a young Irishman and had returned to start a guesthouse in her husband's native town.

As we chatted, the ghost of Wolfe Tone could well have been parading outside in the gathering dusk, for in 1796, Tone, the father of Irish revolution, had tried to pilot a French fleet into Bantry Bay. A storm dispersed the ships; thus the Irish Republic had to wait a further 150 years to be named as such.

Through broken, serrated countryside one may push north through Ballylickey, coldly assessing on the road the economic versus the touristic implications of the Whiddy Island oil terminal, to reach the Pass of Keamaneigh in the Shehy mountains with its stirring song about a tithe battle, thence to Irish-speaking Ballingeary and thence again to lonely Gougane Barra, once the home of St Finbarr the hermit. Here one may tarry at either of the Cronin hotels, later pushing through a forest park into the wooded fastnesses of Valley Desmond—a rare ride this.

In Gougane I visited the island oratory: I also breathed a prayer above the nearby grave of a witty tailor with its epitaph of 'A star danced and I was born'.

This tailor, Buckley by name, was a lovable sage whose mildly pungent anecdotes, as recounted by Eric Cross in *The Tailor and Ansty*, caused a literary storm in an Irish teacup at an hour when insecure authority, insecure scholarship and insecure chastity were at their most depressing nadir in Ireland.

In sheltered Glengariff of the tropical growth, where everything was a little too dreamy for my liking, the merriment of the night had not yet begun in the popular local taverns – Doc's and Harrington's.

I went to a weaver's room where I draped my body in tweeds that cried out to be made into sports jackets. Later I gazed down into the deeps of Poul Gorm—The Blue Pool. As evening faded I took a boat from in front of the Eccles Hotel and rowed out to Garnish Island, there to walk through the unreal, but delightful gardens planted by Annan Bryce, who later bestowed the island on the nation. George Bernard Shaw, for one, overcame the languor of Glengariff to write *Saint Joan*.

Long before the arrival of Shaw, Oliver Cromwell arrived in Glengariff to fling a bridge across a river (they say) in an hour. Views, chamber tombs, a profusion of vegetation, and a climate clement to invalids—this locality lays claim to many marvels.

Should I now proceed almost due northward along the high stone-tunnelled road through Kenmare to Killarney, a road overhung with bare mountains? Or should I move southwest to Castletown Bere-haven along the southern coast road of the Caha Peninsula where rumour has it that the trout in many of the 365 lakes have never seen a lure?

If I chose the latter route I knew that I had a further choice: at Adrigole I could swing north over the Healy Pass coiling past the white Calvary to reach the top, there to loiter in the bracing cold.

Or should I, even more valiant still, continue southwest past Hungry Hill (cf. Daphne du Maurier's novel of that name) where after heavy rain, a waterfall drop-roars 700 feet, through Castletown Berehaven with its nearby Bere Island, once a fortified harbour held post-Treaty by the British and consequently for some years a bone of contention, to the ultimate that was Crow Head?

Dunboy settled the question for me. All my life I had wanted to see the remains of the O'Sullivan Castle of Dunboy, a mile or two out of Castletown Berehaven, where in 1602, during the Nine Years War, defender Mac Geoghegan, finding that the game was up for the Spanish-Irish garrison, (cf. Kinsale) torch in hand had staggered down a cellar steps to the powder magazine with the intention of blow-ing up the castle, rather than surrendering it to Sir George Carew. Geoghegan, mortally wounded, was caught in the nick of time.

Tracing the outlines of the castle on the grass, I thought of the fate of the 142 defenders, none of whom had long survived the siege, for those captured were speedily hanged. I thought too, of the subsequent epic march to the north of Ireland by O'Sullivan Bere and the remnants of his clan.

Near the tip of the peninsula, in the once copper-producing area of Allihies, the sight of Dursey Island across a vicious-looking sound (now bridged by cable car) recalled for me the scholarship of Dursey-born Don Philip O'Sullivan whose books were published while that scholar was in exile in Lisbon.

Hereabouts too, spying a distinctive cottage built against the side of a massive boulder, I told myself that had the Welsh owned such a treasure they would certainly have spared no effort to have it transferred to St Fagan's the Folk Museum near Cardiff.

Still weaving in and out among boulders, I drove north-east along the northern shore of the peninsula. Across fjord-like Kenmare river the Iveragh Peninsula bared its peaks. Passing Lauragh I thought of the stories of my good friend Seán O'Sullivan, archivist of the Irish Folklore Society, had gathered here in his native place, one of the last cultural outposts of a land-mass that extends from Vladivostok to the western coast of Ireland.

The run along the edge of Kenmare River was rich in woods; there was an opulence of growth in the valley bottoms where the brawling of mountain streams was suddenly stilled.

I was now in my native Kerry. I paused to urge myself to be as objective and as temperate as was possible in my comments—quite a difficult imposition indeed.

It was dusk. It was raining. Sitting inside an open window the shoemaker was working late with shining last, incisive awl, aromatic heel ball and smoky candle. He had a face worthy of Leo Whelan, R.H.A.—who had indeed painted a fine picture of a Kerry cobbler.

'How's trade?' I asked.

'Fine!' he said, measuring me slowly.

'Farriers and saddlers are knowledgeable men.'

'Cobblers are more knowledgeable still.'

Almost at random he took up a pair of men's shoes and a pair of lady's shoes. He placed the two pairs side by side.

'These two are courtin'!' he whispered. 'That green mark on the heel of the girl's shoes came off the parsonage gate.'

He took up a heavy brogue.

'This man was at the fair of Molahiffe—cop the cowdung? And this man and his wife were at the seaside on Sunday—spot the sand? This fellow was dancing—notice the polished shoes? This man broke his ankle—one shoe worn and the other unworn.'

As I entered the shop the shoemaker rolled up his apron and settled down for an end-of-day chat. He gave me a lively account of old hotel days in Cork and Kerry, recounting practical jokes played with blue pills and seidlitz powders placed in nuptial chamber pots.

Kenmare of the fine suspension bridge, a seventeenth-century foundation by Sir William Petty, whose descendants, the Landsdownes, had residence at nearby Derreen, once had as basis for its economy an ironworks and a salmon fishery.

Lace is still made in the convent of the Poor Clares; those of recondite ecclesiastical learning will recall an eccentric but brilliant member of this community who once created a furore by leaping over the wall and writing a book called *The Nun of Kenmare*.

Touring New Yorkers are recommended to ride, or walk, up the nearby Roughty Valley to Kilgarvan, birthplace of the late Mike Quill, the ginger-tempered American labour leader, who by his intransigence in settling strikes, made the New Yorkers use their atrophied legs. And if the tourists do so let them not breathe one word against the memory of Mike for he is something of a local deity hereabouts.

And where better to end my Kenmare day than standing in a druids' circle with the local scholar clad in an ex-army camouflaged cape declaiming dramatically against the uproar of a shower?

West-south-west through Templenoe I drove, heading for Sneem and Cahirdaniel, all the while hugging the southern shore of the great Iveragh (pronounced Eve-Rah) Peninsula, and travelling on the southern arc of the Ring of Kerry. Here, English gentlemen, perhaps with memories of tea-planting and high colonial days, and

Dutch businessmen, too, are building homes, hoping to die at last in the gentle woods. Meanwhile we Irish continue to be apprehensive!

The traveller wishing to strike inland is urged to do so via Blackwater Bridge. The river of the name rises in Lough Brin, where Bran, genitive Brin, one of Finn Mac Cool's hounds, died fighting a monster. The river emerges at Moll's Gap, alias Windy Gap, one of the several mountain passes south of Killarney.

Sneem, birthplace of a great wrestler and hideway of General Charles de Gaulle, had as parish priest of former days a Father Michael Walsh, of whom Alfred Percival Graves wrote a ditty called *Father O'Flynn*.

Alfred Percival Graves was the father of the versatile Robert Graves, author of *I Claudius* etc., and of *The Reader over your Shoulder*, a book which is indispensable to anyone desirous of expressing himself accurately in the English language.

Unless I am mistaken, Robert Graves saw service in the British Forces in Ireland during our 'Troubles'. 'He was a gentleman', a guerrilla fighter told me. 'He and I made an informal peace-pact: we then proceeded to talk about literature.'

Two miles to the south-west is Parknasilla where stands the Great Southern Hotel, once the residence of Charles Graves, Protestant Bishop of Limerick, yet another brilliant member of the Graves family.

Near Castlecove and a few miles from the famous Staigue Fort, forking hay in a meadow, was the bright-eyed old man I had come to stalk. For Batt O'Shea was the last *seanchaí* of the area.

As I leaped over the fence one of his daughters nodded in the direction of a hayfork. Keeping as close as I dared to Batty I began turning the hay. Occasionally Batty addressed me in Irish and in English.

When it was time to rest we squatted against a hay-cock. Batty reddened his pipe. His daughter smiled affectionately.

Between puffs, Batty began: 'Did I ever tell you about the time

I operated on my mother for appendicitis?'

'No!' I said calmly (it is contrary to protocol to cast any doubt on the word of a seanchaí).

'I have the appendix above in a jamjar,' he said serenely.

Story after story then. Ancient stories that were Batty's by tradition; new stories he himself had made up. All in all it was a marvellous performance.

Later, I persuaded my friend, Éamon Kelly—for his part of the old man in Brian Friel's Broadway success *Philadelphia, Here I Come*, he was runner-up of the New York Critics Award for the best supporting role of the year—to pay a visit with me to Batt O'Shea. We talked the dawn in.

On Christmas Eve Éamon gathered my sons around the fire.

'Let's see if this story of Batty's will hold 'em . . .', he said. It did!

Presently, on Radio and TV, all Ireland listened to the stories of Éamon. To his unerring ear and eye he had added the actor's technique. So was the craft of the *seanchaí* revived in Ireland.

The circumambient mountains tend to diminish the size of prehistoric Staigue Fort, that saga in stone; once inside it, however, its magnitude is appreciated. Climbing to the top of the unmortared walls by one of the X-stairs, or crouching to enter one of the cells in the interior of the walls, is an experience in reliving history.

I am addicted to stone forts; very dear to me are memories of Mooghaun in Clare, of Dun Aongus in Inishmore of the Aran Islands, and of the Grianán of Aileach outside the City of Derry.

Cahirdaniel lies between the mountains and the sea. Here I stayed for a few days with the then pastor, Father Dillon, a man whose monument stands serried in the trees of Kenmare. Together we explored secret beaches where we found flawless scallop shells, together we read Séamus Fenton's *It All Happened* (a poor title for a rich book dealing with this locality), together we delved into the legends of local saint and scholar, ate lobster, discussed step-dancing and finally scaled almost perpendicular mountains—in a car.

Naturally we also discussed Derrynane, the nearby recently restored residence of Dan O'Connell, the Liberator.

The view north-westward from Coomakista Pass (The Hollow of the Treasure) is rare indeed. Turning my back on Kenmare River with its islands I looked northward over Ballinskelligs Bay. To my left below was Hog's Head, while almost due west of me lay Bolus Head. Under Bolus Head I had often fished with calm, cool David Fitzgerald, a member of one of the famous trawler families of south-west Kerry.

Northwards then, and into Waterville of the fine hotels, and of the equally fine angling, where Charlie Chaplin and his wife Oona, daughter of the immortal Eugene O'Neill, and their children do their summer fishing.

Until 1962 the terminal of the Commercial Cable Company, with its subsequent influx of English engineers ('graphers'), Waterville was referred to by Kerryfolk as 'Little England'. But the memory of folklorist Fionán McColum, at nearby Spunkane, and the Irish speaking areas upriver, vouch for a more authentic Ireland.

Across the bay at Ballinskelligs one sees in summertime the cliff-sides pied with what appear at a distance to be penguins. These are nuns who come here by the hundred to their summer lodges. For a visitor to lure a school of nuns into conversation can be as surprising as it is rewarding. Whatever mental reservations he may have had concerning the sexual problems of the celibate, he may even move to the conclusion that religious sublimation *does* exist, and that on occasion it can make its devotees supremely happy.

'What'll win the drag hunt?' I asked a young countryman.

We were high in the mountainous country north-west of Lough Currane. Close to a thousand people had assembled for the event.

'*The Brehig Hound*,' he whispered, 'But *Filemore* will run him close. They're both local champions.' By his intonation I knew that the man was primarily an Irish speaker.

A hundred beagles from all parts of Munster were led proudly up the field. Earlier in the day 'the drag', a sheep's liver sprinkled with

8 Gouganebarra, Co. Kerry

linseed or aniseed, had been pulled for perhaps 20 miles in a circle of rough country. Motor cars, one bearing a coronet on its doors, stretched out of sight along the mountain road.

Picking up the scent the hounds bayed like incarnate fury.

'*The Brehig Hound*,' I said, tendering my pound note to the solitary bookmaker in attendance. I got odds of four to one against my selection.

A man with an imperial beard dropped a flag. Mad tongue-music skirling, the hounds were off. My friend and I stood on a rock.

Shouts arose on all sides.

'*Filemore* has it!'

'*The Lough*'ll bate the world!'

'Your soul to the devil—watch *Brehig*!', my companion yelled.

Before long the hounds were five miles away on the mountainside.

At last, the rest of the pack having fallen far behind, there were only three in it with a chance. *Brehig* was to the fore, *The Lough* from Cork City was second and *Filemore* was a fair distance behind.

Four hundred yards from home, with *Brehig*, in front, I was counting my chickens as hatched, when the apparent winner went right off the trail taking the *Filemore* hound with him.

'Jasus!' my comrade shouted. His fingers bit through my plastic coat as if it were tissue paper.

The *Lough* came bounding forward to take up the lead. Suddenly *Brehig* discovered his mistake and returned to the point of error. *Filemore* yowled in his wake. By this time *The Lough* was within 50 yards of the winning post. A stream to cross and he was home!

That stream was his undoing. For the city hound stopped to drink! *Brehig* lolloped by, a weary but clear winner, leaving *Filemore* a dutiful second.

His eyes shining at this miracle of recovery my companion turned to face me. As he burst into a torrent of excited Irish, I replied in kind and he almost fell off the rock in astonishment.

The sea surface was calm except where the porpoises turned their

9 Fair Day at Mitchelstown, Co. Cork

black millwheels, as 60 of us left Ballinskelligs Pier in a fishing trawler. We were off to visit the Great Skellig.

We had in our company a Portuguese with a knowledge of Irish history, a children's nurse who lugged along two children in the belief that a day on the high spur of rock would cure their whooping cough, and representatives of various nationalities flushed from the local An Óige youth-hostel. We brought tobacco, stout, and newspapers for the lighthouse-keepers.

As the twin rocks of Skellig came into view, gannets plummetted from the sky and puffins played about the boat. Seals gaped at us and moved away. From the guano-white Little Skelligs, a miniature Fuji Yama, gannets rose by the clamorous thousand.

Close to the Great Skellig I thought of the Danes sacking the Rock monastery over a thousand years ago, slaying the entire community, and taking its treasures to Scandinavia. I thought too, of that quaint survival—a lampoon entitled 'The Skellig's List'—still recited in certain areas in Kerry, which, in doggerel, blisters love laggards who failed to take advantage of a time-lag in church calendar to be married out of season on the Rock.

At last the trawler nosed into a fissure in the lee of the cliff face. On a ledge above, the lighthouse-keepers waited for the boat to rise on the crest of a wave, so that one by one, we could leap into their arms.

This done, we moved upwards on the narrow roadway that wound along the rockside; after a meal in the whitewashed kitchen of the lighthouse building some of us ventured to climb upwards on an open stairway of 600 successive slabs on the cliff-face to reach at last the monastery in its walled-in plateau. As we climbed, fledgling sea-birds hissed and squawked at us.

Above we found a space 300 feet by 100 feet, with cells, oratories, crosses and a miniature church. Pathetically and incongruously amid the age-spotted slabs over dead abbots stood a cross marking the grave of a lighthouse-keeper's wife who had died here in childbirth.

To stand in the enclosure is dimly to gain an insight into the minds of the Celtic monks whose anchoritic code was papally condemned for its severity.

Looking over the sheer cliff, I saw far, far below a boy curled up asleep on the red ribs of a currach. His father, presumably, had moved off in another boat to raise lobster pots.

Standing there I recalled other seapinnacles dedicated to St Michael: St Michael's Mount off the Cornish coast and Mont San Michel in Brittany.

South-west of the high Skellig enclosure, and a little below its level, is a scree called Christ's Saddle. Above this towers the higher of the two island peaks, once the focal point of a medieval pilgrimage of penance. The mind boggles at penitents in their thousands climbing this monstrous crag, shrugging up a rock chimney called The Needle's Eye, clawing up a vertical rock, straddling a stone spindle and finally inching forward above a drop of 714 feet to kiss a cross crudely graven in stone.

The road northward from Ballinskelligs passes through the glen of Finan the Leper, a valley where the world seems completely occluded.

I recall attending the last mass in the old church of the glen, a building that embodied fragments of an early Christian monastery. The church was so tiny that 60 or 70 worshippers crowded it to the door.

I drove into the mysterious cloud that hung low on Coumaneaspuig Mountain and later descended to find Portmagee and the new bridge to Valentia Island outlined in sunlight. Appraising the view I snatched time to consider the plight of the poet who lost his books in the crossing to the island and who bemoaned his drowned library in an Irish song that is still remembered.

Due east then to rejoin the main road of The Ring, a further journey northward of a few miles, thereafter to leave the main highway to drive west to Reenard Point, the place of embarkation for the Valentia Island ferry. The name Valentia is not Spanish: it is simply a romantic rendering of *Béal Inse*, the Irish name for the nearby sound.

A Valentia saga, often recounted, has to do with the making, after four abortive attempts, of the island the eastern terminal of the first transatlantic cable.

The sea cliffs of Valentia rise to 800 feet. At Glenleam, once residence of the Knights of Kerry, there is a disused slate quarry. Latterly the island is renowned for the Gaelic football virtuosity of one Michael O'Connell, who brought the native football code to its highest pitch of graceful perfection.

Cahirciveen town is overshadowed by the mountain of Beentee: the colossus that is its local church, named for the Liberator, is called The O'Connell Memorial Church. Excavated Leacanbuaile Fort, a couple of miles from the town defines a community centre of the 8th or 9th century.

Passing through the town I dallied to discuss current drama with playwright Pauline Maguire, and to sing in a tavern called 'The Plow', one of Cahirciveen-born Sigerson Clifford's fine songs from *Ballads of a Bogman*. In a moment of vexation another of Cahirciveen's literary sons called his native town 'a street of parasitic shopkeepers', but this simply indicated the existence of a minor family disagreement and was readily forgotten.

Kells, a cove to the north-east and a leafgreen, mossy, fuchsialighted, fox-gloved place, is shaped like a horse-shoe and has a beach lying between the points of the shoe.

One moonlit night a friend and I heard through the open window of one of the few houses in Kells, voices rehearsing Synge's *Riders to the Sea*. We walked through an open doorway along a hallway and then knocked softly on the room door. Summoned to come in, we entered a large room to find a group of young women, obviously sisters, reading the play—seemingly for their own pleasure.

My friend and I were handed scripts, male parts were indicated, and the play went on till Maurya's poetic outcry of resignation brought our impromptu reading to an end.

The reading of Synge by the Murphy sisters in such a context was apposite, for the playwright had lived with the Harris family in nearby Mountain Stage and had drawn inspiration from the area.

Relaxing Glenbeigh was just ahead; situated on the edge of an area sorely striken in Famine Days it is now, by an ironic but admirable twist of circumstance, internationally noted for the excellence of its hotel fare. Before reaching Glenbeigh I swung left off the Ring and after a few miles reached bracing Rossbeigh, one of the most photographed beaches in Ireland.

For me, Rossbeigh has always meant a seat by a stone wall high on the cliff road with the exalting and exulting backdrop of the Dingle Mountains across the bay. And my being roused from reverie by a call to a cottage tea and pancakes from a gracious old lady called Molly Lyne long since called to her reward.

But the tranquillity of mind engendered by this area is evanescent: for if there's one thing that makes my gorge rise it is a roadside tourist-trap baited folksily for the naïve visitor. This sometimes takes the form of wicker panniers slung across a donkey's back with a country lad playing the part of nature's unspoiled son of the moorland.

Motor cars stop and seek the ambler's permission to take a photograph. And of course with 'I'll l'ave it to yourself, sir'—there's a tip to follow.

This practice is not peculiar to Ireland nor to my native Kerry: I have seen it in Dinard in France: a girl planted at a window whenever a busful of tourists arrives. Then pseudo-artlessly, she raises her voice in peasant song.

Puck Fair is held at Killorglin on the river Laune each year on three successive days, Gathering Day, Binding Day and Scattering Day, in the second week of August, generally on August 10th, 11th and 12th.

The focal point of the first day is the crowning and enthronement on a high platform, in the presence of 30,000 jubilant spectators, of an overwhelmingly male (or puck) goat alleged to have been captured wild in the nearby McGillycuddy Reeks.

The coronation of the goat is the signal for the commencement of three days-and-nights of revelry. Meanwhile, a horse-and-cattle fair begins on the local green.

As with the Round Towers, Freudian-conditioned interpreters read all sorts of phallic and male-capric connotations into this ceremony.

Chauvinistic authorities, in accounting for the origins of the fair, speak of a vigilant billy-goat (*à la* the Capitoline geese) warning sleeping warriors of the arrival of Cromwell; the more prosaically-slanted state that the ceremonies had their origin in the offering for sale of a single billygoat in an otherwise deserted fair.

In essence, Puck Fair is a venting of a dammed-up energy on the part of ebullient Kerrymen. If one stands outside the circle of earthen enjoyment, one is appalled at the cowdung, the cries of the deformed and at the inordinate consumption of black-brown porter. If one is inside the circle one is enthralled by an untrammelled display of animal spirits.

The travelling people of Ireland foregather here; the authorities try to prevent the banked fires of ancient feuds from bursting into conflagration. And for three days and nights the pubs vibrate with music, most of them remaining open the full round of the clock.

And this seems as a suitable time as any, by moving directly into Killarney, to close the 109-mile-lasso of the Kerry Ring and to admit having given inadequate tidings of the powerful countryside within its noose, with mountain passes like Ballaghoisin and Ballaghbeama —names like blows in the face.

Killarney! Hear its detractors first. They say that for all its beauty Killarney is an untypical gombeenish bailiwick, where every citizen stands poised to fleece the unwary visitor.

This is the facile verdict of asperity. There is much more to Killarney than that.

Take the jarvey on his prehistoric vehicle—the jaunting car. Generally speaking, he is a good-humoured, hard-working man, his mind polished by contact with people of many nationalities. His scale of charges is rigidly controlled. True, he will tell you hoary stories like that of the young man who dived into the mountain tarn called the Devil's Punchbowl and failed to come up: a fortnight later his mother got a letter from Australia, asking her to send on his clothes.

But it's all so naïve as to be close to innocence compared with harsher standards of tourism obtaining in more grasping territories.

Flora? In Killarney the botanist will find arbutus, eucalyptus and magnolia; if he is lucky he may chance upon *Trichomanes radicans*, the rare Killarney fern.

Background? Civil War history has been written in blood on the steps of the Great Southern Hotel: in this building too, the loyal and royal of Kerry immured themselves when in 1867 the Fenians came marching on snow-sodden brogues from Cahirciveen with a tattered green rag fluttering over them.

Fauna? Here are the ancient red deer of Ireland descended from those hunted by the Fianna. In paddocks beside lake-water, graze small black barrel-shaped Kerry cows: over the centuries, this hardy breed has developed immunity to disease so that its milk is reckoned tubercle-free.

Waterfalls? See Torc and Derrycunnihy Cascades. Gracious Houses? See Muckross House with its gardens of rhododendrons and azaleas and pause to praise the bounty of the Bourne-Vincents who bestowed it on the Irish nation.

Excursion? At Kate Kearney's Cottage at the entrance to the Gap of Dunloe you will find that mild-mannered, erudite man, Jerome Coffey—an example of the right man in the right place. The ponies stomp at his door ready to take you through the Gap to the mouth of the Black Valley, with Carntuohill, Ireland's highest mountain, lording it against the sky.

Legend? The ghost of The O'Donoghue rides the lake on a white charger. Ross Castle of the O'Donoghues, quite close to the town, was taken from Lord Muskerry in 1652, because its superstitious garrison believed in the legend that Ross would be taken only from the sea. The Cromwellians learned of this belief, and, under Ludlow, launched floating batteries on Lough Leane. Then, an Irish 'Birnam being come to Dumsinane', the credulous defenders capitulated. In the monastery isle of Inisfallen, close by, were written The Annals of Inisfallen.

Liars? Close to the tall cross in Killegy beside Muckross, lies in an unmarked grave, the mortal remains of the eighteenth century Rudolf Ehrich Raspe, the Hanoverian mining engineer and embezzler, who wrote *The Travels and Adventures of Baron Munchausen*, the world's most renowned fictional liar.

Polite fiction? This is evidenced by the transfer of the locale of Boucicault's melodrama. *The Colleen Bawn*, from the Shannon estuary where the Colleen Bawn was really murdered, to the more picturesque Killarney lake and woodland.

Poets? Still beloved in local memory is racy rascal-poet, Owen Roe O'Sullivan (it is said that he died as a result of having risen from his Killarney death-bed to chase a good-looking servant maid), and his fellow poet, Piaras Ferriter, one of the Norman overlords who became *Hibernicis ipsis Hiberniores* and who was treacherously hanged on Martyr's Hill, close to the Railway Station entrance. Aodhagán Ó Rathaille, too, another fine poet in Irish (as a boy he once read Greek upside down in a bookseller's shop window in Cork), is buried in Muckross Abbey, as also is poet Geoffrey of the O'Donoghues.

There is so much to say about Killarney. But I end my day sprawling on sweet clover among the tombstones of lofty Aghadoe Churchyard, with the right eye of Brickeen Bridge in the distance to delight my senses and the red-roofed Germanic bungalows of the near lake-edge to add vinegar to the dish of my almost perfect day.

He was the wild Colonial Boy, Jack Duggan was his name

So begins the ballad of an Australian outlaw born in Castlemaine, a village not far from Killorglin. The song opens up discussion on other outlaws of Irish blood: Jesse James, whose ancestors hailed from Asdee, Ballylongford, County Kerry and Ned Kelly of Australia, whose father hailed from the slopes of the Galtee Mountains on the Tipperary-Cork border.

West in Inch, a three-mile beach skirts a spit of massive dunes which act as a bar to the great wind, was filmed *The Playboy of the Western World* with Siobhán McKenna as Pegeen Mike, a Welsh Christy Mahon, and all the tinkers of Kerry as extras.

The road west on the southern shore of the Dingle Peninsula runs under the hills and on the edge of the cliffs. Here I saw an Indian wearing a turban walk across a field to a fishing stream; further west a peacock and a peahen greeted me on the roadway. I struck inland by the leap of a salmon stream, and strove upwards through a plenitude of fuchsia to Annascaul, a village on the main road between Tralee (20 miles) and Dingle (10 miles) which is making the most of its perch in the hills. A public-house at the western end of the village was once owned by Tom Crean, who took part in Scott's expedition to the South Pole.

West, ever west. . . . Memories of the patriot, Thomas Ashe from Kinnard, leader of the Easter Rising of 1916 in north County Dublin and who died as a result of forcible feeding in Mountjoy Jail, stir up old recriminations in a land that, 'unfree shall never be at peace'.

Viewed from the end of the pier the huddle that is Dingle town offers an odd artistic unity. The town *qua* town is not endowed with an indelible sense of beauty, but it does hold the key to a vital old-world life. This is especially true when the people from the Irish-speaking area west of the town flood in on the occasion of fair, market or races.

As I walk past the Catholic presbytery I note 'the high house of Dingle' to which Count Rice, an officer of the Irish Brigade in the service of France, planned to bring the ill-fated Marie Antoinette for sanctuary.

And it was in Dingle that I saw the maggie-man. A maggie-man is the chap with the cork-blackened face, who at country festivals, crouches in a barrel provided with peep-holes. Some distance away his wife sells timber balls and challenges the holidaymakers to buy them and knock the head off her husband.

Meanwhile, her husband provocatively bobs up and down in his barrel.

I saw this bloody challenge fully taken up at Dingle Races: I still hear the roar of triumph as the timber ball split open the maggie-man's forehead.

The wife? She was a woman of rare business acumen! For by refusing to allow her husband to wipe his bloodied countenance, she attracted a large crowd and did a roaring business.

But this is not the only Dingle woman I recall.

An old woman sat up in bed in Dingle Hospital. Her hair was carefully combed.

As she sat in state, her sightless eyes vaguely alternating with her ears in sifting the occasions of the ward, a flock of schoolboys crowded to the stairhead and spilled quietly into the room.

As four boys walked forward, nuns and nurses watched carefully.

One of the four boys spoke in Irish. 'Peig Sayers', he said, 'We offer you this small gift as a mark of our esteem . . .' *chun méid ár measa a chur in iúl duit. . . .*

He thrust his gift into the blind woman's hands.

The tears came down the old features. Peig Sayers of the Blasket Islands, one of the great narrators of the wonder-tales of Gaelic Ireland, and a superb natural actress, was on her deathbed.

In gratitude she stretched out her hands to read and caress the boy's face.

Dr Delargy, that great scholar-head of the Irish Folklore Comission, has stated that if all the Fenian tales in Ireland's tradition had been lost, this old woman could have restored them from her memory of oral tradition.

But west it is, skirting the edge of Ventry Harbour where in the legend of prehistory, the King of the World fought a battle with the King of Ireland. The list of prehistoric remains in this locality includes clocháns or beehive-shaped cells, cirques, pillarstones, promontory forts, chamber tombs and cairns, besides some of the most ancient Christian ruins in the land.

Leaving the Fahan group of prehistoric remains on my left, I now head for Slea Head. The road runs under an intimidating cliff mountain with a similar cliff below me and between me and the sea; I splash across a brook which appears to be flowing *over* rather than *under* a bridge, and at last reach the space by the white-washed Calvary at the end, not merely, of the Dingle Peninsula, but of the island that is Ireland and indeed of the continent that is Europe.

Mount Eagle rears above: the road runs *en corniche* along the southern slopes of the mountain. Below me is the coloured sea with its seven islands of wonder.

The Great Blasket Island has produced three eminent writers in Peig Sayers, Tomás Ó Críomhthain and Muiris Ó Súilleábhain. Each wrote originally in Irish, each told in individual idiom the tale of a tightly-knit community in close communication with the elemental forces of sea, stone and sky.

Much of the natural wonder of this area comes through even in translation into English; writers and scholars like Robin Flower of England, Karl Marstrander of Germany, and Professor Von Sydow of Sweden, drew sustenance from the qualities of spirit these islanders displayed.

Tucked under the cliff edge at the very end of the Dingle Peninsula is the pocket handkerchief beach that I love best in all Ireland. Named Coumeemole, its tide is as many-mooded as a woman, so beware that it does not smilingly take your life.

Cows descend the spiral pathway to drink where they have drunk for centuries: if the shoe is occasionally smeared with cowdung, the rock walls of erratic quartz offer compensation in the glint of the Kerry 'diamond'.

Kruger Kavanagh, of nearby Dunquin, is one of Ireland's great personalities. He is a remarkable man with a torrent of knowledge that pours forth in Irish and in English.

Drinking tea in a nearby cottage I glanced out the window; standing amid fuchsia bushes at the gable of his own cottage, I saw fisherman Micheál Ó Gaoithín lost in contemplation.

Micheál, a poet, and son of the great Peig Sayers, illustrates the ancient Irish belief that genius descends from the female line to the male line and vice versa.

'How are you, Micheál?' I said to him in Irish.

'In my mind I am attempting to reconcile a conflict', he said quietly.

'What conflict?'

'The conflict in literature that lies between realism and romanticism.' 'Sometimes', Micheál went on, 'I think that romanticism will win the day. But realism is closer to the truth, and should prevail!'

Out from Dunquin Pier I go with Dr Maurice Harmon, that rare judge of literature, his wife and children: we were Blasket-bound in a black-backed canvas currach.

The Blaskets were hidden in fog. Presently, Dunquin, Ireland, Europe fell away and we rode as ghosts on ghostly water. Orange nylon lines and hooks garishly feathered brought in mackerel to thump the ribs of our frail vessel. At last, cormorants standing on a wraith of rock indicated Beginnish; later we rode into a ghostly cove under the cliffs of the deserted Great Blasket.

Up the lichened slipway we moved with its transverse lines of rock strata. Beside the caved-in schoolhouse mushrooms were luminous. Here Maurice, his wife and children and I sat down and lunched.

Wreaths of fog swirled about us and followed us along the pathway where surprisingly we met a Professor from Harlech who engaged us in conversation about *Twenty Years A-growing*. A collapsing rabbit hole above a ghostly beach almost broke my leg; later still the fog lifted from the face of the sea and there in the east the mainland emerged in sunlit clarity.

Moving belatedly towards the slip to join the others, I found a form as black as Lucifer confronting me on the narrow pathway. I suddenly realized that it was a frogman and recalled with a start that for a considerable time a treasure-hunt had been in progress in the deep-running sound, with the object of finding the treasure of the

Santa Maria de la Rosa, one of two vessels of the Spanish Armada lying for centuries on the ocean floor.

On the mainland again, the climb is ever higher on the road to the north. This is an area of barbaric sunsets, each unique in its ice-blue silver edged with royal purple or with smoking gold. Between me and the setting sun one island resembled a dead prince of Egypt lying in state . . . hands folded on umbilical protuberance, head, shoulders, face, toes—the whole a deflated yet dignified corpse.

Ever upwards to the turn at Clogher Head, known locally as *Casadh na Gráige*, there to view Clogher Strand below me and beyond, sweeping upwards to the sky in ballet grace, Sybil Head and the Three Sisters. In the northwest Brandon Mountain smoked a peaceful pipe above the glazed window that was Smerwick Bay.

Beside Clogher Cove stands the remains of Piaras Ferriter's castle. After 750 years of residence, Ferriters are still here in strength and are still attached to poetry. Tucked away in a corner of Smerwick Bay is *Béal Bán* (White Mouth) where Eileen Ferriter McWilliams holds court in her guest house and where one is likely to meet an archbishop, a Harley Street specialist, an Icelandic scholar, or, as I did once, the members of a noble French family, the O'Mahonys – Wild Geese lured home to Ireland by 'Pope' O'Mahony, now dead, one of Ireland's rarest spirits.

Beyond *Béal Bán* lies Fort del Oro or, in Irish, *Dún an Óir*. The place was so named for a Frobisher vessel laden with pyrites or 'fool's gold', wrecked here in 1578. Today, the fort is merely an aromatic grassy headland most apt for day-dreaming.

In 1580, Fort del Oro saw the massacre of over 600 Italian and Spanish soldiers by the English commander, Lord Grey de Wilton. The bodies were flung in such profusion from the clifftop that the tide lip became choked with dead.

Raleigh and Mackworth were the captains in charge of the butchery: Mackworth was later taken by the O'Connors of Offaly, mutilated and flayed to death.

But Clogher Strand it is! And first, '*Beo go deo!*' or 'Alive for ever!' traditional singer Seán Hoare of Clogher cries out as for the first time he hears his own voice recorded in traditional song. In the room off the kitchen Seán Ó Riada, Ireland's major modern composer, now resident in the Ballyvourney area of Cork and a man skilled in the classical and the traditional modes, had spent night after night composing music to delight audiences yet unborn.

Ballyferriter village with its three or four pubs, a *Garda* Station, a sweetshop or two, a butcher's shop, a guest-house or two, and a hotel, is the centre of an exclusive club comprised of those determined that the older Ireland shall not die.

Here in a dim crowded pub one night many years ago a countryman tapped me on the knee, and whispered *Tá Dylan Thomas anso,*—'Dylan Thomas is here'.

The Welsh poet was part of the frieze of powerful fishermen seated directly opposite me. Not understanding what was said, nevertheless he listened carefully to the ebb and flow of the conversation.

Old Father Tom of Ballyferriter was one of the last of the character parish priests of Kerry and one who provided an antidote to the tonsure-suited boy-priests of today so over-eager to appear 'all things to all men'.

His Roman collar was fastened at the back with defunct sticking plaster. His stock was soiled, his coat was green. His blackthorn stick was too short to touch the ground. His steelrimmed glasses were cracked and misted so that he had to tilt back his head to look at you through a clear corner. His face was white-bristled. His hat was a museum piece. Before someone in ecclesiastical authority got on his trail he had a bright green meat safe nailed to the gable of his church.

High in the rafters inside his church and directly above the sanctuary lamp, swallows—or was it martins?—had built their nests. At the consecration of the Mass the birds sometimes shot through holes in the window and screamed above the worshippers' heads.

On the roadway, Father Tom stopped to chat with everyone who passed. There was a bike called 'The Priest's Bike'—this you borrowed if you wished to get past him in a hurry—the next wayfarer rode it back.

How can I explain to anyone what a beneficent influence this wise, kindly, almost omniscient old man had on me? Scarcely a day passes but I think of him with the deepest affection.

When he died in Tralee, there was talk of his body resting overnight in great St John's Church of that town. But, a rare bravery this in Ireland, his parishioners in the west telephoned the Bishop and said stoutly, 'We want Father Tom to rest in 'Ferriter tonight.'

And they took him over the hills in triumph and rested him overnight in his own church. I like to think that there were ghostly swallows screaming over his coffin in the morning hours.

And now for mention of that perfect overturned (I almost said clinker-built) boat of corbelled unmortared stone—Gallarus Oratory, a vessel of sanctity that requires little caulking after a thousand years. Gallarus is about two miles east of Ballyferriter.

Stand in its gloom until your eyes grow accustomed to the pink hazel colour of the interior, then slowly close your eyes and move back in thought a full millennium, opening them again to imagine yourself a tonsured Celtic monk of the 8th or 9th century.

But we Irish are careless sons-of-bitches, and the pool of water that had seeped through the doorway set me swearing in that holy of holies. (Things are much better now!) To cure my ill-temper, I repaired to the ruins of Kilmalkedar Church, about two miles to the north, a superb example of twelfth century Hiberno-Romanesque architecture, with its most notable carved stones nearby.

And if the Martello Tower-crowned clifftop to the north challenges you, the view from the top will compensate for lost sweat. As a boy, I often took with me on my upward journey by the Camel's Path a stone for the hillside cairn that lies below the tower. The story goes that a camel was employed to draw stones to the tower's building: this was one of the many coastal bastions against a threatened Napoleonic invasion.

Returned to Dingle town through an area remarkable for its geological unconformities the road I inevitably took from thence was via Conor Pass. At the layby at the top of the Pass I looked down on a wide area of landscape festooned with cloud-smoke and shot with rainbow light. Halfway up a mountain flank a deep pool was mendicantly held in a lap of stone. Chilling, odourless mist drove down in trails from Brandon's peak, beneath which lay the silver of lakes, each with its gleaming stream issuing from it.

Suddenly the searchlight of the sun pierced the great grey sky, moved across the unprofitable valley floor and lighted up both the green of aftergrass and the gold of over-ripe corn. For one marvellous minute the sunlight transfigured a red-oxided hayshed.

Due eastward it is, still travelling on the northern coast of the peninsula.

Smell the onions in the wind? That's Castlegregory, sitting at the head of a spit of marram-grown sandy land that thrusts north to the Maharee Islands—isles that have remains both megalithic and Christian. On all sides are neat beaches begging for company.

Here I took time out to go fishing in nearby semi-tidal Lough Gill. Hurray! in my very first cast, the instant my Mepps lure hit the water, I hooked a fighting 2½ lb. trout which I played and killed.

It was in a Castlegregory pub that an old man called Hoare once sang for me a rousing ballad of the 1798 Rebellion, *When the Gallant Frenchmen landed in Mayo*. The singer's surname bridged a gap of almost 400 years; here in 1580 on his way to reduce Fort del Oro, Lord Deputy Gray, in company with Sir Walter Raleigh and Edmund Spenser, lodged at the castle of Hugh Hoare. Hoare's wife, rather than entertain the enemies of her country, ran the wine barrels dry and was killed by her angry husband who (here the cup of tragedy runneth over) later dropped dead in horror.

By way of contrast, Cathair Chonrdoí, a mountain south of Camp village has a tale from the mists of history which concerns a faithless wife who betrayed a hill-top fortress to her husband's foes.

10 An old Kerrywoman

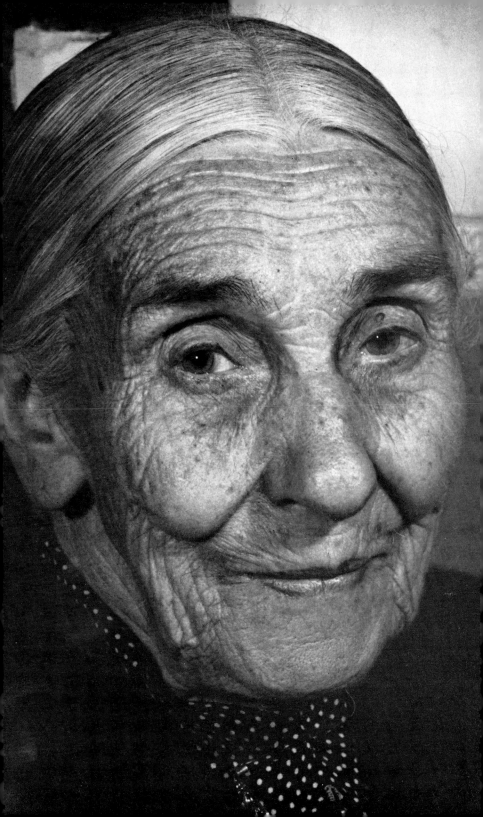

Entering a farm kitchen, 'How do I go up?' I asked.

The startled occupants were so busy disembowelling a mountain sheep, the red of raddled wool mingling with the beast's blood, that the instructions I received were vague.

'How do I go up?' I asked a man standing on the roadside: he told me that he had just returned from Hartford, Connecticut to end his days in his native townland.

'Better not get caught up there,' he said shifting his tobacco quid to the other cheek, at the same time indicating the way to the escarpment, 2,000 feet aloft, above which the fort of Cathair Chonraoí stood.

As we chatted I looked down at a stream flowing at our feet, the course of which I could trace upwards to its source below the summit of the mountain. 'Is this the Finglas stream?' I asked. 'Yes!' the man said. 'That's Finglas – the White Stream.'

I then recalled that the chieftain's wife had sent out secret word to her husband's enemies: 'Attack when the stream runs white!' One night, with the garrison drunk, the woman had overturned churns of milk into the water of the brook. Reading the signal of the white water, the besiegers stormed upwards and took the fort, tying the chieftain to a pillar before putting him to death.

Up I puffed and huffed, struggling through a strange mountain light. For middleaged me the last 200 feet was pure hell! So still was the air that every voice raised in the village of Camp below reached my ears with clarity.

At last, panting, I sat among the ragged remains of the prehistoric fortress. In that piercing purple-blue light it was most evocative. A pit of 1,000 feet yawned below me and the sea showed metallic to the north.

As a menacing bale of cloud moved eastward along the mountain tops, I beat a gut-jolting retreat downwards.

As the daylight waned I looked down into a valley basin called *Gleann na nGealt*, the Glen of the Insane, where all the deranged of Ireland were believed to have once repaired for cure. Later still I stood by the slab-rock in Glenash which, according to tradition, covers the grave of Princess Fais, a woman of prehistory, whose people were here defeated by the mythological Tuatha Dé Danaan.

From the next field a man watching shouted at me: 'I'm going to dig her up and find her go-o-o-old.' Laughing he moved off into the dusk.

There's still a broken windmill near Tralee that I must tell you of, and after that there's a journey to be made to the north of the county.

> *Whoever is goin' on the Amerikay line,*
> *Be at the windmill in ten minutes' time!*
> *Some of ye laughin' and some of ye cryin',*
> *For that's the way till the end of time.*
> *Ding, dong, bell!*

This was the cry of the bellman in the immediate post-famine years as he summoned the starving emigrants from Tralee to board the boats at Blennerville and row out to the open sea where coffin ships awaited to transport them to the New World.

Tralee, a town made famous by a rose, is a bustling place with the accent on the printing industry, the shoe industry and the manufacture of ball bearings. It also brags of some fine tourist hotels.

Sliabh Mish towers above it: on the mountainside is the grave of Queen Scotia, for whom, if legend is not a liar, the Scottish are named. But we Irish were the original *Scoti*: when we crossed the Sea of Moyle to found the new Kingdom of Dalriada, we extended our cognomen into Scotland. Later we abandoned the homeland name in favour of Ir-land or Ireland.

The Earls of Desmond had their major castle at Tralee. The place suffered as a result of the revolt of the fifteenth Earl; on its surrender, the English Denny family took possession of the town. In 1641 Piaras Ferriter reduced it after a bitter siege; later it became a pyre beneath the torches of that almost incredible character, 'Burner' Murrough O'Brien.

In 1583, the last Earl of Desmond was trailed to Glanageenty and there slain by a soldier called O'Kelly, and his head sent off to top a spike on London Bridge. The Earl's grave lies eight miles to the east of Tralee; sometimes when the wind from sea cries around this lonely valley, the local people refer to it as 'The Desmond howl'.

The Tralee of today is concerned with the organization of its annual Festival of the Rose designed to seek out a girl who approximates closest to the ideal—'It was not her beauty alone that won me'—a description of the maiden commemorated in Poet Mulchinock's song, 'The Rose of Tralee'. The Festival spills over to include the whole County of Kerry.

Five miles north-west of Tralee, on the road to Ballyheigue, is Ardfert, once the site of a monastery founded by St Brendan the Navigator. As I visited the village, swing-boats and hobby-horses stood up in violent but vital contrast to the pearl-grey ruined cathedral walls.

St Brendan was born a few miles from the port of Fenit. Legend tells that the plan of his monastery was seized by a crow; following the flight of the bird the saint saw the parchment flutter down to a limestone knoll beside Ardfert—the Height of Miracles. On this hillock the monastery, and later the Cathedral, was built.

Close to the north-west corner of the cathedral a round tower stood until, in 1771, it was blown down in a storm; then, presumably in good old Irish fashion, the stones were taken away to make road metal. Among other interesting ruins in the locality is that of a Franciscan friary founded in 1253 by Thomas Fitzmaurice, first Baron of Kerry.

Not far from Ardfert, beside Banna Strand, is McKenna's Fort, one of the many thousands of circular earthen dykes found all over the Irish countryside, each of which once enclosed prehistoric wattle-and-daub dwellings. In this particular fort, one of the most tragic and noble figures of Irish modern history, Sir Roger Casement, later executed, was arrested on Good Friday 1916, after he had landed from a German submarine.

In the axilla of Kerry Head is an up-and-coming little seaside resort called Ballyheigue, a sunny place with an extensive sandy beach, which, as an item of historical interest reminds one of the looting, by the local landlords if you please! of a valuable Danish cargo of silver, held for safety within the walls of Ballyheigue Castle.

The castle, built for the Crosbie family, still looks eyeless over the great bay.

In mid-bay stands a rock called Mucklach which gave rise to the Irish proverb, quoted of a hungry man, 'He'd eat Mucklach'. Between Mucklach and the shore waves were forever breaking in an otherwise calm sea.

Local people have it that beneath this troubled spot lies a graveyard, once parted from the land by erosion; tradition also tells of bodies being left on the shores to be taken at night by the waves for interment in the subterranean burying-spaces of Church Banks.

Ballyheigue was once held by the Norman Cantillon family who also owned a castle at Ballingarry, five miles to the north. In 1602-1603 Ballingarry Castle was held by Red Garret Stack; later it fell into the hands of the planters.

A member of this Cantillon family made an eminent name as an economist. The name persists in this area even to the present day, as indeed also does the Norman surname Stack, which originated in its Irish context in the Crotta-Kilflynn area to the north-west and for whom Stacks' Mountains were named. Wherever in the world there abides a person with the surname Stack, likely he can trace his lineage back to a north Kerry forebear.

From the top of Kerry head there is a fine view over the Shannon estuary; here also is a coast as natural as it appeared in the beginning of the world. On a coastal monument to men killed in the Irish Civil War appears the unusual name Reginald Hathaway—that of an English soldier who deserted from the British army to fight with the Irish, and later found his death in the ranks of the Anti-Treaty or Republican forces. South of Ballyduff village stands the excellent Round Tower of Rattoo. And Ballybunion lies to the north beyond the Cashen, by which name the salmon-teeming estuary of the river Feale is known.

Let me tell you of the Irish version of the sauna bath—as you may be tempted to experience it in the seaside resort called Ballybunion.

Bladderwrack seaweed rests on the bottom of the bathtub. Mike turns on a tap; the instant the steaming sea-water strikes the sea-weed, the mixture turns into a viscid liquid. As the tub fills, the wrack grows pale—if desired, the brew may be tempered with cold sea-water from another faucet. At last you step in, recline, and experience one of the finest sensations imaginable!

Use the bladderwrack as a slithery-soothery sponge; you are then coated from head to foot in what could well be heated vaseline. Every movement of your body is now a sensuous caress.

Later, rise gingerly from the bath. Careful! Don your bathing trunks. Throw open the door of the little bath-house and, still steam-ing, race down the steps to the beach. Career past the parasols of the visitors and hurl yourself headlong into the breakers. Rise and find that your body has turned boiled-lobster red.

But I double-warn you; don't do this if you have any equivocal zig-zags on your cardiograph!

Ballybunion's twin beaches and its atmosphere of levitation charac-terize a town tagged with what foreigners see as a hilariously funny name.

Along the cliff face above the ladies' beach over the caves, may be discerned a stripe of natural sulphur running almost parallel to the ground. More than one hundred years ago the friction of falling rocks set this sulphur vein on fire, thus giving rise to the facetious reference to the Kerry volcano.

Schoolmaster Liam Browne, whom I interrupted as he was trans-lating Virgil's Aenid into Irish, and I walked the cliff-top beside his house. We saw the phenomenon of millions of starlings forming and reforming, wheeling and diving, above a cliff-cleft where, as its older name in Irish *Scoilt na Druide* (or 'Starlings' Chasm') vouches, starlings have nested for centuries. As I walked along I thought too, of antlers dug up in the strand of Ballyeigh south of the fine golf course where legend also tells that a herd of red deer was once drowned.

But Ballyeigh has far bloodier associations; here early in the last century some of the last faction flights of Ireland were fought. Fireside tales still recall these ferocious encounters.

Pause to view Knockanore (*Cnoc an Áir* or the Hill of Slaughter) to the east, a hill which figures prominently in the tales of the Fenian cycle.

'If your god and my father wrestled on the top of that hill, and if your god laid my father Fionn on his back, then I would believe he was the stronger man.'

So said Oisín to St Patrick after the hero had returned to Ireland, having spent 300 years with Niamh of the Golden Hair in the Land of Ever-Young.

Two or three miles to the north of Ballybunion is the little strand of Beale (Irish *Béal*, a mouth). Ideal for a picnic, its sandhills guard the Shannon's mouth. Here I searched the sky in vain for the vision of Killstaheen, where the old people aver they have often seen as a mirage on summer evenings. 'Once I saw in the sky the image of a young woman hanging out clothes in an alleyway of a south American town,' an old man solemnly assured me.

Running on its monorail the little locomotive puffed to a halt. 'What is it?' the English lady opposite me enquired. I was a boy at the time.

'It's my red hat,' I said dutifully, 'It fell out the window on the way to Ballybunion.'

'Child! Is this train really stopping to recover it?'

'The engine driver is a friend of my mother's', I said.

Meanwhile Paddy Boyle the guard, Jackie Reidy the engine-driver and Michael Walsh the ticket-checker were searching the permanent way: 'Hurray!' the passengers cheered, 'They've found it.' The hat was handed in the window. I solemnly drew it down around my ears.

'Well!' breathed the English lady.

The time was 1919. The train was the Lartigue monorail, joining Listowel to Ballybunion. Years before, Monsieur Lartigue himself had arrived from France to see his ingenious toy come to snorting life. Constructed on the principle of pannier-baskets balanced on a donkey's back, it ran on an elevated V-shaped rail. The windows faced outwards—one side at times into blinding sunlight—and the din of the wheels at ear-level was conversation-killing.

Cross my heart! equipoise had to be established by manipulating sacks of sugar and half-cwt weights. Rascals living beside the only acclivity on the line frequently soaped the top rail and whooped with glee as the train hissed to a halt.

In 1922-1923 the quaintest railroad in the world became a shuttlecock in the bitter game called Civil War. Even at that it survived a few years longer and finally ended its days in the breaker's yard.

There's still a model in the school in Listowel. If the real thing had survived what a tourist attraction it would now be!

You can't believe a man's oath when he talks about his native town: so discount accordingly what I say about Listowel.

In Listowel we have a literary tradition nurtured by a rare bookseller called Dan Flavin who corresponded with Axel Munthe when the young Swedish doctor, then in Naples, had just written his first book, *Letters from a Mourning City*.

Many years ago Dan sent to the Shakespeare Press in Paris for copies of the first edition of Joyce's *Ulysses*; a copy of the massive uncut book he thrust into my boyish hand and said: 'Read that and don't let anyone see it.'

The word *Walpurgisnacht* almost bowled me over. And, wheeoo! when I think of my callow mind struggling with the enormities of Molly Bloom's soliloquy, I feel suddenly assured that boys are tougher than the proverbial hames-strap.

Dan and a fine classical college named for the Archangel Michael, produced a tribe of writers in our small community.

In Listowel we also have, in the last week of September, a week of racing and high-junketting culminating in a wren-boy festival.

Good fishing too in the Feale river, and an open square in which Parnell at a meeting in mid-September of 1891 is alleged to have used the famous words: 'No man has the right to fix the boundaries of a nation.'

A little over a fortnight later, on October 6th, in a remote Brighton suburb, Parnell died, the centre of a divorce scandal that split Ireland for generations.

Close to Ballylongford, on the Shannon estuary, is Lislaughtin Friary, a Franciscan foundation endowed in 1477 by John O'Connor Kerry: a splendid crucifix associated with this friary is in the National Museum. A few miles to the northwest are the massive remains of Carrigafoyle Castle, once owned by the O'Connor clan.

For me, the castle recalls a pleasant encounter on O'Connell Street Dublin.

'What language were you speaking to your friend?' the old lady asked me quietly. I was seated on a chair in front of the Gresham Hotel.

'Irish', I said. After a pause the woman said. 'I'm from Boston. I have saved up my money to come back to my father's land—a place I have never seen. All I know is that he boasted he was an O'Connor of Carrigafoyle. Do you know the place?'

I began to recite a verse attributed to the O'Rahilly of Ballylongford.

> *There wasn't a merrier mansion in Kerry*
> *From Knockanore Hill to the Portmagee Ferry*
> *With plenty of liquor, and money to kick, or*
> *To burn if you wanted to make it go quicker.*
> *For claret was cheaper than paraffin oil*
> *In the time of O'Connor of Carrigafoyle.*

I went on to tell the old lady of the O'Rahilly's death leading a bayonet charge, a few hundreds yards from where we then sat. He who had helped to organize the Irish Volunteers, and confessed himself opposed to the Rebellion, nevertheless threw in his lot with it at the last moment. 'I helped to wind the clock,' he said, 'and I've come to hear it strike.'

From Ballylongford, the road runs along the Shannon estuary to Tarbert on the Kerry-Limerick border. Tarbert is an estuarine port and its neighbouring island has latterly seen considerable development by the Electricity Supply Board. With its bright bustling ferry-boat linking both banks of the Shannon, nothing seems more certain than that it cannot be much longer baulked of greatness.

CHAPTER FIVE

Shannonside

Limerick, Tipperary and Clare

'where the Shannon River meets the sea'

County Limerick is long, low, fertile and estuarine. With its comrade-counties Clare and Tipperary, it has as its hub history-drenched Limerick City, an old Danish town sited strategically at the point of the Shannon where the river ceases to be navigable.

The hills of Limerick are scarcely worth the mention—a few at the western border, the fairy-ridden knob of Knockfierna in the centre and a cluster in the north-eastern corner; for the rest of it, the county comprises a good two-thirds of the Golden Vale.

The tableland that is Clare is shaped like an equilateral triangle having as its base the estuary of the Shannon, on which Shannon Airport stands; freshwater Shannon and wide-spreading Lough Derg form the eastern side, while the western flank, bounded by the growling Atlantic, is guarded on the north by epic cliffs. Its most striking single feature is the Burren, an apparently barren karst-type area of amorphous limestone riddled with caves and subterranean streams which forms the apex of this triangular county.

Mountains in abundance sit on the perimeter of County Tipperary while strong-hearted rivers thrust through its central plain. Its rich land is calculated to set a seaboard smallholder dribbling with greed.

Of the two main roads through County Limerick, one skirts the broad Shannon, the other, an inland highway, moves through the pleasant towns of Abbeyfeale, Newcastlewest, Rathkeale and Adare.

Taking the first-mentioned road and moving eastward from the

Kerry border I make my way up-river along the Shannon, here 'spreading like the sea'.

The day is crystal clear. One is deluded into imagining that one can skim a flat stone for almost three miles across the water to the Clare village of Labasheeda.

To Glin Castle I call to visit the Knight of Glin (The Knight of the Valley) descendant of one of three great Norman families, Fitzgerald, Fitzmaurice and Fitzgibbon, respectively known as the Knight of Valley, the Red Knight and the White Knight. Harvard-graduate, poised, and informed, the Knight discusses archaeology, balladry and history. His people have been there since his progenitor, Thomas of Shanid, built the first motte and bailey in 1200.

A fragment of the original Glin Castle sits dumpily beside the village. Attacked in 1600 by Sir George Carew, Elizabeth 1's President of Munster (Carew's scribe describes the assault in *Pacata Hibernia*) the castle was bravely defended by leaders Dore and Culhane. Carew's men got hold of one of Fitzgerald's sons and tied him to the cannon's mouth. 'Surrender! Or we'll blow your son to pieces,' the besiegers cried.

The Knight answered, and the interests of politeness I paraphrase: 'Tell Carew that the womb from which the boy emerged is still fertile, and with the help of God and his own loins, the Knight of Glin shall not want for sons.'

Foynes, once a transatlantic seaplane base, is a neat port where oil tankers discharge their cargoes, and where, also, children come in summer to attend the local Irish college. This area has been the home of such famous Anglo-Irish families as the de Veres and the Spring-Rices.

A mile south of Foynes village, on the summit of Knockpatrick, a quaint hilltop churchyard with its attendant ruin of a medieval church, marks the place where St Patrick is alleged to have raised his hand and said: 'My blessing on Kerry faraway from me.'

The road now moves inland towards Askeaton, a stronghold of the Earls of Desmond, the ruins of whose great castle still stand in an island in the River Deel in mid-town. On 1579 the town witnessed the butchering of its friars.

A few miles off the main road stands the Agricultural College of Pallaskenry where the Salesian fathers praise God through the medium of fine loam. At Mungret, the twin chimneys of the cement factory come into view: presently a cessation is made on the Limerick quays where Bratt boats from the Baltic tie up at the end of their voyages.

In early medieval times, Mungret was the site of a monastery famous for its erudition.

The classical prowess of the monks of Mungret was once challenged by a rival monastery. Apprehensive of the outcome of such a test, the Mungretians hit upon a plan to discomfit their challengers.

They dressed members of their community as women and set them washing clothes at a ford close to the monastery. As the visiting friars approached, the 'washerwomen' began to gossip in colloquial Latin. Hearing this, the strangers enquired how washerwomen could be proficient in such a tongue.

'Scraps of learning we pick up while waiting on the monastery table', the leader of the 'washerwomen' replied.

This was too much for the oncoming friars, who decamped at once.

The lower or inland road through Abbeyfeale, Newcastlewest and Rathkeale strikes through the heart of County Limerick. Abbeyfeale is a market town which for long insisted on holding calf markets at extraordinary hours of the morning—a cause of commotion and indignation amongst its citizens. The town which once bragged a Cistercian monastery built in 1188 by Brian O'Brien on the banks of the Feale River is also well-known because of its excellent attempts to place the Irish language once more on the lips of the Irish people.

In its square stands a bronze-green statue raised to the memory of Father Casey, a parish priest, who as a village Hampden indelibly stamped the people of West Limerick with the independence of his personal struggle against landlordism.

Between Abbeyfeale and Newcastlewest, the Mullaghareirk hills look uninviting, with the exception of a break at Devon Road. But between this point and the Shannon traditional ways have held a tenacious grip on the minds of the people.

The Munster *Fleadh Ceoil* (Traditional Music Festival) was being held in Newcastlewest. In a fifteenth century hall of a castle of the Earls of Desmond, the *bodhrán* competition was in progress. I was the adjudicator: the wild strumming of this dog-skin, or indeed goat-skin or deer-skin drum filled the vaulted chamber with antique ferocity.

Two Sheehy brothers, obviously champions, had skill, execution and style. Each hand-drum was heated rather incongruously to an electric fire to render its surface taut for drumming.

Later, one summer day in Ballybunion, I saw a seagrass-seller having a strange object beside his green periwinkle cart. 'It's a tom-tom,' he told me, 'that came in with the tide.' I sat down on a grassy bank, held the tom-tom between my knees—there were projections for holding the instrument—and as I wondered how the drum was beaten, I found one of the Sheehy brothers looking at me quizzically. 'Let me try it,' he said quietly.

He placed the African drum between his knees and beat upon it a west Limerick tattoo that soon summoned a delighted crowd.

Newcastlewest has had its poets of a Gaelic yesteryear. The poetry of one, Dáithí Ó Bruadair, is known to many in its James Stephens' translation. I recall the passionate lines beginning:

I will sing no more songs, the pride of my country I sang,
Through forty long years of good verse without any avail,
And no one cared even as much as the half of a hang
For the song or the singer, so here is an end to my tale ...

The legends of mid-Limerick have mainly to do with St Ita, whose nunnery was sited at Killeedy, six miles south of Newcastlewest.

According to a local belief, Ita was privileged to have suckled the Infant Jesus.

Rathkeale, standing in the centre of an area of excellent limestone land, has long been a rallying-place for the picturesque and picaresque people euphemistically known as 'travellers', whose fate is currently the subject of much heartburning in Ireland.

Take any of the sidelanes leading to the left on the main Street of Rathkeale close to the shop with a statue of a Chinaman above a door, (an advertisement for tea, this) and you will presently find yourself in the place where many of these colourful folk spend the winter months.

The travelling people one finds on this eminence indicate the highest standard of living obtaining on the Irish roads. When last I visited Rathkeale the windows of the caravans were bedecked with brass and copper objects for which a ready market is assured.

But there are far less fortunate people wandering abroad in Ireland, their covering against the unpredictable skies consisting of jute sacking or, at best, green canvas, and their commonest bed sodden straw on still more sodden roadside clay. Victuals are picked up any-old-how, and semi-cooked over a fire of green faggot, the smoke from which impregnates every article of clothing the unfortunates wear. Yet, despite the forces of harsh nature and uncaring humanity allied against them, each day in the life of an Irish 'traveller' constitutes a monument to the indestructibility of man.

Adare is reckoned one of the most picturesque villages in Ireland; to me its beauty is merely a re-creation of a pretty English village set down colonially in the midst of the Golden Vale.

The story of Adare is bound up with the Fitzgerald family, Earls of Kildare, who obtained possession of the district from the O'Donovans early in the fourteenth century. After the flamboyant Silken Thomas Fitzgerald had unsuccessfully revolted against the English, the place reverted to the crown. The Fitzgerald castle was finally dismantled by Cromwell.

Adare Manor, now open to visitors, residence of the Earl of Dunraven, stands in mid-village. The place also boasts three friaries or abbeys. The White Abbey, founded in 1230 by an order of

Trinitarian Canons, had as its aim the redemption of Christian captives from the Mohammedans. In the early part of the last century, the sacred building was almost turned into a ball-alley and later still came close to being a market-house; it was finally rescued by the Earl of Dunraven who had it rebuilt as a Catholic church.

Also in Adare are the Augustinian friary, built in 1315 and converted into a Protestant church in 1807, and the archetypal ruin of a Franciscan friary seated delightfully on the banks of the river Maigue.

Unannalled in tourist literature, I continue to find delights in the green deeps of county Limerick; in a recessed cobbled kitchen of a country house, I recall finding an old doctor playing age-old laments on the *Uileann*, or Elbow, pipes; lying by a shallow weedy stream on a somnolent summer day I woke from reverie to see five enormous trout causing minor tidal waves a few feet from my shoes, and once, loitering by the waterfall of Carass, I listened to an old man reciting the poetry of Seán Ó Tuama, an Irish poet and owner of a publichouse near Croom, who is credited having made the first lampoon in verse, known latterly as the 'limerick'. (And oh! how we celebrate each year the Festival of Ó Tuama and his brother poets!)

From Croom it is but a short step to the nearby hamlet of Monaster, a place called for the ancient monastery beside the river. The hamlet was also the scene of a prehistoric fair or traditional gathering.

I was fishing in the Camoge river directly in front of the wind-clean stones of the ruined monastery when I heard a cry for help. Rushing to the roadway above I found that a large swan from the river had mounted the roadside wall and had trundled-flopped ponderously down on to the road edge. There it had spread its wings and advanced on a girl who, petrified with terror, was too terrified to advance or retire.

As, not without trepidation, I rescued her from her predicament, I recalled the classical legend of Leda and the swan.

Monaster saw more interesting sights than this: in 1148 it witnessed the founding by Turlough O'Brien of Thomond of a Cistercian monastery to commemorate a victory over the Norsemen.

In 1370, it saw Brian of Thomond routing his uncle in a bloody conflict, the victor later dragging his kinsman from the sanctuary of the abbey.

In 1580, the village saw the defeat by Malby, the Elizabethan governor of Connaught, of John of Desmond and Papal Legate Saunders who led an army of 2,000 men officered by Spaniards. The conflict had as its climax the beheading of the abbot on the altar steps, the butchering of the monks and the wrecking of the monastery.

To the south, Bruree Village on the River Maigue lies in the centre of a hunting area. Here was reared Éamon de Valera, New York-born son of a Spanish father who had married a Limerick girl named Coll. Dev's magnetic—and for some Irishmen, mysterious personality—straddled Ireland like a colossus from the moment he emerged as a flourdusty prisoner nicknamed 'The Mexican' from a bullet-pocked bakery in the Dublin of Easter Week, until more than half a century later, when he began his second term of office as President of Ireland.

East of Bruree is the once-walled town of Kilmallock, a place with a history as melancholy as any in the land. But as ever, there is the bright thread of a laughter-loving poet to redeem the town, for Andrew McGrath, a Gaelic poet of the eighteenth century, known in Irish as the Tipsy Hawker, streaked Kilmallock's history with the bright vein of peasant laughter.

Today, Mannix Joyce, a scholar-writer of this area, has adopted the pseudonym of the former poet: on occasion, Mannix moves off to Russia or to Algiers whence he sends back despatches to enliven otherwise tranquil county Limerick conversations.

Beside Ardpatrick stands a two-storey thatched public house

where I once saw a solemn-eyed child watch a jackdaw that had flown into my car. How tenaciously the child's wide eyes continue to hold my imagination. Marigolds too, at the base of cottages I recall, as I paused to pay tribute to the memory of the Joyce brothers from this area of tree-clad hills who did prodigious pioneering work in the collection of Irish music and song.

Hospital, named for the Preceptory of the Knights Hospitaller of St John of Jerusalem, is associated with de Marisco, the English Justiciar; the tombs of Hospital go back almost to the Norman invasion of Ireland while *Suí Finn* (Fionn's Seat) among the hills, goes back to the beginning of the Celtic era in Ireland. Knockainy (The Hill of *Áine*) goes one better; it takes us right back to prehistory, for it has associations with the worship of the sun. Until comparatively recent times, mysterious customs involving torches and chanting men moving in a ring around cattle, were carried on in the vicinity of Hospital.

It could well be that the most intriguing secrets of all are yet to be discovered in the area around Lough Gur (*The Farm by Lough Gur* is a minor Irish classic) where in a countryside of character, archaeologists continue to draw surprising conclusions from the layers of pollen found on the lake bed.

Stand at the Crescent by the Jesuit college at the western end of Limerick city and observe the perspective of Georgian houses stretching downwards on a slight declivity to meet the business section at the city centre.

A noble thoroughfare, but perhaps too noble by half; it is as if someone of over-vaulting ambition had erred by providing Limerick with a main artery that could ill brook the presence of closes, bow-ways, alley-ways and cul-de-sacs, all of which vouch for the erratic natural growth of a city.

As is the case with other strategically-sited towns of this nature, (cf. Athlone, Downpatrick and Clonmel) the city's story may be cursorily read in its English Town, Irish Town and Newtown Pery. But Limerick is far older than this tripartite division indicates:

over a thousand years ago, subsequent to its foundation by the Norse, coins minted by Ivar of Limerick were accepted as lawful tender in Scandinavia.

The power of Danish Limerick was temporarily broken at the battle of Solohead, a place close to Tipperary town, by King Mahon of North Munster and his brother, Brian Ború (of the Tribute), the latter destined to be High King of all Ireland and the hammer that pounded the Danes at Clontarf, Dublin in 1014. Subsequently the then Danish-Irish city of Limerick became the seat of the Munster Kings, the O'Briens.

For a time it held the Normans at bay; in 1200, King John caused the fortress now called King John's Castle to be erected, and the de Burgos, or Burkes were placed in charge of the city. The Norsemen were banged out, to live sullenly yet homogeneously outside the city walls.

Bruce of Scotland visited the Anglo-Norman town in 1316; for a considerable time it was menaced by the Irish in the immediate hills of Clare. It saw siege in 1641 when it was taken by the Confederate (Catholic) Irish and was later valorously defended by those forces under the command of Hugh O'Neill.

After the battle of the Boyne and the subsequent siege of Athlone this old city saw its most glorious hour, when as the last bastion of the deposed King James, walls that the French officer Lauzun declared could be knocked down with roasted apples, withstood in 1690 a determined siege by William of Orange and 26,000 men.

When at last, the wall was breached, the women of the city fought side by side with their menfolk. In that grapple 2,000 Williamites died, some of them at the hands of the women.

Every Irish schoolchild can lisp the story of how Lord Lucan, or Patrick Sarsfield as he was known to the Irish, by a commando-style foray on horseback in 1690, captured an English siege train on its way to Limerick and blew it up with a roar that echoes chauvinistically down the years.

The subsequent melancholy treaty 'broken ere the ink wherewith 'twas writ could dry'—was, it is alleged, signed on the large stone that still stands by Thomond Bridge. Thereafter the Irish army was dispersed, many of its soldiers seeking employment as mercenaries on the Continent, where they often raised the vengeful battlecry of 'Remember Limerick!'

The Church of Ireland Cathedral, St Mary's, founded by Dónal Mór O'Brien in the late twelfth century shows evidence of burgundian architecture. King John's Castle built in 1200, bulks hugely above the river but has some odd modern buildings sited within its walls. (*Laus Deo!* correction seems imminent.)

St Saviour's Dominican Church has a statue brought from Flanders in 1640 and presented by a merchant called Sarsfield in atonement for a stain on his family honour. Almost opposite the church is the odd spectacle of what appears to be Doric temple built to house a savings bank.

In St John's Cathedral is a beautiful crozier of 1418 and also an interesting reliquary. Limerick is a place of good bookshops, quayside stacks of white timber and black coal, screaming gulls and overornate churches with that proliferation of red winking altar lamps indicative of exotic devotions.

Many years ago, so the tale goes, the election of Mayor of Limerick City resulted in stalemate. As a compromise, it was agreed that whoever would cross Thomond Bridge first on the following morning, be he mad, daft or abandoned, would be elected Lord Mayor of the City.

At dawn of day, the councillors, attired in their robes of office, stationed themselves at the bridgehead; the first to cross was a sensible simpleton, nicknamed *Seán na Scuab* or 'John of the Brooms', who had trudged down from the hills to sell his crudely made brushes in the city market. Seán was borne off in triumph to the city hall where he was powdered, periwigged and dressed in the ermine of mayoral office.

The changeling rustic was then set up to dispense justice. This he did with peasant acumen.

Meanwhile, Seán's widowed mother set out for Limerick in search of her son. Having sought in scriptural fashion for three days, she was finally advised to seek the counsel of the new Mayor.

The mother created such a rumpus at the doorway of the court-room that the Mayor called upon his minions to drag the intruder forward. 'Who is this woman?' Seán thundered.

The old woman fell at the Mayor's feet, looked up and said: 'Seán, my son, don't you know me?' Her son replied 'Arrah, hush, woman, I hardly know myself.'

It's an unexciting run from Limerick to Tipperary; taking the road that runs through a corridor in the Golden Vale one moves through the village of Cappamore, with, if desired, a diversion through Murroe beside which stands Glenstal Castle of the Benedictines. Continuing on this route through Doon, Cappawhite and forest-embowered Dundrum one arrives at Cashel of the Kings which stands in the centre of county Tipperary.

Further still to the north one may travel from Limerick through Rear Cross and Upperchurch to reach Thurles, the county town of Tipperary. On the flanks of this mountainous stretch of road, if court prosecutions are a criterion, the illicit distillation of poteen has not been unknown. In this locality prospecting firms are already opening up the old shafts in the hope of striking lodes Nevada-rich, as indeed has been already successfully done by the Northgate company in Tynagh in East Galway, where rumour has it that the mineral deposits, mainly silver, are worth £122 millions.

Oola, on the most southerly of the three roads to the east has an Irish name meaning 'apples' ('A big ho, a small ho, a hell and a ha' is how a British Tommy described it). Having passed through the quiet hamlet there is an facile slide into Tipperary, a town that still possesses the Norman motte-and-bailey in many of its surrounding villages. In Tipperary itself there is a weather-stained statue of novelist Charles Kickham sitting patriarchally on one of the principal thoroughfares.

Tipp-town was the birthplace of John O'Leary (*Romantic Ireland's dead and gone—it's with O'Leary in the grave*—W. B. Yeats complained).

In nearby Solohead, where, in 967, the Danes of Limerick were defeated, almost a thousand years later an ambush took place that initiated the Anglo-Irish 'troubles' of 1919-1921.

Perched on the top of Slievenamuck mountain to the south of Tipperary town I watched children fill an assortment of vessels with whortleberries (variously called 'hurts', *fraocháns*, blaeberries or even huckleberries). The children's hands were juice-stained to the wrists.

There too an old man stood beside his unpretentious cottage; he and I together fell into a most companionable silence as we looked down at the eddying chimney-smoke of Tipperary below.

I then dropped down into the Glen of Aherlow, a valley hidden between the Slievenamuck Range and 'the bold Galtee Mountains'. I came upon a beflagged open-air dancing-deck, its bulbs scintillating in the afternoon sunlight. Later I delayed to gossip with a haymaking friend in a meadow walled-in by tall whitethorn hedges. As twilight gathered I rambled aimlessly, aiming an ear at Bansha to the north-east, and an eye towards the peak of Galtymore to the south-west. When the Galtees had revolved to grey green ghosts I reached Lissavernane where, as a slip of moon came up above the hills, the postcard Ireland of nostalgia was a reality.

Cahir with the purple mountains behind it (the Irish name means The Stone Fort of the Fishing) is a well-sited town with that admirable but somehow over-civilized beauty of the English sort. This air of graciousness it shares with the cultured Georgian midland town of Birr.

With its well-appointed hotels, Cahir straddles one of the main crossroads of Ireland; the main Limerick-Waterford and Dublin-Cork roads intersect right on the square of the town. On a rock above the river Suir sits the 500-years-old Butler castle. The Cahir Butlers, a clan which ever inclined to the Irish mode of life, trace their line back to a son of Foreign James, son of the Earl of Ormond, by his niece, daughter of the Earl of Desmond.

In mid-town, beside the singing river, where the rocks of the original stone caher show stubbornly through its foundations, the castle did not prove sturdy enough to withstand successive sieges by the Earl of Essex, Lord Inchiquin ('The Burner'), and Cromwell in 1599, 1647, and 1650 respectively.

In the yard of a mortuary chapel at Tubrid five miles southwest of the town are buried two remarkable priest-Irishmen, Geoffrey Keating, poet, and exponent of classical Irish prose, and Owen O'Duffy who had the temerity to lampoon the pluralist Archbishop Miler McGrath.

From Cahir I roamed downriver along the banks of the Suir where trout sat quietly on tresses of river weed. Through a delectable estate I moved past a Swiss cottage, reaching at last Ardfinnan village with its goose-green and its huge-bulking stronghold first built in 1185 by Prince John of England. Upriver too from Cahir I roamed almost to the gates of Golden, a village that has no aureate connotations since the name simply means *Gabhailín* or Little Fork of the Suir River.

Clonmel lies in the centre of an apple-growing area, and naturally, cider constitutes the local wine of the country. The Comeragh mountains rear behind the streets of the town. Ever a De Burgo (or Burke) town, the family is strongly represented there to the present day.

In terms of history, Clonmel is notable for its siege in 1650, when Hugh Dubh O'Neill and his Ulster troops inflicted heavy losses on the besieging Cromwellians; later the town capitulated, but not before O'Neill and his men had stolen away under cover of darkness.

Laurence Sterne was born in Clonmel, as also was George Borrow who wrote the famous books on gypsy life—*Lavengro* included. Today, the town boasts a falconry, but above all it is the acknowledged capital of the kingdom of the greyhound.

Frieze-coated stout-booted men from all parts of Ireland look towards Clonmel as does the Arab towards Mecca in the hope that one day a greyhound sapling of their breeding, rearing and training will eventually win one of Clonmel's great classic coursing events.

Walking its streets I kept wondering if there were left in Clonmel any descendants of the 500 Walloons brought from Canterbury in 1667 with the object of establishing a woollen industry in the town.

And any telling of Clonmel would be incomplete without mention of that remarkable pedlar-genius Charles Bianconi, who by running the first coach from Clonmel to Cahir in the year of the battle of Waterloo, established the prime regular transport system in Ireland.

Pleasantly on the Suir too, sits Carrick-on-Suir ('God be with you Carrick, where there's neither law nor order' as the old Carrick woman complained in the court of Clonmel), hometown of the Clancy brothers, balladeers, whose singing fame has echoed across the world.

Ever hear how Fionn Mac Cumhaill selected his wife?

He seated himself on a stone throne on the top of Slievenamon (The Mountain of the Women) which lies six miles north-east of Clonmel town, and had the female contenders for his hand race from the base to the summit, the fastest (literally) woman in Ireland being Gráinne, daughter of King Cormac.

On the southern slope of Slievenamon lies Kilcais, famous for the ruins of a small church and a castle, this latter being recalled by every school-child who recites primly in Irish the lines which trans-late: 'What shall we do for timber, now that the woods are down?' This poem, poet Brendan Kennelly movingly recited as panygeric above the grave of his fellow writer Frank O'Connor.

An area on the Kilkenny-Tipperary border is known as the Kickham Country and by none is it held in deeper affection than by James Maher of Mullinahone, one of those rare people who has steeped himself in the lore of the district, and who speaks on it with an authority matched only by his affection for his subject.

In this area I dallied at Melody's pub at the mouth of the Nire valley to listen to ballads made by a local priest. Thereafter I pushed deep into the lovely lost vale until at last a quiet country school set a period to my wandering.

As I walked whistling along I heard the lock-lock of a creamery cart coming behind me; glancing back I saw the pony cart with its

single churn of milk. Seated in the front of the cart was an old man
reading a newspaper.

'You're there!' I began.

'I'm here!' he said drawing up the pony in surprise.

'The churn is warming your shoulder-blades.'

'That's just what it's doin'.'

'What do you do for a living?'

'I take my milk to the creamery. I read the newspaper.'

'The newspaper!'

'I read books too', he retorted. 'More than you or all belonging
to you!'

'I dispute that!'

The old fellow leaped from the setlock.

'We'll talk books', he said holding the reins. 'G'wan out!' he
roared at the pony.

I walked by his side. Sure enough, he had read Chekov and the
Russian Masters, the English Victorians, the New Disruptionists from
the American cities and the Southern Agrarians. The anti-novels
even!

Finally we stopped outside a cottage-farmhouse that was almost
throttled by trees and bushes. The unkempt condition of the place
made me conclude that the old fellow was a bachelor.

'It was pleasant meeting you,' I said. 'Here we part.'

The old man took off his hat and looked at me. 'Come in and
delay with me,' he blurted softly. 'I'm forty years waiting for a
fellah like you to come along.'

In the 3rd or 4th century Eoghantacht tribes, possibly refugees from
Irish colonies in Wales, took Cashel and its fertile surroundings as
swordland and later established lordship over Munster, acknowledging
the supremacy of Tara at a still later date. On occasion some of these
Eoghantacht Kings were also church dignitaries and this fact tended
to give Cashel an ecclesiastical visage which contributed to its acceptance in 1101 as see of the Archbishops of Munster.

The Danes took Cashel in the mid-tenth century but the valour of the Clare *Dál gCais* under Mahon and Brian redeemed it. Subsequent to the murder of Mahon, in 976, Brian became King of Cashel and his O'Brien descendants held it until the arrival of the Normans in 1169.

During the period 1127-34, Cormac McCarthy erected the delightful Cormac's Cathedral, one of glories of Hiberno-Romanesque architecture. In 1169, Big Dónal O'Brien began a new cathedral: here in 1171-2 at a synod summoned by Henry II of England, the kings and church dignitaries of Thomond acknowledged Henry's claim to rule Ireland.

Dónal O'Brien's cathedral was subsequently replaced in the thirteenth century by a more imposing building, the work of three successive archbishops. Later still Edward Bruce held a parliament on the rock.

In 1495, Great Garret Fitzgerald, Earl of Kildare, when called to account by the English King for having burned the cathedral, replied, 'I wouldn't have burned it, sire, only I was sure that Archbishop Creagh was inside!'

Cashel was again burned in 1647, this time by 'Burner' Murrough O'Brien, who butchered the clergy and used the chasubles and copes as horse cloths. In 1686 the cathedral was rebuilt for Protestant use, and in 1749 it was finally abandoned as a place of worship by Archbishop Price who stripped the cathedral of its roof. His excuse for doing so? 'I found the Sabbath climb to the top of the Rock far too arduous!'

But climb one must to the summit of St Patrick's Rock, and, entering by the gateway, walk past the hall of the Vicars Choral and the crutched St Patrick's Cross, to move into the cathedral proper.

Within, altars, tombs and monuments abound; here the 12 apostles are cut in stone; there on a stone tomb chest in the north transept are a group of stone mourners. Moving through mysterious wall passages, clambering up echoing stone stairs one emerges on top of what is locally called 'The Square Castle', to view above the remains of Hore Abbey and St Dominic's Abbey a circle of country-side that defines the fertile heart of Munster.

Descending, if one searches, one may find the tomb of Miler McGrath, who had himself appointed Archbishop and then proceeded to haggle in benefices until he had accumulated almost eight in all; meanwhile the papally-approved Archbishop of Cashel, O'Hurley by name, was hunted, captured, and put to death without any pretence at trial.

The stone roof and ornamental tomb chest of Cormac's Chapel merit the closest attention. Polychrome painting once covered walls that now battle with lichen so that in its heyday the interior must have been most attractive.

At the north-east of the cathedral stands a perfect round tower while within the great building there is a lazar-squint (or is a croft?) that twins with the legend of a lazar-house in a grove of trees on the road to Cahir.

As for Cashel town itself, I am not sure that I admire the bright tympanum of the church of St John the Baptist, nor the ranked statues in its interior. However, as I was married in this church, with my wife coming from a house in the shadow of the Rock, a house that once saw a strange brooding genius called John Davis White edit a local newspaper, I cannot, or dare not, complain!

But I do recall delightful days in Cashel, dallying for hours in the cathedral with Joe Minogue (his son, Billy, is now the third Minogue Keeper of the Kings) or strolling on the edge of cornland, the ripe stalks reaching high above my head, and each dusk bringing me upon the Rock from a new point of the compass.

I had been travelling in a sawney-go-easy bus from Cashel to join a train on the main railway line at Goold's Cross. At a crossroads the vehicle was flagged down by an agitated old lady, who asked the conductor if somebody had been given a parcel for her by a chemist in one of the towns through which the bus had passed.

A Johnny Appleseed seated at the rear of the bus stood up and deferentially handed the conductor a brown-papered parcel that obviously contained a bottle. This the conductor handed to the lady; immediately he raised his hand to ring the bell.

'Wait!' the old lady said as she tore the paper wrapping off the packet. She then held the bottle up for all to see. There were only a few spoonfuls of the medicine left.

'The hoor drank it!' the old woman wailed. She rushed into the bus and began to pummel the messenger, who, his eyes fixed in front of him, sat swaying beatifically as if he had his existence in a realm above all conflict. 'Tisn't the first time he did it either!' the old woman yelled.

Dundrum with its pine forest, reminded me of the twinkling tree-trunks of Bavaria. About Holycross, with its ruined Norman twelfth century Tironian, later Cistercian, abbey, now in the process of being restored for use as a parish church, the beech trees were translucently green. Here was once treasured a relic of the true Cross presented to the monks by a grandson of Brian Ború who had received it in 1110 from Pope Pascal II. Set in a shrine of gold encrusted with precious stones, the relic was for centuries the focal point of pilgrimage. The *sanctum sanctorum* where the relic was kept is still arbitrarily identified in a building that has unique features to its carvings in black limestone.

To understand an important facet of Ireland, one must understand the Gaelic Athletic Association.

Originally founded in Thurles in 1884 by a group led by Michael Cusack, a Clare schoolmaster, and inspired directly or indirectly by the Fenian Brotherhood, the G.A.A. has as its proximate aim the cultivation of native games, Gaelic football, hurling, handball and rounders and as its remote aim the preserving of the national characteristics of Ireland.

Bitterly attacked by its criticis, the Association precluded its members from playing rugby, soccer and hockey and has won an astonishing measure of popular success.

To visit Thurles Sportsfield on the occasion of the playing of a Munster Senior Hurling Championship, say, between Cork and Tipperary, is to see exuberant Ireland at its very best.

The G.A.A. has recently renewed the century-broken links binding it to Australian football which traces its descent from Gaelic football.

Mention of Templemore, the town under the Devil's Bit Mountain (Tourist titbit: 'The devil bit that hole up there out of the hilltop and spat it southward to form the Rock of Cashel!') inspired me with a recrudescence of boyhood awe. For once, as a child, in the grip of an obscure fever I woke to find myself douched with 'miraculous' water from Templemore where a japer had persuaded a credulous public, but not indeed the incredulous clergyman who later unmasked him, that he had seen statues bleeding in the local church.

Nenagh (The Fair or Assembly) was for long a hide pulled asunder by Irish-O'Brien and Norman-Butler wardogs, with O'Kennedys and O'Carrolls yapping loudly on the outskirts of the tugging match. Its ponderous 100 feet high Butler donjon ('The Nenagh Round') still conveys a sense of abiding force. Nenagh was also the site of one of the most important Franciscan houses in Ireland.

The town has excellent hotels and is currently engaged in a valiant effort to exploit its proximity to Lough Derg on the Shannon River by organizing boating and fishing trips thereon.

Because of the sheepruns on the mountain range to its south, Nenagh was once famous for its sheep fairs. Latterly, the efficient but far more prosaic system of auctions in enclosed marts is slowly but surely driving the traditional spitting-on-the-palm-and-marking-the-beasts'-rump-with-the-end-of-a-cowdung-loaded-stick clean (!) out of business.

Roscrea, once a Butler stronghold, is sited on the gap between the Devil's Bit and Slieve Bloom Mountains. The main Limerick-Dublin road passes right through the holy ground of St Cronan's monastery; the weather-eroded, rain-eaten west doorway of the church still indicates in defiant grandeur its individual Irish version of Romanesque.

In keeping with the thought of the rodent centuries one may move to the Cistercian abbey of Mount St Joseph, a couple of miles from the town and watch silkworms consume mulberry leaves.

At Roscrea I swung south-west, first to see a thatched house in the picturesque village of Puckane, thence to move to Portroe on isletted Lough Derg, thence again through lovely country to Tipperary's Ballina which stands on the opposite bank of the Shannon from Killaloe in Clare. As a result of the forking of the river to form the head-race of the Shannon hydro-electric scheme, the falls of Doonass on the Shannon have almost vanished. Yet I found here on the Shannon shore gentle, reedy and pleasant back-waters as a consequence of which, slightly drowsy, I again entered the county Limerick.

In an upstairs room in a tall house in Castleconnell beside the river, an old alert man, his arm and leg stroke-wounded sat in front of a huge lens behind which a naked bulb shed its light on a book by Emily Brontë . Not an easy man to interview, but when I sent up the name of a mutual German writer friend I was shown in at once. We talked in the context of the Irish story of fifty years before. His admiration for his friend Casement was unbounded. As secretary of the Irish Volunteers, and co-founder of Fianna Éireann, Bulmer Hobson, since dead, had played a major role in siding with Professor Eoin McNeill in cancelling the Easter Rising.

Later, riding into Limerick, I drew the car to the side of the street to greet an old friend, who as a young medical student, accompanied by the woman who later became his wife, a member of the great rebel Limerick family called Daly, had clawed his way up to Dublin to fight in the G.P.O.

Clad in green pullover, brilliant-eyed and laughingly alert, Éamon Dore, a full 54 years later, was bouncing off the pavements of Limerick as if still full of the joy of living.

Both men were part of the Irish story. Each took a different decision more than half a century ago. The years had justified Éamon Dore to the full.

Over the Shannon from Limerick City and into Clare, a county that I find has an acutely personal appeal for me.

Furze, lilac, broom and whitethorn were in bloom together.

The lace of cow-parsley decorated the road edges. Moving almost due north I hugged the right bank of the Shannon until I reached Killaloe.

Here I spent a pleasant couple of hours roaming in St Flannan's Church of Ireland cathedral *olim* St Mary's Catholic cathedral (founded 1182) and later paused to ponder on St Mo-Lua's Oratory rescued from Friars' Island which was submerged in 1929 in connection with the Shannon scheme; the oratory was later re-erected beside the Catholic Church of Killaloe town.

Above the weir in Killaloe the water lay quiet in an arm of the river. Downstream, the Shannon was harnessed in the hydro-electrical scheme that had revolutionized Irish life. On Lough Derg the Mayfly was up and, everywhere, boys with leather-hasped boxes of perforated tin and bearing strong rods were leaping on to the thwarts of clinker-built fishing boats. Upstream drowsed *Béal Ború*, once the fortress of Brian Ború.

To the north-east lay Scarriff, a most civilized town dedicated to drama and the manufacture of chipboard. North of Scarriff stretches a region of desolation and character lying about and amid the Slieve Aughty mountains. It is worth pushing north east to Mountshannon (a 30½ lb. trout was once caught here) to see even from a distance the holy isle of Inis Cealtra. Complete with round tower and a frieze of ruins, some of which date from the 7th century, the island makes a striking picture against the lake background.

On the southern rim of the Slieve Aughty mountains lies the village of Feakle and due north of it lies Lough Graney; both village and lake are associated with Merriman the Poet.

Respect for the Rabelaisian poet Bryan Merriman has grown with the passing years. His masterpiece, *Cúirt a' Mheán Oíche* (The Midnight Court), is an earthen no-holds-barred indictment by the wanton young women of Ireland of all unrandy Irishmen reluctant to mate. In their poetic ire, the women drag the narrator-miscreant-protagonist before their queen at a midnight court and describe the predicament they find themselves in as a result of certain physical deprivations. Needless to say, the women demand that restitution be made.

I was on the open-air platform at Feakle on the day that the long-delayed memorial stone to Bryan Merriman was unveiled. Previous to this there had been objections born of insecure gentility.

Feakle's claim to fame is many-headed for the village also finds time to be proud of the memory of a 'witch' called Biddy Early (even Daniel O'Connell visited her) who owned a magic bottle, a drop from which was a nostrum for all ills. A conflicting legend states by looking into the bottle Biddy could foretell the future. And fame also has been Feakle's portion as a result of the finding in 1948 in Gorteenreagh of a hoard of gold artifacts of the late Bronze Age.

From Sixmilebridge where, in 1723, Dean Swift was allegedly refused meat on a Friday, I pushed due south past a graveyard shaped like a coffin and reached once-forested Cratloe, formerly the haunt of Freney the Highwayman. Cratloe oaks also supplied the roof for Westminster Hall. Thence I headed almost due west for Bunratty and all that name connotes.

Bunratty castle itself, now accurately restored and open to the public, is flanked by a pub called *Dirty Nelly's*, metamorphosed with nice business acumen to *Durty Nelly's*; this castle constitutes one of the showplaces of Ireland. Possibly MacNamara-built, it was for long the residence of the O'Briens, Earls of Thomond. Renuccini, Papal legate, who visited the place in 1646, inordinately praised its appointments and gardens.

Three miles north of Newmarket-on-Fergus is Dromoland Castle until recently seat of Lord Inchiquin and now a luxury hotel; here was born in 1803 William Smith O'Brien, leader of the Young Ireland Movement. The 'baronial' castle stands on a large estate which incorporates inside its south-east entrance a large stone hill-fort called Mooghaun: I hope that one day some learned and wealthy institute will scientifically investigate this ancient trivallate fortress.

The plaque on Quin Abbey declared that the Franciscan monastery had been founded by Síoda MacNamara, whom my mother, God rest her, most resolutely claimed as an ancestor of hers. This typical early fifteenth century monastery has incorporated in its fabric an

Anglo-Norman castle of de Clare, the solid towers of which are still plainly to be seen. Suppressed in 1541, the friars of Quin remained in the area almost until 1820.

But I found that my errand in the territory of my MacNamara forebears was not yet at an end, for in the name of what I choose to call 'integral tourism', I had previously scripted an entertainment for a castle in this area – something that the Irish literary purist is quite scared of doing.

In finely-restored Knappogue Castle outside the village of Quin, the medieval dinner had ended. Silence had fallen on the 150 guests. In the banqueting hall the lights slowly dimmed while in a nearby room young men and women stood ready to enter the larger hall and tell within the small compass of place and time the story of Ireland.

As a slender reed of music cried in the castle recesses the pageant began. Successively Celts, Danes, Normans, English and mere Irish played their parts in the little pageant which I had enlivened with music, dance, mime, tableau and song.

Praise is due to the Andrews family responsible for the discreet restoration of the castle.

Ennis of the twisty streets is where you have to meet your friends and where you can't avoid your foes. It's a cathedral town with a fine classical courthouse. Here on the banks of the river Fergus stands a ruined Franciscan friary founded in 1250 by an O'Brien of Thomond; it contains some excellent panels from a MacMahon tomb of 1470.

The most famous progeny of Ennis were Mulready the painter, (1786-1863), Dermody the boy-wonder poet (1775-1802), who burned out his body and spirit in riotous living, and Harriet Smithson who married Hector Berlioz the composer. The town still prides itself on the fact that it elected O'Connell as standard-bearer for Catholic Emancipation and that for 42 years (1917-1959) it was the headquarters of de Valera's own constituency.

Ennis also produced a great clown called Johnny Patterson, son of a nailer, who 70 or 80 years ago, was the idol of Irish country audiences.

The road between Ennis and Kilrush is straight, long and lonely; you may if you wish take the coast road which twists south west by Killadysert and Labasheeda. West Clare was once served by a belovedly humorous narrow-gauge railway, the engine of which still survives as a showpiece at Ennis Railway Station.

At Lissycasey, on the 'upper road' the traveller stops at a public-house to drink a famous eggnog. Its restorative qualities are reputed once to have saved a judge's life; he repaid the debt by granting the original proprietors a licence to sell liquor, which in addition to eggflips they do excellently to this day.

Five miles to the east of Kilrush, at Killimer, the Clare terminal of the Shannon ferry, I stood on a flagstone above the grave of the Colleen Bawn, a beautiful girl called Ellen Hanly murdered by drowning in mid-Shannon, and on whose sad story Gerald Griffin had based his novel *The Collegians*, Benedict his opera, *The Lily of Killarney* and Boucicault his play, *The Colleen Bawn*.

Kilrush is a centre of traditional music; there I found Louis Marcus, the Cork film producer, in the process of making of what later proved to be a very striking film called *Fleadh Cheoil*. A feature of the film was Louis' adroit use of the heavy rain which fell at the height of the festival.

From the town may be seen Scattery Island, site of a 6th century church of St Senan. As the island lay athwart the track of Viking settlers it was an easy prey for the intruders. Kilrush itself seems poised on the edge of some mysterious adventure. The houses are quite large and were built probably to withstand the winter gales that funnel through the Shannon's mouth. Its twin town Kilkee, with its hotels squatting like polished nails about the horseshoe of Moore Bay, was bright with the apparel of summer visitors. Kilkee in authentic Victorian nomenclature likes to style herself 'the Queen of Irish Watering Places'. However this does not detract from her undoubted beauty, although again the name of nearby Intrinsic Bay, called for a ship called Intrinsic wrecked here in 1826 does somehow set my teeth on edge.

From Kilkee I made an excursion southwest to Carrigaholt. By the little harbour of Carrigaholt in 1588, seven ships of the Armada rode at anchor for four days sheltering from the storm that proved so disastrous for the vessels of that great fleet. Close by, a MacMahon castle told its normal tale of summary hanging and led my memory step by step to Lord Clare, later a marshal of France, whose feats at Fontenoy are the subject of a heroic poem by Thomas Davis. These old tales I discussed with Victor Tobin and his wife in the O'Curry Irish College on the edge of the sea.

I confessed myself disappointed with the natural Bridges of Ross formed by erosion of the cliffs near Moneen but found recompense in a church near Kilbaha where is preserved a portable altar called 'The Little Ark', in which, in penal times, mass was offered on the part of the beach between high water mark and low, the local landlord being powerless to remove the altar from this no-man's-land. As a finale in this truly isolated peninsula where the thatched houses are still plentiful I pushed out to the end of Loop Head and as the sun went down I surveyed the Kerry mountains across the Shannon mouth.

'There's always singing at Casey's of Quilty,' Ciarán Mac Mathúna of Radio-Telefis Éireann told me. Ciarán should know as he's a man who has done much for traditional music. So to Quilty I hastened, but when I got there on Sunday, on the dot of two o'clock in the afternoon, Casey's was closing its doors.

That night I slept in O'Malley's of Spanish Point, a village composed largely of the summer residences of religious communities.

As I walked across the beach that tranquil night everything seemed preternaturally still. And yet it was on these same sands in September 1588, that O'Brien and Clancy (this latter a member of one of the hereditary learned families of Thomond) butchered the floundering sailors of the shipwrecked Armada.

For me the bloody images were held in equipoise only by the quiet memory of the dead Irish poets Ó Coimín and MacCruitín buried in the nearby graveyard of Kilfarboy. MacCruitín especially is of international stature: for almost ten years he worked on research with Dean Swift, previous to which he is credited with having been tutor in France to the Dauphin, son of James II and Mary of Modena.

At twilight the following day, a car, its rack festooned with bamboo poles, pulled up outside the house; out piled the Heffernans from Kilmeedy in Limerick, friends of my friends, complete with 15 dozen mackerel caught with rod and jigger.

'If you're going fishing,' one of them, an American priest, said, 'go to Baltard beside Doonbeg—there's a ledge on a rockface with deep water below it. If you have three jigs you'll often kill three mackerel at a time. Don't slip in—the ledge is slippery with mackerel blood.'

However having had my share of gore in the memory of dead Spaniards, I went up to Miltown Malbay where at evening as I entered the town, I heard cries from the sportsfield. There I found two teams of brawny lads locked in stubborn stalemate in the final of a tug-of-war contest.

Just then there came an explosive cheer from the playing-field. I knew at once that the tug-o'-war deadlock had been ended. The cheer too was signal for the beginning of festivities connected with yet another festival—that of 'The-Darling-Girl-from-Clare'. Miltown Malbay began to thrum with life. The people began to sing. In a pub I fell in with an Englishman and his French wife.

'Jacques wishes to enter for the Talent Competition,' she told me diffidently. 'He plays the Jew's-harp.'

'Go right up on the platform,' I told the would-be competitor. Jacques was even more diffident than his wife. Would the Irish deny him the reward of his virtuosity? Or ridicule him?

At last Jacques was persuaded to mount the platform where he got a rapturous reception. That man could play the Jew's-harp! Later, when his name was announced as winner, he received as first prize something quite typical of Ireland—a barometer. We all whooped with joy.

By God! life was good. Into the pub then with me to drink to Jacques' health, to chat with an Irish-Australian *seanchaí* (I doubted if the fellow could pronounce the bloody word) and later to return singing to my cottage bed. In the morning I awoke to find a streaming sun in my eyes.

Where was it I bought that vari-coloured tweed hat? In Lahinch of the long beach of course. 'It will make you dashing!' Margaret Barry had said. The 'dashing' decided me so I bought the tweed hat. It was made out of a purple, green and gold tweed woven I'd say, by Albert Millar of Clifden, and as Margaret placed it on my head she smiled archly and said, 'When it gets old and battered you'll simply love it.'

Hat askew on my head, I went down the promenade to buy *dillisk* or seaweed, and freshly boiled periwinkles at Healy's.

In Lahinch, a grown-up fishing village, then thronged with vivid holidaymakers, but with its old-world roofs of slabbed Liscannor stone still betraying its plebeian origin, the prime topic of conversation was golf. But for me, for whom golf is a piddling pursuit fitted only for the mentally, physically, and morally obese (I reserve the right to alter that statement someday). Lahinch is a place where to walk the crude yet powerful bastion of the promenade on a wild day is a fine experience.

With pioneers like Bushnell, Fulton and Brun, a man who greatly developed the submarine was John Holland born in nearby Liscannor in 1841; his health failing, as a Christian Brother he went to the United States, where financed by Fenian funds to the tune of 60,000 dollars, he designed an underwater vessel called 'The Fenian Ram' which he successfully tried out in New York harbour. His aim was to design a craft that would break the power of the British fleet and thus help to liberate Ireland.

A few miles to the east is Ennistymon where, through an archway of the main street, I saw framed above an angry falls in the little river Cullenagh the Falls Hotel gleaming white against an emerald background. This was once the home of Caitlín MacNamara, wife of Dylan Thomas.

Standing in this town of the graveyard on a hummock, with its painted pubs and summer-merry west-Clare life, I was reminded of the sad but glorious journeyings of the Welsh poet through America, an odyssey terminated by his death of 'an insult to the brain'.

North-eastward out of Ennistymon I roved to make an oval-shaped detour through Kilfenora, Killinaboy, Corofin and Dysert O'Dea thence almost due east again to Ennistymon. This oval in the heart of Clare encloses a series of archaeological pleasures that can barely be hinted at.

In Kilfenora, the cathedral of St Fachtnan and its churchyard have notable features that include crosses and effigies. Three or four miles to the east are the enormous ruins of the O'Brien castle of Leamaneh where once Red Mary MacMahon, on being confronted with the corpse of her husband Conor O'Brien, slain in battle, said, 'Take him away! Dead men are no use to me!' She held her lands for Sir Donat O'Brien, her son, by offering to marry any Cromwellian officer nominated by General Ludlow—and nominated is not an inapposite stud-word! Red Mary later married an English soldier called Cooper and thus preserved the O'Brien inheritance.

Near Kilnaboy, north-west of Corofin, is the famous Tau cross which, shaped like the axilla rest of a T-crutch, has two heads carved on the face of the transom: exhibited in the Rosc International Exhibition of Modern Art some years ago, its presence tended to prove that abstract art is nothing new. A national sensation was created when this cross, whether it is of Christian or pagan origin is uncertain, was carried off by a coterie of angry Claremen who objected to its temporary removal to Dublin from what they reckoned its natural habitat. An excellent plaster cast of the Tau Cross is in the National Museum.

The dying sunlight of the afternoon rimmed with fire the High Cross of Dysert O'Dea, three miles to the south. Once the site of a hermitage, Dysert O'Dea was also the scene of a decisive battle in 1318 between the native O'Briens and the Norman de Clare, the Irish victory being important since it set a stop to further Anglo-Norman incursions into Thomond.

The road northwards out of Ennistymon rides into an unprepossessing stretch of bogland so I doubled back to Lahinch and took the cliff road that moves westward through Liscannor and, having passed Birchfield House, swings northward against a determined acclivity.

Here I took time out to marvel at the naïveté of the tenants of one Cornelius O'Brien who, on their landlord's instructions, raised a monument to his honour. Still musing I raised my hat to the dripping recesses of St Brigid's well where, on the Saturday before the last Sunday of July, crowds that include many Aran Islanders, gather to pay 'rounds' and later indulge in merrymaking at Lahinch.

Rampart after rampart of uncompromising cliffside sliced jaggedly down, down, down; the troubled sea is so far below that its cliff-foot brawl is but a rumour of remote battle carried upwards on a fitful wind. This indeed is Moher.

Gulls mew about the monstrous cliffside; listening through the lattice of the wind one hears their cries as if they were children quarrelling in the faraway. On the cliff-edge, upended flagstones keep the unwary from pitching over while below cliff-level there is a platform of stone upon which once stood what must have been an exciting stone picnic table. Beside one's boots, flagstones jut vertically out of the grass, perhaps in places to be levered out like grey leaves sliding out of a volume of time-foxed vellum.

One climbs to the highest part of the 750-feet cliff. Cattle raise their heads to trumpet through the unglazed windows of an O'Brien tower, built about 1835 for the convenience of visitors. After the sun has gone down, enormous gulls, each stationed at a discreet distance from his neighbour, begin solemnly to stalk the cliff-top fields.

I drive north-east from Moher, and after a mile or so, come round a bend of the road upon one of my favourite views in Ireland.

In the north, Galway Bay, the Aran Islands, and the distant Twelve Pins of Connemara are ranged out for my delight. Beside me are trim cottages; some are thatched but each has its outhouse roofed with flagstone. Fisherstreet village lies below; beyond it is Doolin Point with boulders everywhere strewn and barbarous parallelograms of nude stone.

At Doolin the Aran Islanders come ashore walking quietly on rawhide shoes to drink and dance a step maybe at gentle Gus O'Connor's pub.

From this area I find it difficult to drag myself away. Once I spent a whole day here saving hay in a meadow: as I worked in the air shot with larksong I felt as rich as Damer.

Inland now, and over the Spectacle Bridge to see the white walls of Lisdoonvarna gleaming in mid-bogland.

Lisdoonvarna is synonomous with the gay gravity and the grave gaiety of rural Ireland at its best. It is beloved of the thousands who come here each year (with September as its peak month) to drink from the famous sulphur, iron and chalybeate springs and then most discreetly to frolic before winter mists wrap up the western coasts.

Lisdoonvarna Spa then with its singing pubs, its inordinate consumption of water that smells of hard-boiled eggs or rusty nails and the wonderful air of its uplands. Lisdoonvarna with its parish priests, its farmers, its rural officials holy, whole and wholesome. It stands out in affection like an old church (or, indeed, an old pub) that in its Gothic mahogany conveys a sense of security that elsewhere the novel years have set at nought. Match-making in the old astringent sense is no longer a feature of the town's natural life but the place does still vouch for quiet and gracious romance.

In this context, I must say: *Haud inexpertus loquor*. For once, as a hard-to-please young man I visited Lisdoonvarna for a day and stayed there two laughing months, and from thence brought myself home a wife. . . .

The Burren, with Mount Elva as its most striking feature, can be said to be famous and infamous, beloved and abhorred. It is difficult to avoid quoting a comment, probably falsely attributed to Oliver Cromwell! 'Burren? Not enough wood to hang a man. Not enough water to drown him. Not enough clay to cover his corpse.'

Though infamous, because of its apparent barrenness, the wealth of its antiquities includes cairns and chamber tombs. Its subterranean lakes have lately been surveyed for the first time by a team from Bristol University. It is beloved of botanists because of the rare flowers—*adantium capillus veneris* is one—that grow in the crevices of its rocks.

At Ballyvaughan, on the north-western edge of the Burren, I asked an O'Loughlin man (O'Loughlins were the traditional chiefs of this area) how people—or even cattle—lived on those apparently barren hills.

'The word is exist,' O'Loughlin said in mild reproval.

'Exist,' I amended contritely.

'Strangers like you think there's nothing there but bare stone. Yet, if you climb those hills you'll find ravines of sweet grass that offer shelter from the wind while the hoarded summer heat from the limestone warms the cattle all winter long. Farmers in the Burren just let their cattle run. I keep 20 milch cattle up there, Poll-Angus mostly. They never give me trouble. And they never fail to hold the bull.'

I spent a long while on the top of Corkscrew Hill looking at the inset of Galway Bay to the north, trying to find the smoke scrawl of Galway City and tracing hills upon hills far beyond Black Head and on the Connemara shore. Immediately below me was a green oasis having as its centre a house called Creagan's Castle, beside which a pair of cream-coloured Connemara ponies with dark manes, were running wild.

Flying into Shannon from Atlanta via London, Dick Dodd had joined me on the road. The pair of us walked up the road that led to Corcomroe Abbey, founded in 1180 by Dónal Mór O'Brien, which lies almost exactly halfway between Ballyvaughan and Kinvara.

Before us, in the bizarre light under an altar archway, prone on a tomb lay what is traditionally believed to be an effigy of an abbot, both tomb and effigy crudely cut from stone.

But these were merely stage props in a drama that had already begun to take shape before my inner eye. For I had been imaginatively transported to the Abbey Theatre in Dublin where *The Dreaming of the Bones*, that powerful Yeats play which owes much to the *Nō* Theatre of Japan, was being enacted.

The scene of the play is laid in Corcomroe Abbey: it has to do with the story of Dermot MacMurrough who became King of Leinster, carrying off in 1166 Dervorgilla the wife of Prince Tiernan O'Rourke while her husband was on a penitential visit to Lough Derg in County Donegal.

The play tells of the ghosts of the dead lovers forever wandering in the Irish countryside vainly seeking the forgiveness of even one Irishman.

Finally, here in Corcomroe they encounter a young man on the run after the Easter Week Rebellion and beg his forgiveness. The use of chanting and masks in the play leaves an indelible impression.

For Dick and myself the abbey with the cloud-capped hills above it and the backdrop of tomb, cross and effigy must inevitably abide in powerful memory.

CHAPTER SIX

West Ireland

Galway and Mayo

But—hark!—some voice like thunder spake
'The West's Awake! The West's Awake!

Lough Corrib drives its wedge deep into county Galway and splits it into two separate areas that diverge widely in texture and configuration: the east is a fertile plain stretching over low stone walls to the Shannon, while the Irish-speaking west (Connemara) is distinguished by peaks called the Twelve Pins with winding valleys between and swaths of bogland that move moodily to an indented coastline. Everywhere there are merry rivers, islands, and lakes.

County Mayo, which is sib to Connemara, offers an added dimension of coastal variety with St Patrick's holy mountain south of Clew Bay as centrepiece. Within the confines of Mayo lies Ireland's largest island—Achill. The scenery inland is not a whit the less diversified than that of Galway.

Everywhere in west Ireland the keynote is wildness and the recurrent emotion of the traveller is that of discovery.

A few miles south of Gort in County Galway a fingerpost to the right read 'Lough Cutra Scenic Drive'. This had of course to be explored. Presently I found myself in tranquil country. On both sides of me the hedges dripped hay. There was a castle, a lake, and a general beauty of landscape. Above all hung an utter silence. Lough Cutra Castle, now in the process of restoration, remains in the memory because of its noble rooms.

Gort, once an O'Shaughnessy town, which lies in the centre of an area of high literary interest, was seat of the 6th century King Guaire of Connaught.

As I strolled in the quiet town, a Persian cat from the hotel in which I stayed kept following me and insisted on rubbing his head affectionately against my trouser's leg. A joker publican had a notice in the window which read 'Free Drinks tomorrow!' At Mass in the local church, the following morning, the priest gave a scholarly sermon, semantic and dialectic aeons removed from the Kiltartanese the Abbey Theatre-conditioned enquirer expects to find in the south of Galway.

Alas! Lady Gregory's house at nearby Coole is down. The noble house in which, to some extent, the fortunes of the Irish National Theatre were plotted to fruition, is razed to the ground. Valerian triumphs over its broken walls. The Seven Woods of the Yeats' poem have sickened and sorrowed. A moment of national aberration and something priceless has been lost.

There is an avenue of light-seeking cedars: there is also an immense copper beech incarcerated in an iron cage, on the bark of which visitors read the initials of Lady Gregory's famous guests: W. B. Y. (William B. Yeats), G. B. S. (George Bernard Shaw), S. O' C. (Seán O'Casey), A. E. (George Russell), and many more. De Maupassant too was once here to walk pondering under the noble trees.

In nearby Kiltartan village I looked hard at the people who passed me by and thought how in her plays, Lady Gregory had jelled their moods and manners forever. Remembered with especial affection in her one-act play *The Workhouse Ward* with old Michael Meskell and his crony-foe hurling insults at each other, the pair becoming unexpectedly reconciled on the edge of parting, and again reverting to vituperation as the prospect of their leaving the workhouse recedes.

Five miles or so to the north of Gort, on the main Gort-Galway road, another fingerpost indicates Thoor Ballylee; traversing a hummocky road that runs eastward one finds beside a pebbled stream and a ruined mill, the bulk of a Norman (de Burgo or Burke) Tower. Here W. B. Yeats lived for some years.

I visited the place some years before in the first darkness of a summer's night. Drawing up at the thatched English-looking cottage that crouches beneath the tower—the cottage windows had jalousies and there was a door that boasted a latch—I found the place closed and barred for the night.

For a time I prowled in that truly Norman hollow. Leaning over the bridge I heard trout rising under the bushes. Lighting a match and holding it high I made out the legend cut on a stone inset in the castle wall.

> *I, the poet William Yeats,*
> *With old mill-boards and sea-green slates*
> *And smithy work from the Gort forge,*
> *Restored this tower for my wife, George,*
> *And may these characters remain*
> *When all is ruin once again.*

On this occasion I came with daylight. The door swung open at my touch. Inside, I saw a Spanish-looking girl sitting reading at a table.

'It must be lonely when no one comes?' I asked.

'Yes, indeed', she said quietly.

It has a rare atmosphere, this keep for which Mary Hanley of Limerick provided the zeal and edge requisite for its renewal.

Mounting the spiral stairway and peeping into the bare spacious rooms I kept thinking of three other Marys whom I associate with Yeats: Mary O'Malley of Belfast, whose contribution to the production of Yeatsian drama in that city has been monumental, Mary Watson of Sligo, who recites the poetry of Yeats with such rare feeling, and Mary Hynes the miller's daughter from Ballylee, a young woman beloved of Blind Raftery the picaresque poet.

> *I am Raftery the Poet, full of hope, full of love,*
> *My eyes without light, my quietness without torment.*

This I quoted as I moved upwards, peeping the while into white spacious rooms.

On the top of the castle I leaned over to look down on the stream below. The spire of Gort was a pencil point in the summer haze.

Approaching Louhrea I found songs battling for the foreground of my consciousness. One was by Pádraic Fallon, a talented son of Loughrea, whose integrity will not allow him to push his literary wares, another was by the eccentric Bard of Thomond (Michael Hogan of Limerick)—but this latter perhaps may have to do with a different Loughrea. I also recalled the short stories of Loughrea's Séamus O'Kelly, whose masterpiece, *The Weaver's Grave* adapted by Micheál Ó hAodha of Radio-Telefís Eireann, had won the Italia Award for Television plays. *The Weaver's Grave* I reckon the third greatest Irish short story: for me Joyce's *The Dead* and O'Connor's *In the Train* fill first and second places.

Loughrea of the powerful chimneys was quiet and restrained. A muted pig-fare was in progress. There were blue carts galore. The air was pierced by the squealing of suckling pigs. A line of tinkers, their faces harrowed by rough living, sat on a stone wall beside the carts.

I noticed a tinker boy, recurrently trailing a whiplash in a pool of maroon animal piss and ritualistically flaying the face of a stone image set in a nearby wall.

I came close to the lad; in the intervals of his scourging, I read beneath the stone head the legend of Stoney Brennan. Mention was made of his curative powers.

'Who was Stoney Brennan?' In a nearby 'privy' I asked this question of a toothless pair of old men who were solemnly relieving themselves.

The pair convulsed with glee.

'He was hanged for feckin' a turnip,' said one.

'He was a quack doctor,' chuckled the second.

'He didn't stale the turnip at all,' said the first.

'If he had, he'd have some satisfaction an' he gurglin',' said the second.

'Come here a Friday night,' said the first old man.

'You'll see thousands dancing out there in honour of Stoney,' said the other.

'He'll never die out in Loughrea!' both chuckled together as I went away.

The stained-glass windows of St Brendan's Cathedral were impressive. Beside the Cathedral, the gateway of the medieval town has been adapted as a small diocesan museum; Father O'Callaghan, the administrator, trusted me with the key. Chalices and old vestments, crosses from penal days and ancient rosaries—they were all there.

Afterwards, I went to visit the Carmelite Abbey. In the old abbey nearby—not very wisely restored—a brown-robed monk walked into a small compartment in the ruin, where rows of votive candles burned before a statue of the Virgin Mary.

The heat was intense and the smell of burning wick and consuming wax almost overpowering. Here, since 1300, at times despite sharp persecution, devotion to the Virgin has gone on without break.

As I emerged into the sunlight, I thought of the French general, St Ruth, decapitated by a cannon ball at the—for the Irish—fatal battle of Aughrim in 1691, his head and trunk buried by torchlight in this abbey.

I thought too of the naked bodies of the 7,000 Irish dead, laid out in files at the end of the bloody Aughrim day. 'The dogs of Aughrim' have gone down in local lore for so addicted to the taste of human flesh did they become that for years afterwards they hunted in packs and even attacked travellers.

O'Kelly has manure that is neither sand nor lime
But fine straight soldiers who'ld do deeds with the pike.
They have been left in Aughrim, file on bloody file,
Set out like so much horseflesh on which hungry dogs could
*   dine. Och, Ochone.*

Aughrim of the O'Kellys! Some day I'll go back to Aughrim and handle the mementoes of the battle that an old friend, Martin Joyce, has collected in the miniature museum of his school.

East Galway is flat. At evening the setting sun strikes in raddle-red through the lace of its stone walls. Excellent tillage country, its main towns, Athenry, Ballinasloe, and Tuam, draw sustenance from the good earth.

Athenry (Ford of the Kings) with its nearby head-quarters at Craughwell of the famous hunting pack 'The Galway Blazers', I found sunk in midsummer sleep.

This somnolence was in contrast to Athenry's murderous history; in 1316 when the Burke-Birmingham Anglo-Norman alliance inflicted a bloody defeat on the Irish under King Phelim O'Conor, the dead on the battlefield numbered more than 8,000 and included almost all the native Irish chivalry of Connaught. The town saw subsequent sackings, one by Red Hugh O'Donnell in 1598.

Under the stilts of its high castle, and in the shadow of its broken walls, a train whistle sounded like the peal of cannon.

Ballinasloe on the Galway-Roscommon border is noted for its fairs, the quality of its limestone and the artistic appointments of St Michael's Catholic Church. Its great fair is held in early October.

Tuam of the sugar beet factory was once the seat of the O'Conors, Kings of Connaught; it presides over an area rich in ringforts, some of which boast souterrains. Since the time of St Jarlath in the 5th or 6th centuries it has been a place of ecclesiastical eminence and is now the metropolitan see of the province of Connaught. The famous Lally, or O'Mullally, of the Irish Brigade in France whose nephew Lally-Tollendal was Marshall of that land, had his ancestral home some five miles north of the town.

Galway City is a wholesome, glittering, bright-minded, narrow-ribbed laughing kind of city. Irish-speaking Connemara keeps the mill-wheel of the town gaily revolving. Its many links with Spain are probably authentic but over-stressed.

In Eyre (now Kennedy) Square, I thought of writer Sean-Phádraic Ó Conaire, ex-British civil servant turned writing rambler, complete with black and green cart, scribbling stories under rainy hedgerows, making long treks through the midlands to Dublin city, there to climb the railings of St Stephen's Green and make a nest for himself with the wild ducks on the tiny island in the lake.

Poor Phádraic, the first writer to attempt to modernize the short story in Irish, was the subject of a fine poetic panegyric by F. R. Higgins which begins as follows:

> *They've paid the last respects in sad tobacco.*
> *And silent is this wakehouse in its haze.*
> *They've paid the last respects and now their whiskey*
> *Flings laughing words on mouths of prayer and praise.*

'Where's Sean-Phádraic?' I asked the man working inside a picket fence for I had searched in vain for the puckish statue that for me symbolizes the city. 'Dumped in the Corrib,' the man shouted.

'Dumped!'

'What did that ould scribbler ever do for the liberation of this country?' the worker went on, and then added with a smile: 'There was talk of planting him with his back to the jacks. But he'll go plumb centre in a place of honour. The President of America and ould Paddy Connary, a bloody good double.'

And Sean-Phádraic was later replaced plumb-centre.

With four or five hundred other people, mostly tourists, I leaned over the parapet of O'Brien's Bridge to watch the salmon in the Corrib River below. It was a sundrenched Sunday and the traffic was desultory and muted.

Below was the wonder of a platform of salmon in an unpolluted river bed in mid-city. In rows, in ranks, in side-long wedges, in echelons, the fish were outlined in pea-green water about two or three feet deep at this point.

Outside Corbett's in Mary Street I found two street musicians, one with a banjo the other with a fiddle. They were playing *The Coolin*, the most plaintive of our Irish airs. These were the Dunnes, men with whom I had soldiered with on many a raucous night at the southern festivals.

12 A live hen awaits a buyer in the open-air market

I left them and went downstreet. The musicians then struck up *The Valley of Knockanure* in my honour and indeed in memory of our mutual friend—the absent John Wilson. This ballad which I had made on an older incomplete version is sung widely in Ireland today.

By the wall of the *Cois Fharraige* (By the Sea) room in the basement of the Great Southern Hotel stood an impish, daemonic and powerful bronze of *An Craos-Deamhan* or Hunger Demon; on another wall stood what appeared to be a weather-antlered yew tree.

The girls in attendance were native speakers of Irish from Connemara. They were amateur actresses of note and traditional singers as well. As one of the girls began to sing *Dónal Óg*, a song that I find passionately disturbing, I intoned my own translation of the verse in which a young girl complains of unrequited love:

> *You took the east from me: you took the west from me,*
> *You took the gentle moon and stole the staring sun,*
> *You've tattered the heart that beats in the cage of my breast.*
> *And even denied me Christ the Virgin Mary's Son. . . .*

'We're not saying definitely that Christopher Columbus prayed in this church before he continued on his voyage to discover America.' The woman who addressed me with such a preoccupation for accuracy was arranging cards in the Church of St Nicholas-of-Myra in Galway.

As I gazed up at the ribbed and vaulted roof, 'What we *do* say,' she went on, 'is that legend has it that Columbus *may* have called to Aran to take on a pilot, and that he *may* even have called to Galway. If he *did* call to this city on a Sunday, and if he *did* have a mind to worship, the church at which he was most likely *would have* prayed, is this, St Nicholas-of-Myra.'

A convolute statement this, and prudently hedged in by provisos.

13 Cormac's Chapel, Cashel, Co. Tipperary

As Kerrymen we are not quite so temperate in our claims as to who discovered the New World. St Brendan!—who else?

One needs the exercise of a further mood of caution in accepting the words of a tablet on the wall of the yard of this same church. The legend states that in 1493 a Mayor Lynch acting from a profound sense of duty, hanged his own son from a nearby window and that this callous act was the origin of the verb to lynch. Closer to the bone of scholastic truth however is a further Nicholas-of-Myra claim—that Scribe An Dubhaltach Óg Mac Fhirbhisigh compiled part of the Book of Genealogies in this storied Abbey of St Nicholas.

Galway City had its origin as a Burke settlement wrenched from O'Flaherty land and brought to municipal fruition by the efforts of fourteen tribes of Anglo-Norman burgesses. These conscience-stricken burgesses later had cut in stone over the west gate a prayer which read: 'O Lord, protect us from the ferocious O'Flaherties.' They also had an edict aimed at the mere Irish which hopefully decreed: 'Neither Mac nor O shall swagger in the Galway streets.'

Chief among the burgesses were the Lynch clan, who had a reputation for scholarship. Lynch's Castle, at the junction of Shop Street, and Upper Abbey Street, is now the Munster and Leinster Bank.

An Taibhdhearc is Galway's famous Irish-speaking theatre where such great actors as Micheal MacLiammóir and Siobhán McKenna have acted. Here also many of the Abbey Company have begun their careers on the stage. As I had been there many times before, however, I decided to move on and soon found myself in Salthill, the resort suburb to the west of the city, where anglers in their scores were casting mackerel lures into the sea. It is not uncommon for a thousand mackerel to be caught by line when a shoal moves close to the shore in Salthill.

I had visited Salthill on many previous occasions, the most memorable being the day on which the Irish-speaking people of Ireland gather to watch the *currach* men of the western coast compete for mastery of their craft. I recall the black-tarred canvas canoes cleaving the waves and the mesmeric effect the moving oars had on the spectators. In the pubs the tide-roar of singing was as loud as the roar of the sea.

On the morrow I had arranged to go to the Aran Islands. I reached the quay as the boat was casting off, its passengers animated by a spirit of adventurous gaiety. It was easy to get to know everybody on board and soon we were chatting together like old comrades. There was a Federal Judge from Kansas and his lawyer friend, two priests, an American film-maker and a group of courteous but shy islanders talking together in Irish.

We had also on board an islandman dressed in brown pin-striped suit who had married a London barmaid and was taking her home in triumph, and an internationally-famous architect determined to study the cliff-fort of Dún Aengus.

The boat allowed us five hours or so on the main island of Inishmore: another boat serving the three Arans would allow time to visit the smaller islands of Inishmaan and Inisheer.

After leaving the quay, scalding coffee was served. To the south Black Head loomed; to the north stood ranked the mountains of Connemara.

After a few hours chugging, the islands came into view and presently we saw the crowds gathered on Kilronan Quay on Inishmore. A file of jaunting cars and traps stretched along the pier. The pierhead was gay with yellow cylinders of gas, the fuel which now tends to supplant the turf or peat formerly imported from the mainland. With the passing of the peat has also passed that anachronistic vessel called the Galway 'hooker'.

As the gangway clattered down I clucked to a jarvey, thus engaging a side-car for our excursion. Once ashore, a party of us set off for the village of Kilmurvey on the other end of the island above which the great fort of Dún Aengus is poised.

A side-car or jaunting car will, at a pinch, take six people, two at each side, one perilously dangling his legs from the rear with the jarvey crouched in his crow's nest in front. At a pinch, I said, for four is normal and five is tolerable.

The sun shone brilliantly. On the roadside were stone monuments erected by the islanders to the memory of their dead forefathers. As we jogged along I chatted in Irish with the jarvey: we spoke of Robert Flaherty, maker of the film *Man of Aran*, of Barbara Mullen and Maggie Dirrane who took part in the same film, of Liam O'Flaherty, the island writer in Irish and in English whose short stories and sketches of island life are unsurpassed, and of other writers like Máirtín Ó Direáin and Máirtín Ó Cadhain. We also mentioned Galway's own Walter Macken, but recently dead, and for climax we spoke of 'that melancholy man John Synge' for whom life on the islands was especially fruitful.

As the reaping-hook of Kilmurvey beach came into view with a scant three or four holiday-makers lolling upon it, the horse dragged to a halt. Descending from the vehicle we moved upwards on foot over the parallels of blue limestone where the rock-fissures underfoot held miniature bushes espaliered on naked stone.

I plucked some wild flowers growing in the crevices: gentian, clover, heart's-ease and sea pinks. Rubbing a wool tuft to a thread, I tied my nosegay of flowers together to make a corsage. As an island child appeared from nowhere I offered her my bouquet. The child gravely accepted the gift.

Rain so fine that it could well have been sea-spray had begun to swirl about our faces. Looking back I found that the file of side-cars and traps on the roadway below had diminished with distance.

Dún Aengus was now immediately above us, that broken fortress the origin of which has puzzled archaeologists. Generations have asked if this was the place where the *Fir Bolg*, one of the aboriginal peoples of Ireland, had made their final stand against invaders.

Arriving almost at the clifftop I glanced downwards and to my left to discover a roaring bay far below. From a ledge on the cliff-face above this bay a fishing line glistened out and down in the erratic sunlight. On the ledge I saw a venturesome angler perched; recurrently the spray bloomed upwards from a shattered wave to cast its gauze about his figure. After the spray had drifted off, the sea-angler and his sunlit line stretching to a mid-bay area surfaced with brown scum-foam, were recurrently discovered.

But all the ramparts of the coast seemed dwarfed by the sheer cliff on which Dún Aengus itself was hung. About the stronghold *chevaux de frise* formed a vicious battery of rocks angle-embedded in the ground so as to serve as the bayonets of a monstrous age. The tunnel-pierced walls of the horseshoe-shaped rampart held within its semicircle an outcrop of stone that could well have once been the focal point of the fortress.

Gulls wheeled and lamented. The air was latticed with the bickering of songbirds.

I stayed there for a long while with the wings of legend beating around me. Later, from the rampart, I noticed how in the valley to the north a resolute planter, by tumbling several puny stone walls, had once made fields in the accepted sense of the word and had later built himself a 'great house', now in ruin. But beyond this novel estate, stone room after stone room, flattered by the name of fields, stretched to the island's edge.

Arrived back at Kilronan we paid the jarvey and moved into a cottage pub where fishermen, their faces wind-bright and their ganseys dark blue, conversed bilingually. Joining in the conversation I ventured to remark that footballer Joe Keohane was a 'big man and able to use every ounce of his weight' whereupon the biggest fisherman I had ever seen, probably accepting this as a compliment to himself, got up and moving across the floor said: *Tá an ceart a't* ('You are right!'), at the same time solemnly squeezing my hand much as the valiant tailor of legend squeezed cheese in the pretence that he was squeezing stone.

In a field by the pierhead, the shaggiest ass I have ever seen—matted curtains of hair floated from the sides of his belly—frolicked about in an absurd chase of a pair of heifers. I entered a nearby bar.

In the company of a brace of proper female Bostonians I drank and chatted about Dorchester and Marblehead. 'I came here for a day—that's two months ago,' one woman said as she sipped her drink.

Through the pub window I could see the ridges of the islands of Innishmaan and Innisheer. The sight recalled for me memorable days and nights spent on both islands, but especially on Innisheer, the smallest and most easterly of the three. Innisheer lacks a pier sufficiently large to take a mail-boat; as often as not getting ashore means going over the side of the mail-boat and down into the bounding currach of Rory Ó Conghaíle to be borne high on a wave crest to the beach.

Innisheer! I recall its school invaded by sand, the island lads with their long, white homespun trousers and the women with their black shawls worn over red petticoats. The abundant onion garden of Tomás – that too I recall, and the smell of boiling tar as the boat-maker prepares to weatherproof a currach. Nor do I forget the wreck of a coastal steamer rust-reddening the rocks and the Sabbath river of people flowing between the unmortared walls of the little roads.

So, standing at the pub window, I sent greetings over the sea to Innisheer: to its young brown-haired priest, to Andy the Dancer who can also make a currach dance on a violent sea, to Orla Knudsen the erudite Dane who, in search of solitude, reached that haven and, renting a cottage on the edge of the dunes, revived the almost dead island craft of making *crios* belts out of brilliant-coloured thread, to the laughing teenagers from the summer school, to the basking shark that almost became a pet of mine, to the dune-top graveyard with its carpet of Our Lady's Bedstraw and its occasional wild orchid, and above all to Seán (*an tSiopa*) Ó Conghaíle, a man who, by common assent is acknowledged to be the island king. His wife, sons and daughters—how they have welcomed me across the years; at times when I was tense and exhausted they have even placed a cottage at my disposal, and most courteously left me to uncoil. Food and drink, music and laughter, comradeship and conversation, the reading of poetry and the listening to records that connote the authentic voice of the Irish west, these blessings I owe them in fullest measure. And these blessings I acknowledge in gratitude.

Leaving Galway city, one may, if one wishes, move north then north west through Headford and Ballinrobe to cross the isthmus between Loughs Partry and Mask, spying on the other side of the lake Irish-speaking Tourmakeady set between the Partry mountains and the water, to reach, at last, Westport in County Mayo.

This seemingly prosaic road I have often travelled, staying perhaps a night in a fisherman's inn where the food and service was a delight (the name of one is Alderford if you wish to seek it), or at a gracious great house (the name of one is Lisdonagh House east of Headford if you must know) where the welcome, the atmosphere and the company proved superb. In this area fishing is an angler's delirium— and oh! the morning smell of those trout frying on the edge of an inlet of Mask!

But this temptation to move north I resisted, and with Maurice Hayes drove past Salthill and its mackerel-shoals to Spiddal ('Spiddal' is a corruption of 'hospital') where we came upon one of the most remarkable men in Connemara. Máirtín Stándún has, through his business genius and hard work, built up a business in Spiddal employing 30 or 40 people, which makes and sells the products of his native Connemara—Aran hand-knit ganseys (sweaters), crioses or woven belts, souvenirs of marble, bolts of tweed. The language of the store is Irish and the accent is proudly and unequivocally on things that are our own.

Twenty miles west of Galway on the coast road, the then parish priest of Tully, Father Tadhg Moran, took time out to show us the little wonders of his roadside church. The chalice had insets of rare enamel—the work of a Glenstal Brother—indicating virtuosity in an art in which the ancient Irish excelled. The chasubles of local báinín and tweed with inserts of *crios* or woven belt material, were exquisite.

As we left Tully we ran into a storm. Hitherto, I had seen Connemara in moods that were milk-mild. Now I was to see her scowling face. As we travelled west a storm howled down. The red sand-stone road before us seemed touched by scorch. Mountains and lakes reared in a mimicry of their image in the paintings of Paul Henry. Mackintoshed roadworkers huddled in the shelter of rhododendron clumps. Red-raddled sheep cried like infants. The car turned a bend and, in a land almost bare of trees, struck a fallen branch, so that we narrowly avoided a mishap.

Later, the day brightened. We pushed through Costelloe and drove south west for Carraroe.

Fiche bliain ag fás . . . Twenty years agrowing, twenty years in blossom, twenty years decaying, twenty years not caring whether there or not.

This is how the Gaelic proverb records the four spans of the life of man.

Fiche Bliain ag Fás or, in its English translation, 'Twenty Years A-growing', is the name of the Gaelic classic written by Maurice O'Sullivan of the Blasket Islands. As a young man, Maurice had joined the Civic Guards and later died in Connemara. We found his grave near Carraroe by the rocky shore.

As we came to the edge of the sea our pathway through the dusk was perilous. At last we reached the graveyard we sought. Under the brow of the awry huddle of crosses we found, amid the rocky clay, the grave of Muiris.

'*I ndil-chuimhe Mhuiris Uí Shúilleabháin*', the cross road. 'In loving memory of Maurice O'Sullivan, author . . .'

Just then we saw on the rocks between us and the sea, a pair of lovers seated on a rock, their figures outlined against the water. A sliver of moon came up and on its reflection in the shifting water the head of a seal appeared. The seal, the sea, the lights across the bay, the lovers, the rocky shore, the natural graveyard—Muiris Ó Súilleabháin was laid to rest in a place as natural as his own Dunquin.

At Screeb of the fine beach we found ourselves in a dilemma as to which road we would take. Due north to Maam Cross, there to talk angling with Holmes Peacocke whose inn sits at one of the crossroads of Connemara, or swing west and then drive south into the Rosmuck Peninsula, an area which has profound historical associations for Ireland? As usual, we compromised by doing both. Racing north to have a drink and gossip about old times with Holmes, we then retraced our steps to the landmark of the turf-burning electricity generating station at Screeb and thence moved westward to Rosmuck.

The land grew still more boulder-strewn. I saw the white hillside cottages where as a young man I had danced and sung all night long. This was then an area where poteen or home-distilled whiskey was common. Nora and Cáit and Eileen, my laughing partners of the long ago, where were they now?

At the gateway to the Rosmuck Peninsula, beside Gortmore and on the edge of Lake Alliveragh where a red-shirted lad filled a donkey pannier with turf, I cupped my hands about my eyes and peered through the window of Pearse's cottage where the Irish leader had repaired to hatch the overthrow of a government and to dream of a Gaelic Ireland.

When last I saw this cottage late in the decade following the establishment of the new Irish state it was then occupied by the local lady teacher and her niece who often invited a bunch of us young hooligans, grappling with the intricacies of the Connemara dialect of Irish to make the rafters of the historic cottage ring with twilight reels. Often in mid-frolic a knock would come at the door and a group of hushed visitors, headed perhaps by an old pastor, unable to believe his senses, would enter and stare at us. 'National blasphemy!' their eyes accused. Sanctimoniousness printed on our faces, we would sit quietly until the visitors had departed. Whereupon the kip-of-the-reel started again.

I thought that if the reincarnated ghost of Pearse had come up out of one of the bedrooms—as I sometimes expected him to do—he would have approved of us rather than of the visitors.

Nuns in a car, white posts to keep vehicles from tumbling into lake water, a quarryful of donkeys, woodbine claws, foxglove turrets and fuchsia tassels, a nesting swan on an island, a hotel in an island, red petticoats hung out to dry on writhing bushes, sheep against the grey stones of one of the Bens—that was the Connemara as we continued to encounter it.

This and more we experienced on that stout peninsula on our way to Carna, Glinsk and Cashel. The rock edge where land meets sea is here marked by yellow-orange seaweed. This area is dedicated to St MacDara: boats passing his island five miles to the west of Carna dip their sails in his honour.

In mid-bog beside Glinsk we came upon an unusual tinkers'

encampment on the roadside. The camp itself was larger than its south-western counterpart with the l' poles and ridge poles as thick as a man's arm. In all, it had the crude effect of an eastern pavilion. The man's name was Laurence, his wife was a Maughan. ('It's me surname—Laurence', he explained.) At his feet were a pile of newly-made tin gallons that flashed in the sun. He had a blue van and a pony and cart. Scattered about the ground in a kind of crude order were mirrors, combs, ornaments and hideous 'sacred' oleographs.

North then to Recess to visit the showrooms of an industry built around green Connemara marble. Everything from cufflinks to fire-places was on show and a sense of design indicated. On the southern shore of Ballinahinch Lake is Ballinahinch Castle, once home of one of Ireland's great eccentrics, 'Humanity' Dick Martin, a founder of the R.S.P.C.A.

From Recess, if one wishes, one may go first north, then north-west to Kylemore through Glen Ina hard by lovely Lough Ina, travelling between the Bens and the Maumturk mountains to short circuit the round road that lies to the west.

We stopped on the high street of artist-and-botanist-beloved town Roundstone, a place of dunes and beaches (Dog's Bay and Gorteen are beautiful) with Errisbeg Mountain high over us. This town was founded in the 1820's by Scottish fisherfolk attracted there by the abundance of crayfish and lobster in the locality. Kate O'Brien the novelist lived for some years at the Fort above the harbour. I slept that night in a roadside cottage after a pleasant meal and a glut of evening singing.

North of Ballyconneely, where in 1919 aviators Alcock and Browne crash-landed in mid-bog at the end of the first-ever flight across the Atlantic, there is a sense of the world opening towards the north. West of the oxygenated highway lies glittering Coral Strand on Mannin Bay. Later still, harbouring some slight delusions that we were drifting in the South Pacific and not a little sated with solitude, we entered the triangular-shaped town of Clifden, founded by the D'Arcy family and now the Connemara capital.

A bunch of English country mummers, somewhat like exotic birds, were hyperconsciously dancing in an open space in mid-town. On their garments sequins glittered. After watching them for a time I went off to visit Albert Millar who weaves tweed and sells báinín ganseys in his fine store in mid-town. As I entered, Albert handed a gansey to an America saying, 'Take it with you! If you don't like it, or it doesn't fit, pack it back.' 'Okay!' the American said; then incredulously: 'Aren't you going to take my name?' 'Off you go!' Bobby replied, 'I have never been cheated so far.'

North-west by the upper road overlooking Clifden Bay are some superb views. Omey Island dedicated to St Féichín may be reached on foot at ebb tide. Cleggan, when we reached it, seemed bare and open; there, in a house in tune with the locality, resides Richard Murphy, a major poet, and once owner of one of the last of the Galway hookers. He is the author of a memorable poem on a local fishing disaster.

From Cleggan one may go to Inishbofin Island, there to stay perhaps at Day's Hotel and talk with the O'Tooles and Schofields. Possessed of further valour one may even sail to the lonely island of Inishturk with its neat harbour and ask the islanders to recount the legends of the *Beoir Lochlannach*, or Danish beer.

The story of Inishbofin goes back to the Synod of Whitby in England in 663, when, after acrimonious wranglings, Bishop Colman of Lindisfarne, with 30 of his intransigent Irish-English monks of Northumbria left the gathering in high dudgeon, and retreating to Inishbofin, then the ultimate western point of European Christianity, founded a monastery. Thus was ended the native Irish authority extended for centuries from Iona over the English Church north of the Humber.

Danish beer? On lonely Inishturk the Irish ran to earth the last Dane and his son, both of whom were possessed of the secret of making heather ale. The Irish chieftain brought the pair to the top of a forbidding cliff and threatened to throw them down if they refused to tell the secret. 'Throw down my son first,' the old man whispered, 'I would be ashamed if he heard me reveal the secret.' The young man was hurled down. 'Now you may throw *me* down,' said the old man equably. 'I was afraid that if you hurled *me* down first my son would tell you what you wished to know.' At Letterfrack in the middle of nowhere, a cattle fair was in progress. With a knowledgeable man of the locality, I discussed the foundation of the village by Quaker Ellis in the nineteenth century. Letterfrack is quite fiercesomely situated beneath intimidating mountains.

Surgeon Oliver St John Gogarty, wit and author, had a noble house at Rinvyle, in the vicinity of which are a ruined church and a well dedicated to seven daughters of a Welsh king. The Anti-Treaty forces burned the Gogarty house, thus understandably drawing the vengeance of the rather vituperative St John on their heads. For de Valera he reserved a special measure of witty spleen: 'Dev can certainly be called Hibernian since he resembles something uncoiled from the Book of Kells.'

Exquisitely rebuilt, the Gogarty house, now a hotel, was a welcome oasis for Maurice and myself. The air of the west had honed our appetites to a fine edge. We were late for dinner, but the young chef stretched a point for us. After a satisfying meal we tottered to a bank of rounded stones above the beach at the rear of the hotel, and nesting ourselves down like belly-taut dogs, dozed the doze of the just.

When later we awoke at full sunset the off-duty chef was standing beside us. 'At dinner,' I began sleepily, 'someone mentioned a miraculous catch of fish?' 'An English visitor came here for a few days ago,' the chef replied; 'she had never wet a line before. The river was in flood and the sea-trout were running. The lady was given a rod, a line, a hook and a supply of worms. In one hour she had killed 75 trout and one peal salmon.'

From Rinvyle we moved south-east through Tully Cross to strike the main road a little to the east of Letterfrack; thence after a short run, with the Twelve Pins almost set due south, we reached Kylemore Benedictine Abbey set dramatically beneath steep Doughruagh Mountain (1,736 feet) and beside Kylemore Lough.

As we arrived on the loughside we saw, directly in front of the Abbey, an angler in a boat playing a salmon. The hooked fish swirled almost contemptuously about. I walked along the lakeside to where in a little mausoleum the Henrys—husband and wife, lie buried. Built originally in 1852 by Michael Henry, surgeon and financier of Manchester and London, to please his wife, formerly Margaret Vaughan of County Down, the castle carried with it 9,000 acres of mountain, lake and bogland. The building cost £1¼ millions and is lavishly castellated. It was once a place of onxy fireplaces, oak balustrades, bevelled mirrors, stained glass windows and pelmets of gilt.

Mrs Henry, 'a queenly woman', died in Cairo of 'Nile fever'. Her husband survived her by 36 years and saw his empire crash as a result of the failure of his mines and the attrition of lawsuits.

Destroyed by fire in 1959—the granite walls of Kylemore Abbey stood staunchly against the flames—the Benedictine nuns who had bought the place after World War I took advantage of the catastrophe to redesign the 70-roomed building with due regard to its requirements as a school. The ballroom where the Henrys once held court is now a Benedictine Choir. Around the building, hydrangeas, fuchsias and rhododendrons bloom in profusion.

This Abbey (of Iershe Damen) had its origin in Ypres in Belgium in 1598 and was an offshoot of a Benedictine Abbey founded by Lady Mary Percy, daughter of Thomas, Earl of Northumberland, martyred at Tyburn in 1572.

On one occasion the nuns of Ypres returned to Ship Street in Dublin; after the Battle of the Boyne, however, they fled back to Ypres. War recurrently raged around their abbey until German guns destroyed it wholly in 1914.

The dramatic history of this foundation is interwoven with the Irish Brigade formed in France by the remnants of the army of James II in 1691 and placed at the service of France after the Siege of Limerick. This unit persisted until 1798 when, subsequent to the French Revolution, it was scattered throughout Europe.

Entering the Abbey, one finds under glass, a faded dark blue flag with a harp in red-gold. This was the original flag carried at Ramillies in 1706 when Lord Clare's Dragoons turned an apparent rout into an attack.

Striking Killary Harbour, Ireland's most perfect fiord, was truly a delight. Some miles west of Leenane we found the water lapping the foot of Mweelrea and its brother mountains. On the tranquil surface of the fiord a black boat drew its net in a circle about a point on the northern shore. Only the thump and creak of the oars broke the stillness. The fishermen's voices came clearly across the water. After the final lowhanded hauling, there was the sudden upended bag of squirming silver fish.

We then raced out a few miles to Aasleagh Falls on the Galway-Mayo border, where the Erriff river, in full-blooded spate, tumbled in brown power into the drowned estuary that is Killary Harbour.

Reluctantly, Maurice had to take off for his native North of Ireland; I was left to my own devices.

From Leenane there was a run I simply had to take: it thrusts right into the heart of the Joyces' Country which lies for the main part on the broad isthmus between Loughs Mask and Corrib.

Let me see if again I can call that journey to mind: southeast and uphill into Maam valley, there to fork left at Griggins, past Aille Dubh waterfall, along the north shore of Lough Nafooey, thence to Finny and Clonbur on the isthmus proper, and finally to nip over the Mayo border into Cong, which place, with its sound not unlike that of a bell, provides a full stop not merely in my itinerary but in the history of Ireland.

I loitered for a long time in the bogland above Lough Nafooey, that most secret of lakes. I examined stones, wool, heather and clay. I chewed grass, smelled bogland air, watched windflaws on the surface of the lake, identified peaks, wondered where little roadways rambled to, and in sum had a lazy and rewarding day.

But I am to tell you about historic Cong.

First I must mention the nearby mock-Gothic Ashford Castle on Lough Corrib, an impressive building erected for the Guinness-is-Good-for-You-family which incorporates a de Burgo Castle dating back several centuries as well as a French chateau built by the Oranmore and Browne family.

The castle is now a superbly-appointed hotel owned by a member of the famous hotelier clan, the Huggards. Much of the lovely and uproarious film *The Quiet Man* with its redheaded heroine (author Maurice Walsh, my neighbour and friend, was addicted to redheads) was shot in this locality.

Now let me be confoundedly annoying in the Irish mode by stating what did *not* happen here—except in the pages of bogus history. The legendary battle of Moytura, in which two of the major aboriginal tribes of prehistoric Ireland, the *Firbolg* and the *Tuatha dé Danann*, (Belly-men or Bag-men and Ancestors of the Fairies!) fought for supremacy, almost certainly did *not* take place here at Moytura as some authorities would have it. The real battle of Moytura took place near Kilmactranny in County Sligo.

St Féichin of Fore of the Wonders founded a monastery in Cong early in the 7th century. An Augustinian Abbey, also a semi-university – the restored North doorway may be seen on the village street—was founded in 1128 by King Turlough O'Conor; Rory O'Conor, last High King of Ireland, compulsorily retired by the Norman invaders, died at Cong in 1198. Members of Rory's family, including his daughter who was queen of Ulster, are also buried here.

The famous Cross of Cong, one of the glories of the National Museum as well as the Shrine of St Patrick's Tooth and the *Cathach* of the O'Donnells, this last a jewelled casket made to hold a copy of the Vulgate attributed to St Colmcille, are other treasures associated with this area.

The Cong district once abounded in highwaymen and duellists. As an idiotic relief scheme dreamed up during the famines of 1846-47, a canal linking Loughs Mask and Corrib was undertaken. The originators overlooked the porous nature of the local rock formation: after five years of backbreaking labour in which the lake bladders kept piddling down through the strainer of rock, the project was abandoned. To compensate you for any sense of vicarious disappointment at this outcome, let me hasten to tell you of the Monks' Fishing House where, in days of monastic greatness, a trapped salmon, by ringing a bell, notified the kitchen that it was ready for the spit.

A visit to the clean-stoned ruin of the Franciscan-Observantine monastery of Ross Errily where it sits in beauty by the reedy river Suck, a short distance from Headford and to the east of mid-Lough Corrib completed my rather arbitrary ramble. I spent an unique hour high on the monastery tower. Killursa, a monastery in this area, is associated with a whimsical monk-saint called Fursa, a disciple of St Brendan, who is also associated with Burgh Castle in Suffolk and Revonne in France. Fursa, a precursor of Dante, wrote 'Visions' of heaven, purgatory and hell which frightened the timorous of medieval Europe. The Irish novelist Mervyn Well has written whimsically on the Fursa legend.

This monastic excursion completed, I returned to Cong and, hugging the northern shore of Lough Corrib, passed through Cornamona and Maum returning eventually to Leenane where I was advised to wait for the sheep fair in August—that is if I wished to experience authentic enjoyment.

But for me it was over the border into County Mayo, again passing what was now a sedate Aasleagh Falls, and then travelling due west under the peaks of Devil's Mother and Bengorm. Here as I sped west by the shore road I found Lettergest beach and Callary cove. Delphi too! south of Doo Lough—a place most classically named.

Keeping Doo Lough and Mulrea mountain on my left and the Sheffrey hills on my right, I rode into Louisburgh and thence sped south-west to Killadoon. Before entering the hotel I stood for a moment in the dusk relishing the prospect: Mulrea mountain was now on the southern skyline while in the western ocean stood the bulks of Inishbofin, Inishturk, Caher Rock and Clare Island.

As night fell I walked alone on the torn edge of the sea. Taking up an amber bottle that had been washed ashore, I looked at the last of the sunlight in the low west and dreamed myself into a new world of brown-orange fantasy.

14 Fowl and butter market, Co. Galway

Darkness came down on me as I walked on thundering Killadoon beach. I though that the full-blooded sea must surely break its bounds: the limits of so mighty a beast could hardly be determined by an apparently arbitrary tide-lip. It was no surprise to me therefore, when an incontinent breaker, cresting over the backs of its fellows, sent me clattering up seven ramparts of stones. Woolly black cattle with white heads gaped at me through their horns.

In the morning, in search of a place called Silver Strand, I went southward along what seemed a cul-de-sac. Following the road to its pebbly end I crossed a red-bedded stream on stepping-stones and then turned seaward to experience the full-throated welcome of a connoisseur's beach.

'D'you think he'll make it?' I asked a man at Roonagh Pier, four miles due west of Louisburgh.

The man looked out at the boat rising and falling on the irate sea between us and Clare Island. 'Chris'll make it,' he said. 'He couldn't make it yesterday—the sea was mad rough. Today, I'm here for the island mail.'

I was dubious. Noting which, 'Be easy in yourself!' the mailman said. 'Chris'll make it!'

We turned our back on the sound and squatted at the edge of the pier. The sun shone.

When at last the boat came in there were three teenage girls in Aran sweaters, obviously holiday makers, sitting on the deck. There was also an island girl going to Coventry, her doleful mother accompanying her as far as Louisburgh. And, of course, there was Chris O'Grady in beret and gansey. The quay gained a little life.

After Chris had returned from Louisburgh with some messages, we got on board and pushed off. Chris handled the boat expertly amid mighty waves. After half an hour or so of turmoil we tied up in a little harbour under the shadow of what is known as Granuaile's Castle, now used for storing lobster pots.

As I moved along the sandy road that led to Chris O'Grady's hotel, a postman came towards me riding soundlessly side-saddle on a

15 Sharpening a scythe on Achill Island

donkey. 'How are you?' I asked him. 'Reasonable', he said reining in his mount. 'Is that all?' I asked; then we both went off into an involved conversation about nothing at all.

Across the sound on which mackerel shoals beat out daft patterns, the whole panorama of the western coast from Achill in northern Mayo to Slyne Head in Galway stood up in backdrop supreme. The holy mount of Croagh Patrick lorded it in the middle with an elongated sierra of peaks spread on either side.

Queen Granuaile, or Grace O'Malley, a name which poetically has come to connote Ireland, had little connection with Clare Island, except that, according to legend, she was buried in Clare 'abbey', a few miles west-south-west of the harbour.

Grace, a pirate and a plunderer, lived from about 1530 to 1600. The day her son was born she is alleged to have come on deck with a blanket tied around her waist to fight side by side with her crew against—of all the people—the Turks. 'I dismiss you!' she told one of her husbands, divorcing him on the spot. She went to London to visit Queen Elizabeth. Legend tells that she slept with the cable of her ship tied to her bed-posts: a more colourful version says that the cable was tied to a cord and the cord to her big toe.

I loitered upwards on the western hill of the island. The island's only rusty motor-car followed me. ('Who'd pay motor taxation when the roads are like dirt tracks?'). Three children came running in my wake. One said: 'I'll show you a school—there were only three children there before it closed. See that wall dividing the boys from the girls? We called it the Great Wall of China.'

Walking slowly along I came to a hollow, where beside some houses, a stream, its edge brilliant with St Anthony's Fire, had once been canalized to drive a mill. I went onwards until I reached the deserted lighthouse on the clifftop: beside it were white-washed cottages that seemed the epitome of isolation.

That afternoon I walked the road along the southern shore. Above the thatched cottages gulls mewed like cats. At the sea edge below was a large rock black with cormorants. Sparrows were every-where. I followed the anachronistic telephone poles through bare land strewn with loosestrife, meadowsweet, and horse daisies. As

I went I inhaled air that demanded to be gulped open-mouthedly.

At last I came to the abbey ruin. The arms of the O'Malleys were carved on the sanctuary walls; I craned my neck in an effort to trace the lichen-eroded paintings (a donkey? a hound? St Joseph?) on the ceiling. Within the walls of the ruin ancient dead O'Malleys lay under native flagstones: outside, modern dead O'Malleys lay under headstones of black marble with lettering of gold. I climbed a claustrophobic little stairway in the abbey to find an overcroft above the chancel.

A youngish man was working in a garden nearby. I noticed tattooing on his forearms. 'I was in the mines in Derbyshire,' he told me. 'I stuck it out through the toughest air-raids in London.' He looked long at Caher Island and at Innishturk beyond it. 'My wife is from the Irish midlands. We met in Southampton. We get on fine here.'

On this quiet island I found so much to delight me that I had difficulty in leaving it. On its north-eastern tip was a high crescent-shaped peninsula of rounded stones: some of these were as big as roc's eggs, others were smaller but perfectly ovoid. Some more were mottled, others the colour of rusted iron.

I also found myself looking forward to the island night when, in the small pierside pub, I would stretch up my hand among the many articles hanging from hooks and touch the low ceiling. There I recited poetry in the company of a kindred spirit called Mick Micky O'Malley. 'A scholar is out fishing,' he said with a smile. 'When he comes in he will challenge you to a duel of knowledge.' The schoolmistress verified this. But Mick Micky was scholar enough for me.

When at last Chris O'Grady's boat took me to the mainland again I felt a sense of loss at parting from a people who in the pre-TV era had spent their winters reading. And had profited thereby.

For breakfast in Louisburgh I had dollops of sea trout. The night before, heavily-scented country girls had gathered in for a *céilí* in the local hall – the organization known as *Muintir na Tíre* was doing its best to keep the west alive. Past the Old Head and Lecanvey I rode between Croagh Patrick and the sea; past Abbey Murrisk then and into Westport where a cargo of white timber shone on the quays.

Westport House, open to the public at certain times of the day, was closed for the night. I looked vainly through the gates at the great house and saw that an inlet of the swan-bearing sea had been semi-trapped to provide the place with an ornamental lake. The meeting of the natural and the artificial was noteworthy—something I had already noted at Muckross House in Killarney. I visited the house the following morning and noted the treasures.

Westport is excellently laid out (James Wyatt, 1780) complete with a Mall where, God prosper him, many years ago a dentist relieved me of a toothache that threatened to trepan me. The town claims the title of premier sea-angling centre in the west.

The last Sunday in July was at hand so I remained there for a day or two waiting for the thousands to arrive for the annual pilgrimage to the top of Croagh Patrick. Presently the people began to flood into the town in tens of thousands. They squatted everywhere.

On the vigil of pilgrimage day the host of old and young, ugly and beautiful, wealthy and poor, some of whom were even bare-footed, trudged, hitched, rode, cycled westward to Murrisk, and from thence climbed the peak of quartzite where St Patrick once prayed and fasted. All night long that trudging went on with pauses for prayer at traditional 'stations'. As dawn broke over the archipelago of islands in Clew Bay the grey-faced pilgrims heard mass and received Communion.

God forgive me, I funked the pilgrimage. But next year, or maybe the year after that, who knows but that I may rise to the holy occasion.

At Ballintober which is roughly some nine miles east of Westport and seven miles due south of Castlebar, I came upon the famous Ballintober Abbey.

Inside the Abbey I met Father Egan, a man blazing with the

cause of fully restoring 'the Abbey that refused to die'. The phrase is his own. His success, apart from hard work, of course, is a tribute to the power of those six words.

This Augustinian Abbey was founded in 1216 by King Cathal O'Conor of Connacht and, despite Cromwellian efforts to destroy the place, mass has been offered within its walls without break for over 750 years. It is of one age with Notre Dame cathedral and was built on the site of a patrician foundation. Theobald of the Ships, son of Grace O'Malley by her second husband, lies buried beneath the sacristy floor.

Father Egan has also been instrumental in having a commemorative stamp issued in honour of Ballintober Abbey. On the walls, the restored areas are clearly outlined in lead. As the work proceeded, unearthed stones were carefully laid aside for examination; some bore the incised colophon of the medieval mason. One mark resembled a swastika, another a stylized shamrock.

The stone of Ballintober shall praise Father Egan for centuries to come.

Back again at Westport I moved due north along the shore of Clew Bay. Presently the Irish-Romanesque church of Newport bulked against the sky. It has a Harry Clarke east window of stained glass, one of the last he designed. Beside the dripping roadway stood an I.R.A. Memorial. Dark clouds had gathered above the town and the backing of grape-purple air rendered church, memorial and landscape intimidating.

For me nearby Burrishoole 'Abbey' and the O'Malley Castle of Carrigahooley revived keen memories of my good friend Ernie O'Malley. Fighter, writer, Ernie O'Malley of Burrishoole, Westport, County Mayo, red-headed and with chiselled features, was the revolutionary *par excellence*. Ruthless for the right, scholarly, ingenuous in certain ways, as a medical student he had lived with a 'Peter the Painter' in his hand. He was reputed to have had nerves of steel; his face bore the horseshoe prints of rifle butts where he was battered while he was a prisoner in Dublin Castle. Indomitable Ernie, too. Refusing to compromise, he was high in command of the Republican forces in the Four Courts in Dublin when the Civil War ripped Ireland wide open. Subsequently he had spent years in Mexico studying primitive art.

I remember Ernie telling me of incidents he had never put into his book *On Another Man's Wound* (in the U.S.A. this book was called *Army Without Banners*). In the United States, Ernie was admired even by gargantuan Thomas Wolfe, the writer.

I was now travelling due west along the northern edge of the bay and on the road to Achill Island. On my right hand the Nephin Bay Range of hills kept pace with my itinerary. Near Mulranny a yellow river thundered down from the heights. Rossturk Castle loomed up between me and the western horizon. Travelling on the southern shore of Curraun Peninsula I soon reached Achill Sound.

Sweeneys of the Sound sell everything one can think of. Behind the bar hangs a painting of Brendan Behan with a spotlight on it; for a moment it made me think that the bould Brendan had been canonized. Not far away stands a secondary school where a brave man, not without being misunderstood, I wager, had pioneered education for the benefit of the islanders.

In Achill itself there is a dramatic deserted village on a hill flank. You may, if you are fortunate, find amethysts; there are also enormous rhododendron clumps. Some of the hotels have ballad-bawling sessions that I would have relished in my salad days. From the top of Croaghaun mountain a cliff falls almost sheerly 2,000 feet to the sea. There are beaches a-plenty; the Minawn Cliffs are highly impressive as also is the tiny village of Doogort with its skull-capped hayricks and its beach that glows green and orange. Finally, black asses with white bellies, snow-white cottages, black peat ricks, white crosses and black cattle all make up the chequerboard that is Slievemore mountain. I moved on to Keem Bay.

On the cliff road above Keem Bay a gust of wind came down on me as I got out of the car and, crawling to the cliff face, looked over and down. The sea below was crazy. The currachs employed to net the sharks, were huddled in the lee of a rock. The parent boat was somewhere in hiding. The lookout man had abandoned his post on the cliff-top. Hopes of seeing a shark threshing in the net dwindled in my breast.

But I did later see a row of sprawled black-curled dead sharks in Porteen Harbour. There the liver is cut out and the oil extracted.

There followed a desolate return over Achill Sound, the over-looping of the peninsula of Curraun, the bouncing down to Mulranny again, thence north to Ballycroy where the rhododendron again appeared in a characterless bogland. Then mile after miserable mile—or, if you wish, mile after magnificent mile, of loneliness.

A square-shaped area called Erris, with Bangor Erris, a village beneath a quarry clawed out of a hillside, as its capital, starkly occupies the north-western corner of County Mayo. By long odds, it must be the most desolate district in Ireland.

And yet, if I were a man who loved stark solitude or who saw splendour in the steel blade of a lonely river, perhaps it's there I would find solace.

It was as if every force of nature was in conspiracy to daunt me as I swung north-west towards the Mullet Peninsula. The noon sun was wiped out by battalions of jet clouds. The purple air, that had previously intimidated me beside Newport, again made its appearance. Rain began to fall. Fall? it flogged, it flayed downwards releasing a million pitchforks on the roof of my car and raising an ear-splitting drumming. At noon, even with switched-on headlights I could scarcely see where I was going. Behind me I could dimly discern the lights of a fellow-traveller close on my tail.

Hitherto I had had some idea of swinging inland towards Bellacorick to find that musical bridge on the parapet of which one can play the diatonic scale by rapping it with a stone; a lightning flash and its almost concomitant thunder peal ended any notion of such an excursion. It seemed as if the ghost of Red Brian Carabine, the seventeenth-century Erris prophet, with his predictions of fire and disaster, had risen from the grave to shower maledictions on my head.

And yet, in Ireland, it is a mistake to take the weather seriously.

Suddenly the sky opened to reveal a tender shade of blue, and as I entered the isthmus to the Mullet proper, the whole western world was laughing at my previous discomfiture.

Presently I reached Belmullet.

In Belmullet a man called Pat Healion talked to me of the problems of his town. It needed a briquette factory, he said. A pretty girl 'amened' that. Others who came up began a vivid conversation. I suddenly had the feeling of being in contact with an isolated but independent people, some of whom have even gone to jail as a protest against the condition of their roads. As I mentioned history: 'Go down to Michael O'Donoghue the headmaster—he lives in American Street,' I was told. 'American Street?' I echoed. 'It's named for a Jack Reilly, the American,' came the reply.

Michael O'Donoghue was standing in his doorway. He responded to the stimulus of a greeting in Irish. Seated before a huge fire he talked and I listened.

'In the dawn of time, Ferdia came from near here.' (*When Cuchulainn and Ferdia fought, there lacked no pride of warrior courtesies*). 'Another thing,' he said. 'You'll read in the history books that 2,000 years ago King Dáithí the Raider, was killed at the foot of the Alps. I query the authenticity of that legend. There's a mountain called Alp here in north-west Mayo and local folklore tells of a giant called Dáithí. The story of King Dáithí being killed by a thunderbolt near Switzerland is moonshine.'

In a lull in the flow of talk I said: 'I was once at an O'Donoghue clan rally in Killarney where labourers, taxi-drivers and American millionaires, all came marching along. It was interesting to see the high tobacco-knife nose repeated in their faces like a motif in music.'

'We O'Donoghues came originally from south Kerry,' Michael said. 'We marched here after Kinsale with O'Sullivan Beare.' (A mere 360 years were spanned by that sentence). 'As a reverse process the McSweeneys, professional gallowglasses, originally from Scotland, came from the north and settled in the south.'

We talked on giants, landlords and on the invasions and evacuations of Ireland. 'You should see Charlie Cawley the blacksmith in Church Street,' Michael advised as we parted.

'You made pikes in 1916?' I asked Cawley, a small intense man of 80, working in his forge.

'Pikes?' he shouted. 'My father John Cawley also made them in 1867. His father Christie Cawley made them in 1847 and his father before that made them again in 1798. For 170 years that anvil has sung the song of freedom.'

The man was as intense an old man as I have ever seen.

'Have you time to listen to a story?' he went on. 'Sure!' I said.

Using the chant of the traditional story-teller Cawley told me a story of a smith and the devil. The story ended with the devil changing himself into a sovereign and the smith sledging him on the anvil till the coin howled for mercy. Passers-by stopped to hear the tale. Presently the forge door was crowded.

I'll be back to Belmullet; back to see the last nesting place in Ireland of the phalarope, to see the churchyard where legend says the people are (most sensibly) buried standing upright, back also to trace the history of the French Lavelles who (the name also may be of Gaelic origin) Michael O'Donoghue told me, first landed on the islands of Inishkea.

Are we Irish foolish to do what we do with our vast resources of bogland? We dig up the turf, dry it, save it and burn it unconcernedly. I reckon we could put it to better use say as a versatile auxiliary to horticulture. Every load of turf I see on the road on its way to fire or furnace I interpret as an unenconomic destruction of the soil of my fatherland.

I would rather that we relied in fuller measure on hydro-electric power which uses the natural forces of falling water. Of that, God knows, we have plenty in Ireland.

This was the train of thought that brought me east to Glenamoy.

Thirteen miles east of Belmullet and thirty-six miles west of Ballina, right in the heart of a vast moorland, one chances upon a man-created oasis of growing rich waving grass.

This is the Glenamoy experimental station which seeks by experiment on this type of boggy soil to discover if worthwhile agricultural produce can be won from a land typical of three million acres in Ireland. If successful, this should prove a boon to the Irish economy.

In Germany, I had seen areas in the apparently profitless Lüneburg Heath, when properly treated, provide high crop-yields.

Drainage and manuring were prime problems to engage the attention of *An Foras Talúntais*—the body charged with this Irish experiment. The yield of cereals and potatoes consequent upon the application of various manures was carefully noted.

Standing at the door of the main building with Mr P. J. O'Hare, the officer in charge I looked at that apparently endless moorland.

'A grim landscape,' I commented.

'I thought the same when first I came here,' the man beside me said quietly. 'As the local people, especially the girls, told me the story attached to each ridge in the landscape the whole area came alive for me. Now I am able to identify myself with it in all its moods.'

Cogitating on the wisdom of this observation, I passed Belderg which sits beside a breach in a particularly formidable coast wall, and at nightfall entered Ballycastle.

The hotel at Ballycastle was once a coastguard station; the bedroom into which I was shown clearly indicated that the building had been constructed with an eye to defence.

In the darkness I walked to Ballycastle Pier. Above me gleamed the lights of the little town.

Out at sea the headland called Downpatrick had been cloven as with a great axe so that the northern light showed through the cleavage. 'What happened to the headland?' I asked one of three lads standing by. 'Doonbriste—the Broken Fort?' he asked in return. 'Yes,' I said.

'There's telling on that,' he said darkly. 'A farmer couldn't divide his land between two sons, so St Patrick split it for him.' 'The man wouldn't convert to Christianity, so St Patrick cut him off,' the second lad amended. 'Foolishness!' said the third. 'There's a soft vein there and the sea ate it!'

'Puffin' holes too,' said the first of the three. 'And a channel that I often went through in a boat,' said the second. The third mentioned a 'ground sea' which seemed to be the terror of local boatmen.

In the sea close by a seal appeared.

'That devil won't let a salmon up the river,' said the first bitterly. 'Throw a stone at him!' I advised. 'I'll throw no stone at a seal,' growled the second. 'Nor me, neither,' said the third. The replies carried undertones of superstition.

There was no moon, only the faint light on the face of the sea. We fell into a companionable silence.

Beside Ballycastle and close to a megalithic tomb has been uncovered the remains of a house possibly 5,000 years old. The phrase 'as old as time' kept recurring to me that night on Ballycastle Pier.

Surrounded by her grandchildren, Mrs Marion Walsh of nearby Heathpark leaned her still-youthful head against a marble mantelpiece.

Her grandchildren stopped to listen.

'General Humbert and the French landed at Kilcummin in 1798,' she said. 'The "loyals" ran, but the country people welcomed the French with cheers.' (*When the ships we'd been wearily waiting, sailed into Killala's broad bay*).

'The people here couldn't understand a word the Frenchmen said. Then the local girls spruced themselves up. They wanted an excuse to visit the French lads. So they killed cockerels, drew them, dressed them, and going up to the camp offered them to the soldiers as presents. (That's what the girls did also in Synge's *The Playboy of the Western World*.) Whatever brightness was in the feathers, the Frenchies liked their colours, so they stuck them in their cockades. Then they kissed the girls goodbye and marched off singing to capture Killala.'

My anticipation whetted by this tale, I moved on to Killala, which proved a minor disappointment. For someone, probably with an eye to future business, had crowbarred out the rock on which General Humbert had first set foot and had dumped it at the back of a shop. My single reward at Kilcummin was to meet the handsomest, swarthiest, most dynamically attractive girl I have ever laid eyes on. I wished I had been a young French soldier just landed in Ireland and that she, or her great-great-great-great-grandmother, had offered me a trussed chicken as a token of Hiberno-French affection!

Below Ballina town the 'Strong God of the River Moy' loitered in pools most eminent in the annals that chronicle the coming and going of salmon. As a boat moved sharply in the main stream the line of net-corks in its wake extended until it had assumed the shape of a giant hairpin. Worked by four men, a winch drew one end of the net inshore towards the low wall on the Sligo side of the river. The men at the other end of the net rope staggered in the strong current. Then, in the ever-narrowing noose of floats, fins appeared, leisurely, puzzledly sailing. A last low-held powerful jerk and the struggling confused mass of salmon tumbled on to the grassy stones.

'Two thousand in one haul,' a shopkeeper told me when describing a former miraculous draught of fishes. 'The whole town was called out to help.'

Where now? Southward to Foxford to see the woollen mills conducted by the Irish Sisters of Charity? And there to renew acquaintance with the birthplace of F. R. Higgins, a poet I once greatly admired. Thence perhaps to drive westward as far as admirably sited Pontoon between Loughs Conn and Cullen, thence again to swing east to Swinford or even south to the tall gravel pits about Kilkelly, whence I could roam north to Charlestown for a yarn with Johnny Hassett, sparing a smile for the memory of the cast-clothes man outside his door who, with a wink in my direction, once told a crowd of fairday farmers that his wife was 'burnin' oil and that he was thinking of tradin' her in for a newer model.'

Feeling unusually adventurous I could again seek out that annual gathering on the shore of Urlaur Lough, nine miles north of Ballyhaunis, where once I blundered into a 'patteran' or patron day ceremony complete with swing boats and wheel of fortune, raucous but admirable and set under the ruined walls of Urlaur Dominican abbey.

But still, except in fancy, I am in Ballina, so I decide to move north along the coast on the western side of Killala Bay through Enniscrone and Easky in County Sligo where after a slight divagation into Leitrim I would journey north-west, eventually to call a cessation among the mountains of Donegal.

CHAPTER SEVEN

Sligo, A little of Roscommon and the Hills of Donegal

'Come away, O human child!
To the waters and the wild'

YEATS

Sligo has many physical advantages: individuality of landscape, a coastline of legend, and lakes that for beauty rival those of Killarney. It has strong associations with William Butler Yeats, the poet, and with the spirit of a horse-woman countess turned rebel of the rebels, Constance Markievicz.

Monaghan of the dumpy hills provides a succession of views over rolling countryside made bright with lakes. This was once the territory of the MacMahons, a northern clan not to be confused with the MacMahon sept of Clare. Today, its coarse fishing resources draw anglers from many parts.

And then there is *Tír Chonaill* or Donegal, kin in the clipped speech of its inhabitants and in its configuration to the people and braes of the Scottish Highlands. Its great-hearted valleys and leonine headlands are most typical of the western Irish coast. Donegal is a county that is truly rewarding.

The instant one crosses the border of County Sligo one hears the voice of Yeats murmuring: 'Beware that they do not drive the living imagination out of the world.'

To me, clean-boned Enniscrone, or Inishcrone, a town on the east side of Killala Bay seemed composed of houses oddly addicted to the colour blue. Waves sluicing across pocked tables of stone, high dunes and a generous prospect implied that one day the town would be a major resort.

On the pier I met an old friend, Michael McKeon, whose people were pilots in Killala Bay: Michael spoke of a local fishing disaster when, without warning, a storm rose out of a clear sky. The tale told of a sudden plummeting of the barometer and a Cassandra-like prophet at a pier-head whose warnings some fishermen fortunately heeded, and others unfortunately did not. We also spoke of the Mac Fhirbhisigh family of nearby Lacken or Lecan, who, under the patronage of the O'Dowds, for 400 years gave Ireland professional historiographers, genealogists, and poets. And we also recounted the legend of the O'Dowd man who married a mermaid and reared a fishy family.

The low-lying road that runs east out of Easky through Dromore West to Skreen has on its edges some of the last thatched houses in Ireland. This north-facing shoreland is as clean as a bone in sand: I find, however, and here I speak as a casual traveller, its people oddly unresponsive as if sparks had not been struck from their metal.

Close to Easky, which has a ruined castle of the Hebridean Mac Donnell gallowglasses once in O'Dowd service, I saw beside a new school a large ice-age split rock. Here I had a desultory conversation with a smiling girl who told me of Fionn MacCumhail's vain attempt to cast the crag into the ocean, whereupon in his rage the hero struck it with a second stone and split it. There is also the legend that the split rock would close on an unjust man and crush him to death, so I discreetly kept my distance from the fissure.

On the roadside near Skreen I stopped to examine a monument to MacFhirbhisigh the scribe: on my asking an old man about it he drew me aside—even the roadway was deserted—and told me with bated breath that the unfortunate scholar was murdered by Planter Crofton because 'he had witnessed a rascal doing something private with another man's wife'. Whereupon we looked deep into one another's eyes and together hummed our disapproval—whether of the Peeping Tom, the moral lapse, or the slaying, I'm not quite sure.

My eye noting the clear waters of a stream near Skreen I soon came upon beautiful Beltra under Yeats-beloved Knocknarea Mountain. Beltra has cairns and megalithic graves and is associated with heroes with euphonic names—Lewy of the Silver Hand is one that comes readily to the tongue. From Beltra I travelled east past the falls at Ballysodare and into the city-town of Sligo.

Sligo I found in the throes of the International Yeats' School, an event held in mid-August each year. Here scholars from the ends of the earth come to dissect, to analyze and to synthetize the poetry, plays and essays of Yeats.

The prospect of encountering so many eager-beaver professors and students rather daunted me: however the tranquillity induced by the sight of Nora Niland serenely presiding over her old-world library-museum calmed me considerably. What's more she told me exactly what was afoot in the city.

Thereafter Sligo with its firm devotion to the arts was mine to loiter in, to savour and to enjoy.

Set with strategy and beauty between Lough Gill and the sea, Sligo, the second largest town in Connaught, dates from 1245 and the erection there of a castle by Maurice Fitzgerald, Lord of Naas. Entrenched in Sligo, Fitzgerald considered himself well placed either to move south-west into Connaught proper or to thrust north into Donegal.

For centuries, the story of Sligo resolves itself into a struggle between the Normans and the allied forces of the O'Conors and their overlords the O'Donnells.

From the higher ground in the city Knocknarea may be seen to the west: to the north lies the oddly-shaped table-flat hill that is Benbulben, its western end shaped like the prow of a Spanish galleon. In nearby Killasbugbrone was once preserved in a special shrine the tooth of St Patrick, which he is alleged to have lost one day as he entered the little chapel there. After a series of adventures the tooth now lies in the National Museum.

16 Heavy traffic on a County Sligo road

I entered Sligo Town Hall just as one of the most colourful personalities in Ireland, biblical-looking Eoin O'Mahony of Cork, popularly
known as 'The Pope', was ending his lecture.

If ever there was a knight-errant of medieval Europe reincarnate
in Ireland it was surely Eoin. In the intervals of lecturing in the
United States, he stamped round the land, a self-appointed and
popularly-acclaimed ombudsman, pleading for amnesty for political
prisoners, guiding people through the maze of the Irish literary
renaissance, tracing genealogies, even offering himself as presidential
candidate, and in general, animating the Irish scene by his affable,
erudite, whimsical, resolute and humanitarian presence. And finally
fatally wasting his physical resources in the process.

After Eoin's lecture had ended we retired to an upstairs room in
a local club where some inadequate balladeers were holding the
floor. The singing ended as 'The Pope' occupied what appeared to
be his gestatorial chair whence for hours on end a torrent of literary
reminiscence flowed from his lips.

In the quiet streets in the early hours of the morning I made
a wish for Sligo and its citizens: that the Summer School may not
succumb to the cut-throat competition that characterizes much of
international scholarship. For dissection of poetry may be carried
to the extremity where one slits the skylark's throat to see what
makes the song.

I slept that night at Jim McGarry's house in Collooney (Jim—book-
lover, horse-lover) with a statue of Captain Teeling high in the
darkness above me. Teeling, an aide-de-camp to General Humbert,
had shown outstanding courage at nearby Carrignagat in an engagement with the militia.

'Get up at once!' Jim shouts at dawn of day. 'Today we attend
mass at the Well of Tobernalt.'

Into the car then with me, my head sleep-loaded and Yeats-loaded.
From the summit of Cairns Hill the 'embroidered cloth' of Sligo—
town, mountain, lake, sea, sea-shore—is seen spread below. We
detour to Carrowmore in the vicinity of which once lay the greatest

17 Near Kilkieran, Co. Galway

concentration of megalithic graves in Europe (160 once, now less than 30), a nation's treasure house abominably wasted.

On an open field beside the lake a concourse of people has assembled. Booths flap, glistening tea-urns blow geysers of steam into the morning air, white aprons shine, and cars like beetles are ranked between us and the water.

Parking our car we move forward to the focal point of assembly, a natural rock-altar on a cliff face. Here is offered each year a commemorative mass to recall the many masses offered on this slab in Penal Days when the laws decreed that the head of a priest carried the same reward-tag as that of a wolf.

The area is enlivened with bird song. From directly beneath the now-decorated altar clear stream water rushes noisily.

I begin to enumerate the powerful forces that had once held sway in this area.

Prehistory extending backwards to 2,000 B.C. had left its vestiges in numerous pagan burial grounds, in the crannógs on Lough Gara's lake-bed and on the battle-site of Moytura already mentioned in connection with Cong. Legend also tells that Queen Maeve (the English call her Queen Mab; the Welsh, Queen Maud) lies buried under an acre-cairn of stones on top of Knocknarea. Early Christian Ireland is here vouched for by the presence on nearby Innishmor, or Church Island, of the ruins of a 6th-century church, beside the gateway of which, in Our Lady's Bed, pregnant women once prayed to be preserved from death in child-birth. The literary Ireland of Yeats has pursued me all the road from Sligo, while a more recently rebellious Ireland is implicit in the hoof-thuds of the Countess Markievicz's blood horse which must certainly have galloped across the very field on which I stand. Mercantile Ireland, dusted with the flour of the Pollexfen mills, where the young Yeats gained abiding impressions from his mother's kinsfolk, is not wholly absent.

A choir now begins a hymn in Irish. Bearing the dressed chalice, the priest emerges from the woods. An ash tree in full foliage provides a baldachin for the altar.

Four thousand people focus their eyes upon the priest. From the booths comes the clang of a churn lid. The opening words of sacrifice crackle over the loudspeaker. A chalice noises on stone. A swinging blue tit looks down from wires overhead. Presently the priest gives a brief sermon. He isn't sentimental about the Penal Days. The thousands file forward for Communion in the woods.

After mass there is a bustle around the booths. Laughter too, as strongly brewed tea cascades from the spouts of earthenware teapots. With new-found comrades we chat and poke fun. The sun trundles up the sky. I bend down to pluck a perfect mushroom that has lain untouched amid the boots of the throng.

Sligo, with the superb ruins of its Dominican friary kept plucking at my sleeve but I had to be off.

First I travelled south-west to Tubercurry where a few enthusiasts have built up an oasis of drama, thence I went east to Ballaghadereen, and later travelled up and over the hilltops and finally down into the pleasant town of Boyle in County Roscommon.

Set at the foot of the Curlew mountains, Boyle boasts a beautifully-ruined Cistercian monastery dating from 1161, which for long was under the patronage of the Mac Dermots of Moylurg.

On Trinity Island on Lough Key are the ruins of a Premonstratensian Abbey; here too is buried Sir Conyers Clifford, English President of Connaught, defeated in a pass in the hills above Boyle by O'Donnell and O'Rourke. (*And fleet as deer the Normans ran, through Corrshliabh Pass and Ardrahan*). Clifford's head was tossed across a barricade as proof that the English jig was (temporarily) up. Here also are buried the ill-fated lovers Una MacDermot and Strong Tom Costello, the usual entwining trees forming a lovers' knot above their graves. Their love is enshrined in a famous traditional song in Irish.

MacDermot of Moylurg is the historic patronymic in this area; his castle on Castle Island ('The Rock') inspired Yeats. Even now, gazing across the lake to where the great building shines in the sun, the sight would inspire all but the pauperized of spirit.

On Trinity Island, based on still older records, were compiled the Annals of Lough Key; these were later copied on 'The Rock' by Brian McDermot in his own handwriting. Here also the MacDermots, patrons of literature, entertained the musical and literary giants of a now vanished Ireland. Plunder and slaughter, arrows in the throats of princes, poetry, devastation and delight—all are reflected in the turbulence of Lough Key's annals.

Lough Key today is a pleasant retreat. Even as I watched from a clifftop I saw that quite close to a wind-flawed patch called Devil's Half-Acre an angler had hooked a great trout.

One final place of pilgrimage before again turning northeast to Sligo town; close to the reedy shore of Lough Meelagh in Roscommon with Loughs Arrow and Skean to the west, I entered the mossy churchyard of Kilronan, a place associated with the erudite Ó Duigeanáin family—some members of this clan still hold their traditional erenach lands granted them as a perquisite of lay management—and there found the grave of the last of the Irish bards, Turlough O'Carolan (1670-1738), who having called for his harp and composed his *Farewell to Music*, died at Alderford near Ballyfarnan at the house of his benefactor McDermot Roe.

A sense of desolation pervaded musical Ireland at the news of O'Carolan's death. From all parts of the west and upper midlands, harpers and musicians, tattered and adorned, thronged to pay their last respects to the acknowledged king of bards as he lay in state in the wake-room. Ten harpers vied with one another in playing laments above the corpse. For four days and four nights a majestic if barbaric mourning-feast, with echoes going back to the Celts of the Danubian Basin, continued until the corpse stank to high heaven and the mourners were reluctantly forced to place it in the clay. A large number of proscribed priests came out of their hiding-places to chant above the open grave.

Standing beside O'Carolan's resting place one is stirred by a sorrow and a pride that holds elements of the maudlin and the magnificent.

The melody of *The Star Spangled Banner* is believed to have been composed by none other than the redoubtable O'Carolan himself. I never see the O'Carolan's harp, preserved at Clonalis House of the O'Conors Don, without recalling the minstrel's funeral.

On returning to Sligo my first pilgrimage was to Rosses Point five miles to the north-west and thence to Lisadell which lies to the north and across Drumcliff Bay. In Lisadell, of landlord or 'ascendancy' stock, were born the rebel Countess Constance Gore-Booth and her sister Eva the poetess, both of whom allied themselves with the Irish tenantry and against the rule of 'gigmanity'.

At first, the underprivileged country people found it difficult to believe that the sisters, flamboyantly riding to outlawed assemblies, were sincere in their convictions. At a point-to-point meeting four riders bent on trimming Constance's pride tried to crowd her on a bank and so cause her to come a cropper, but she outwitted them even though she had to leave her tattered skirt on a post in the process of doing so.

Later, while studying art in Paris, Constance married the Polish Count Casimir (de) Markievicz: the couple then returned to Dublin and became a force in literary circles. In the Irish capital, she mingled with the young poet-revolutionaries. To help light the fire of rebellion she organized a national boy-scout movement—Fianna Éireann.

In the rebellion, 'Madame', as she was called, was second-in-command of the College of Surgeons' garrison in St Stephen's Green. The open Green, its amateurish trenches exposed to fire from the roof of the Shelbourne Hotel, was a sitting duck for British snipers. The Countess, an excellent shot, is credited with having killed four of them.

On the surrender she was sentenced to death, a sentence later commuted to penal servitude for life. She was the first woman in the world to be elected to any parliament but did not take her seat as she was in prison. Released on general amnesty from Holloway Jail —her letters from prison make fascinating reading—she received a rapturous welcome in Dublin where she now enjoyed the stature of an Irish Joan of Arc.

Her later career oscillated from jail to 'on the run'; in the Civil War she took the anti-Treaty side and again found herself in prison. In 1927, having given all her money to the poor of Dublin, she died in poverty in a public hospital ward.

The house at Lisadell is neither impressive nor beautiful except perhaps in a massive and uncompromising way. The ends of its great ground-floor Long room or Music room are rounded; what with oil paintings and souvenirs of arctic journeyings the place resembles a museum. Yet, at evening as the sun strikes through the western windows, the great room seems to take fire as if the blazing spirit of 'Madame' were once again abroad.

In Sligo—town or county—W. B. Yeats can never remain remote from recollection.

The poet died at Roquebrune in France in 1939; in September 1948 the Irish Government brought his body home and had it reinterred in the graveyard of Drumcliff where the stump of a round tower and a sculptured cross vouch for ancient eminence.

Here beside the church where his grandfather was rector (1811-1846), W. B. Yeats lies under a plain slab on which appears the enigmatic epitaph he wrote for himself: 'Cast a cold eye on life, on death. Horseman pass by.' Over all is Benbulben, the flat-topped mountain, its flanks stained an unusual shade of green.

In Drumcliff, I walked among the spotted stones. Presently, I spied a laneway leading surreptitiously to the north. Walking between its high-hedged ramparts I found myself on the bank of a stream. Here except for the natural noise of the hurrying water there was no sound. Sitting there I recalled that at nearby Cúl Dreimhne in A.D. 561, 3,000 men were killed in a battle occasioned by, above all things, a breach of copyright by St Columba (Colmcille).

This is the story of the battle: St Finian alleged that St Columba had copied his hymnal without permission. Columba refused to bow to the judgement of High King Diarmuid: 'To every cow her calf, to every book its copy', and called upon his kinsmen for aid. Issue was joined with the royal forces and the Columban army won! Columba's subsequent sorrow on seeing the battlefield dead, his exile to the island of Iona and his missionary labours in Scotland and northern England are important even in a European context.

On the road north into Donegal through Grange and Cliffony one may take a boat to Innishmurray there to turn the cursing stones on a troublesome foe. An English visitor did just this for Hitler!

A coastal townland called Streedagh once saw a hundred bodies washed ashore from the wrecked Armada. But such tales are forgotten in the high life of summer Bundoran, a seaside resort drawing its devotees from Northern Ireland and Scotland. At nearby Bundrowes, Franciscans, previously ejected from Donegal, compiled in the period 1630-1636, the Annals of the Four Masters.

I am now in a huge black boat rowing across angry lake waters. The boat carries 150 pilgrims. Before us on a mid-lake island I see, as by miracle, a floating basilica.

The lake is Lough Derg in County Donegal. In a cave—*Caverna Purgatorii*—in this island, tradition says that St Patrick did penance over 1,500 years ago.

Lough Derg means Red Lake: a monster killed by St Patrick is believed to have reddened the water with its blood. Here also tradition says that God granted the saint a vision of Purgatory.

It is raining heavily as we approach the island that, if medieval record is correct, cowed criminals, terrified soldiers, attracted knights-at-arms, quizzed theologians, and inspired Dante.

As we reach the little pier, the sun emerges to light the rocks and the great basilica door. We now see the barefooted pilgrims praying – surely a thousand of them—their insteps and ankles splashed with the black sand-mud of the island. Some, moving in what appear to be hypnotic penitential circles, stumble barefooted over jagged rocks.

Many of the pilgrims, both men and women, are fashionably dressed. Some are possibly small farmers or tradesmen. One, surprisingly, is a Chinaman.

On the third day one leaves the island physically more dead than alive, but spiritually more alive than dead. For those weary of physchiatry and the mumbo-jumbo that looks to a Utopia where the world's ills are offered facile solution, the exercises of this remote island may offer a new dimension to thought and to being. For there, on a diet of boiled brackish water seasoned with salt and pepper, one is given an odd clarity of vision. But it is not a place of lugubriousness; by and large one's fellow-pilgrims are as gay a bunch as ever walked the road to Canterbury.

Sited due north of the dunes at Finner, Ballyshannon is the true gateway to Donegal. There I decide to visit Dorrian's old-world thatched pub on the higher part of a town that sits above the River Erne where it drains Lough Erne. This old pub could well provide a fitting setting for *The Playboy of the Western World*.

But how can these pubs hold out much longer against the elegancies of the lounge bar?

I once asked a cynic why it was that in the older Irish pubs of the south the counter of the bar proper was higher than the grocery counter.

He considered for a moment and then said: '(a) It's to ensure that the drinks won't be spilled by men jostling, (b) it's also to make certain that the brimming glass has not far to travel from counter to mouth, and (c) it's to cover up the secrets of drink-mixing that go on behind it.'

The new hydro-electric scheme by which the Erne River is harnessed at Cathaleen Falls, is, to one as stage-conditioned as I am, a perfect setting for Denis Johnston's play *The Moon is the Yellow River*. Behind plate glass in a quiet room, salmon and trout revolved indolently in pea-green water as they awaited their turn to climb the watery stairway to the dammed-up water overhead.

The O'Donnells of Tír Chonaill, who fought unceasingly to control the river crossing at Ballyshannon, might not have had the leisure to fish for salmon, but Allingham, (1824-1889) the local poet who wrote a jingle called *Four Ducks on a Pond*, as well as a nostalgic piece about his native Ballyshannon which he called Belashanny, seeing these temporarily incarcerated fish would almost certainly have rhymed them down the centuries.

The progenitors of these salmon also fed the monks of the Cistercian Abbey of Assaroe which, nobly ruined, lies a mile to the northwest of the town. To venture further back into prehistory,

Partholán of Scythia and his followers, who, 1,500 years before the time of Christ, landed on an island below Assaroe Falls, must surely have consumed steaks cut from the salmon of the winding Erne.

A flawless beach such as Belalt Strand off Rossnowlagh which lies due north of Ballyshannon makes me sad, for I feel that it is only a question of time until it is raped by development. The sand-dunes of the Irish west too must cause concern to the thoughtful; the sooner these playgrounds of the future are nationalized the better for the Irishmen and Irishwomen of tomorrow.

The nearby ruin of Kilbarron Castle, sited precariously on a rock above the coast, was once held by the O'Sgingins, official historians of Tír Chonaill. In 1580, this seat of learning passed by marriage into the possession of the O'Clerys; right well did the new owners uphold tradition, for of the famous Four Masters, two bore the surname O'Clery.

At Ballintra where I wished that the inhabitants would paint the exteriors of their houses, I rejoined the main road. In an adjoining demesne, the Ballintra river does some lively gymnastics in an area known as The Pullans.

Donegal town, once headquarters of the O'Donnells, has interesting ruins in Donegal Abbey, founded in 1474 by Nuala, wife of the great ·Red Hugh. It also has the ruin of Donegal Castle, as well as a memorial to the Four Masters, and St Patrick's Memorial Church of the Four Masters. After the Flight of the Earls (1609) the area was planted by Sir Basil Brooke, who laid out The Diamond or Market Place in traditional English style. The repercussions of this plantation are still with us more than 360 years later.

From Donegal town one has the choice of striking north-east and inland through Barnesmore Gap, Ballybofey, Stranorlar to Strabane, or of travelling by the coast road, beginning with Mountcharles, otherwise known as Tanatallon.

As ever, the coast it is by an overwhelming majority!

With a blessing on the memory of Séamus MacManus of Mount-charles, author and storyteller, I entered Inver, a fishing village where lies buried the body of Thomas Nesbitt (born 1730) who invented, above all things, the gun harpoon for whaling. Thence the road lead to Dunkineely and Killybegs, this latter a fishing resort much akin to Dingle in County Kerry.

In Killybegs I stood beside the loom of the hand-tufted carpet factory and watched the pattern grow row by row. Raising my eyes to look through the window I saw below me in the harbour the herring trawlers swing almost imperceptibly at their moorings.

Beyond Kilcar and Carrick on the road to Glencolumcille, Slieve League rears up like a horse and appears to neigh appreciation of epic cliff scenery, with the view from *Amharc Mór* (Great View) on the cliffs of Bunglass as the zenith of its splendour. Thence Slieve League may be seen sliced sheerly 2,000 feet to the sea. But forward to Irish-speaking Glencolmcille with its old associations with Colmcille, its patron, and its modern associations of an unusual priest.

Name? McDyer. Vocation? Parish priest of a place where legend says that Bonnie Prince Charlie once lay in hiding. Avocation? Fighter for economic sufficiency. Highly romantic nickname? (Or so sensational papers would have us believe.) Left Hand of God. Courage? Limitless. Accomplishment? To have bridged the fatal Irish chasm between thought and deed. *Modus operandi?* Bull-dozing and cooperation: *Locus operandi:*—immediate—a long scree or valley 15 miles long. *Locus operandi*—remote?—Ireland as a whole. Population of parish? 1,000 or so. Outlook for same? Bleak. Livelihood? Meagre. Enemy? Apathy—domestic and national.

This priest fought the impoverished soil. He saw to it that electricity and tarmacadamed roads enlivened the dying valley. He pioneered collective farming. A canning factory and a tweed factory employed women who would otherwise have drifted to the factories of England. He talked, inspired, led, argued, cajoled and to a great extent smashed cynicism. He took off his jacket and began to build a hall. His parishoners joined him in the fight. Win, lose, or draw, Father McDyer deserves a handclap from all Ireland.

Hightailing it now E-N-E to pleasant Ardara which sits in the centre of a tweed-producing area, whence all roads that lead outward into the major world break through gaps in the mountains.

Glenties, reckoned the tidiest town in Ireland, was white-frock-clean with its red geraniums all aglow. On the road north-west to Maas, the dramatic, if as yet distant, view of Gweebarra Bridge indicated the way to the Rosses and the Donegal Highlands. At Maas, rumour of a beach to the west proved irresistible: sure enough, beside Narin-Portnoo, there is coastal beauty, which having viewed and savoured, I doubled back to Maas and thence moved northwards through Lettermacaward to Dungloe and the Rosses.

Traversing this uncompromisingly stern landscape, it is easy to appreciate how the Irish language has survived amid boulders that provided a natural physical barrier to Anglicization. The question of the Irish language, its utility, its fate, its future in a possible merging of European nations is currently being keenly discussed in Ireland.

Through the medium of the English language the Irish profoundly affected the spiritual atmosphere of the United States, Britain, Australia, New Zealand and to an appreciable if somewhat secondary extent, of Africa and even of distant Korea.

But we simply dare not, without incurring future native, if not indeed, world condemnation, dispense with such a valuable source of world experience as our own language. Without any doubt, the word 'international' postulates or embodies the national.

Tales such as *Déirdre of the Sorrows, The Fairy Palace of the Quicken Trees*, and *The Fate of the Sons of Uisneach*, must find a place in any international cultural array. And these are but part of the inheritance embodied in the Irish language.

So imposing is the Bank of Dungloe, and such is the measure of financial confidence it exudes, and so convincing is its innuendo that the surrounding countryside is plagued by highwaymen, that I almost hammered on its doors in my haste to deposit my every copper in its vaults.

Apart from the bank, the town has been sung into national fame by the revival on the part of a folk-group of an old song called *Mary from Dungloe.*

The coastline that rims the Rosses to the west is indented: interesting islands such as Aranmore lure you over the water with a promise to tell a tale of the Four O'Donnell Pearls. At Burtonport, herring is still king. Crolly is famous for dolls—real dolls that is—while in the area known as Gweedore, boulders cry out for sculptors. Gweedore village I passed and repassed in an effort to find Áine Nic Giolla Bríde who has made a contribution to Gaelic drama by her valour in building an Irish theatre in such a secluded part of the land. As I shuttled to and fro, I recalled that my first introduction to Donegal came through the novels of Patrick McGill and his, for then, raw stories of Irish potato-diggers in the bothies of Scotland. Peadar O'Donnell, that man of many parts – literary, revolutionary, political, sociological, followed later. And any mention of Donegal must evoke memories of Paddy the Cope (the co-op), that doughty pioneer of economic cooperation.

They were playing darts in a roadside pub—four young Irish teenagers, one with a tatooed forearm, clearly for the greater part of the year engaged in 'the building line' in England just as their grandfathers before them were tatie-hoking in Scotland.

Wearing wrist straps, pale blue shirts, a plenitude of hair, Irish-speaking with the good old soldier's word ejaculated at each failure to cast the dart into the centre of the cork-and-wire circle, they swaggered, drank and were typical of the half-generation, neither Irish nor English with none of the better characteristics of either race.

I left them and moved across the rooftop of Ireland to Gortahork where Seán Ó Heochaidh emerged from his bungalow to recount some of the folklore wonders which he had collected in the locality. Behind him in the sky sat the white cone of Errigal, its shining quartzite reminding me of a Japanese print. Its sister peak Muckish promised a rare view from its summit. Seán advised an expedition to Traighmacroarty thence to walk across the sands to Donegal's Inishbofin. But time was master and the road brooked little delay.

Clochaneely of the Irish college loomed up: with it came a tradition that Balor of the Mighty Blows, the Formorian ruler of Tory Island, had beheaded a man named MacKinley and left his blood crystalized in the centre of a crag in the locality.

Through Creeslough of the song (*They're cutting the corn in Creeslough today*) to Carrigart, with nearby Rosapenna with its beach and golf-course, southward to Milford with the Fanad peninsula and its spectacular examples of coastal erosion seen across Malin Bay. Westward from Milford is Rathmullan where, in 1587, Red Hugh O'Donnell, then 15 years of age, was lured on to a merchant ship and taken to Dublin Castle. Resentment of this act engendered a war that lasted for eight years. In 1607 Rathmullan was also the point of departure for the Continent of the Ulster chieftains after which the Plantation of Ulster was resolutely begun. And at Rathmullan too, in 1798, were landed Wolfe Tone and the survivors of the 300 Frenchmen captured together with the battleship *Hoche* in a sea-fight off Lough Swilly. Subsequently, Wolfe Tone, the man who first laid down the principles of Irish separatism, was found dead in his cell in Dublin, his throat slit. Murder or suicide?—history still argues the point.

Near Newtowncunningham, with Maurice Hayes again as co-pilot, I began to search for the historic fortress called the Grainán of Aileach.

'Aw', said the huge man whom we questioned on the roadside near the village. 'You're lucky men you met me. I'm the mon to direct you to Grainán Fort.'

'By a short cut!' he shouted, as unceremoniously he dragged open the car door and sat on the back seat, depressing the whole vehicle as he did so. 'There are people who'd direct you by a road where you'ld break your springs,' he went on. 'Not me! I'll guide you on the tar all the way.' He sighed his satisfaction, then: 'Turn your car right aroun',' he ordered.

'Isn't Grianán of Aileach to the North?' Maurice mildly remonstrated. 'Right aroun', the newcomer insisted. 'I was born and r'ared in this locality. Every stick of it I know. You're in safe honds.'

We drove south. He took us into switchbacking by-ways where he called on old friends 'just for a wee minute'. He stopped to examine cattle grazing in the fields. 'Yon's good', he commented, then ordered us to proceed. People standing at crossroads he greeted with a kind of staid hilarity. 'A good job you met me,' he repeated after each encounter. 'I'll take you right around at the back of Grianán Fort.'

When at last a signpost indicated that we were close to Stranorlar, a breath of suspicion blew across my face. Maurice Hayes's silence I now realized was touched with amusement. Our new-found guide must have noticed my anxiety, for with his next roared direction, if the sun was any indication, we were heading north again. After an hour and three quarters of convolute driving he ordered us to stop.

'A few miles down there,' he said airily. 'And there y'are!' Departing he shook hands with each of us. 'A good job you met me,' he shouted as he clumped away. 'An' God's blessin' on ye!'

We drove on. After a few miles the countryside was vaguely familiar. We realized we were again entering Manorcunningham— this time from a different direction. We also realized that we had given a playboy a joyride around north-east Donegal.

Round and round we spiralled on the new road that led to the fortress on top of Grianán (Sunny Room) mountain. Evening had come. As we reached the hill-top a chill wind blew. The evening light turned the stones of the triple fortifications to gun metal. Here it was, then, the Grianán of Aileach, stone brother to Staigue Fort in Kerry and to Dún Aengus in Aran. And though it had been imperfectly restored, it was still broodingly powerful and aloof, and evocative of an age when with the first chink of European dawn, this place may well have been a temple of the sun.

The building of the fortress, according to the Four Masters, took place in 1500 B.C. and it was subsequently developed as a stronghold of the O'Neills. In 1101 A.D. it was partially destroyed by Muircheartach O'Brien, king of Munster, in revenge for the destruction of Kincora by the king of Aileach.

After the partial demolition of the fort, each horse-soldier of the O'Briens balanced a pair of stones on his saddle bags and bore them south to Kincora. I can never visit the cathedral at Killaloe without giving credence to the (probably fanciful) tale that some of the cathedral stones came from the destroyed Grianán of Aileach.

Dusk had fallen. North-west on the mainland, beside Inch island, daylight ebbed from the loughside meadows. In the east the chimney-smoke of Derry hung above the houses. West across Lough Swilly house-lights came up in Rathmelton. In the south the Foyle river was a twist of silver paper. In the full-blooded north, peak beyond peak beyond peak the mountains stretched into farthest Inishowen.

CHAPTER EIGHT

The Heart of Ireland

'...a quiet water'd land, a land of roses'

Poised on Grianán Aileach and ready to move across the Foyle into the six counties of Northern Ireland, I ask myself if I dared forget to visit the Irish midlands which constitute the heart of Ireland, an area for me enclosed by a circle drawn with a radius of, say, 30-40 miles with Athlone as its centre and embracing sectors of the counties Westmeath, Offaly, Laois, Galway, Roscommon, Leitrim, Cavan and Longford.

This is an area which—the Slieve Bloom mountains on the Offaly-Laois border apart—lacks a mountain range of consequence: it compensates with drumlins, erratic but gently rounded eskers, lakes galore as befits a natural basin, rivers that fill and drain these lakes, and rich pasturage where Hereford cattle, 'beef to the heels', gaze benevolently at the wayfarer. Its most notable topographical feature is the river Shannon meandering indolently southwards amid its low-lying callows.

I viewed the midland drumlins from the air on one of the rare days when Ireland was snowbound. Through winter sunshine I saw on the tops of very many of the hillocks below me clearly defined by snow and shadow the ring marks of ancient forts; some had triple concentric earthworks but all were evocative of the Ireland concealed in the mist of prehistory. From such an eminence I was also enabled to appreciate the vital position occupied by county Westmeath's Athlone, set south of sprawling Lough Ree, and guarding one of the most important river crossings in the land.

In the twelfth century Athlone comprised part of the O'Conor

18 Half-door in Donegal

Kingdom of Connaught: this necessitated the erection of a bridge to provide access to kingly Meath. In 1200 the Normans were in possession of the place and later constructed the castle which still stands at the bridgehead. Recurrently suffering quite dire misfortunes of siege and capitulation. Athlone's bravest hour was in June 1691 when, with the breached bridge and Irish town on the west bank both held by 1,500 Jacobite soldiers, it endured the most severe bombardment recorded in Irish history: later it crowned its endurance by the feat of a Jacobite soldier called Custume who, with a handful of volunteers, broke down the arch which had been repaired under cover of darkness by soldiers of the besieging Williamite army of 21,000 men, then under the command of de Ginkell.

Today the citizens of Athlone have much in common with the not-so-far-away town of Loughrea in as much as both populations eat, drink, sleep, wake, talk and walk in terms of drama each May during the final stages of the All-Ireland Amateur Drama Competition.

On another level Athlone is making a bold bid for prominence and prosperity: the game- and coarse-fish in the reed- selvedged lakes of central Ireland are valuable to the national economy: in recent years angling enthusiasts especially from the upper English midlands are now discovering the area in increasing numbers.

Nine miles due south of Athlone on the left bank of the Shannon is Clonmacnois, where in 545 A.D. St Ciarán founded a monastery which, at the pinnacle of its fame, could truly be called a university and as such was liberally endowed by kings of Ireland.

This sanctuary inevitably attracted the unwelcome attentions of the Danes and later of the Anglo-Normans. It survived the harshest of calamities until 1552, when the English garrison of Athlone marched south, seized the sacred vessels, and razed the monastery. A subsequent attempt to restore the cathedral in 1647 evoked another bloody response from Cromwell's army: after this the cathedral, the chapels, the high crosses, the towers and the slabs were abandoned to the curlews and the grass.

19 Fiddler and home-made fiddle

Conscious of desolation refined to beauty by weather and time I wandered at evening in Clonmacnois. Presently I was joined by an old man, obviously the keeper of the place and the lover of every one of the 400 inscribed slabs the enclosure contains.

In the course of our conversation the old scholar mentioned that St Ciarán's father had hailed from Donegal in the extreme north of Ireland, while his mother had come from Ciarraí Luachra on the Cork-Kerry border in the extreme south of the country.

'How could a man from the north meet a girl from Kerry in that remote period?' I asked. 'Kerry must have been as remote from Donegal at that time as the Middle East is from Dublin now!'

'Ciarán's father and grandfather were chariot-builders,' the old man replied. 'Consequently chariots and horses were readily available to the saint's father as a young man. Nowadays, the adolescent borrows his father's motor-car to go on a jaunt; in those days, at the first of summer, the young Irishman of spirit secured a horse and a light chariot and wandered all over the island. At night he slept rough with his mantle over his head. True, the country for the most part had only the rude cart-tracks one sees nowadays in cowboy films, but even at that time there were serviceable bridges, bridle paths through the forests and causeways across the bogs. Then, as now, there were long stretches of firm beaches on the coastline. That the river fords were well known is evidenced by the numerous Irish placenames containing the word *áth*, a ford. Imagine the countryside around you without any fences and you have the Ireland of 1500 years ago. So it was that father of Ciarán, in his wandering, met and fell in love with a girl who lived not far from Killarney.'

I found this simple interpretation of history convincing.

Still moving downstream through Shannonbridge, thence south east to Cloghan thence again south west one arrives at Banagher in County Offaly where Anthony Trollope, while stationed there as a Post Office Surveyor in 1841, wrote his first two novels, both with an Irish setting.

Across the Shannon in County Galway and five miles north-west of Banagher, set more or less in a loop of the river, is Clonfert, where in the mid-6th century St Brendan founded a monastery later to be associated with many famous names in Irish ecclesiastical and literary history. Ravaged twice by the Norse and destroyed by fire on four separate occasions, in the twelfth century it evolved into an Augustinian priory. The richly ornamented doorway of the tiny cathedral which dates from the mid-12th century shows Irish Romanesque at its most superb.

Birr, its bright square pied with flowers, lies at the six o'clock mark of my midland clockface. Here in post-hunting revels the local huntsmen set fire to Dooley's Hotel; thus originated the name of The Galway 'Blazers', a pack known the length and breadth of the land.

In the nineteenth century a Father Crotty of Birr anticipated the use of the vernacular in the mass by more than a century and was almost excommunicated on the head of it. A tall column erected in 1747 in Emmet Square with the idea of placing a statue of the 'bloody Duke of Cumberland' on top was later left unfinished when it was pointed out that if Highland troops were posted to the town, the statue of their oppressor would act as a red rag to a bull.

Once the centre of the territory of O'Carrolls of Éile who had their principal castle in the town, the Birr district was in 1620 included in the confiscation of O'Carroll land granted to Laurence Parsons of Leicestershire.

For some years Birr was known as Parsonstown: the Parsons family lost and regained it in the varying fortunes of war. As Earls of Rosse, the Parsons family provided pioneers in many fields of endeavour and were liberal in their outlook. The third Earl (1800-1867) won fame as an astronomer and had telescopes constructed to his own designs. The Birr Observatory which he founded has recently celebrated the centenary of its establishment.

It's due west now, and again I cross the Shannon at Portumna, a scrupulously neat town sited at the head of Lough Derg. Portumna was once the seat of the Clanricarde Burkes (*and glory guards Clanricarde's grave*) who secured vast tracts of land by inter-marriage with the native O'Maddens.

195

The Slieve Aughty hills are to the south-west as again I swing north to Ballinasloe, a place which tempts me to add a postscript to my mention of its fair during my previous Galway itinerary.

In the Ireland of today the battle of fair versus mart has been indisputably decided in favour of the mart.

The Irish fair was an unusual phenomenon indeed.

The farmer, his wife and sons, had to be out of bed at two or three o'clock in the morning. To the accompaniment of the barking of sheepdogs and the roaring of drovers, there began the bizarre drive over the darkened countryside; cattle running in all directions had to be headed off by the more agile of the sons and the more vociferous of the shepherd dogs.

A notorious hazard of droving was the intermingling with other herds of cattle: the frenzied extrication was executed to the accompaniment of the rat-tat-tat of ash sticks on the rumps of the beasts.

At last the farmer, his frieze coat often loaded with a bucketful of rain, reached the bedlam that was the fair green, whence the fair itself had overflowed (most apposite of words) on to the streets of the town.

There the beasts were corralled against the backdrop of a brightly-painted house ('They show up great against paint!'), with the result that the carefully-tended house-façade was soon dung-bespattered.

If the townsman protested—understandably the publican never did—he was told with pungent embellishments that 'the bloody townies were dependent upon the fairs for their living and that where there was muck there was money!'

Presently, the well-shod buyers, bamboo sticks under their arms and red raddle-sticks in their hands, moved to and fro, shouting, haranguing, cajoling, refusing, departing and inevitably returning. If a few pounds remained to be haggled over, a middleman appeared out of nowhere with his plaintive cry of 'Don't break my word!'

Eventually, to the accompaniment of ritualistic spitting on palms and shouts of 'Let ye be said by me!' the bargain was clinched.

For the farmer, the buyer then scribbled a chit which could later be presented for payment at a local bank.

Then began the adventurous procession of the cattle to the train, which necessitated passage through a 'custom gap' where tolls were paid to the patent holder of the fair; it was only when the linchpins fell into place on the doors of the cattle-wagons that the farmer could breathe a sigh of relief.

Later he met his wife who had come leisurely riding into town in a pony and trap. When the chit was cashed, much money-clucking took place under the tent of the farmwife's shawl. The sons were given moderate hansels while the farmer himself sidled off to a pub run by a man from his own district to have a few drinks with his friends.

Later still, he bought articles at stalls or booths set up in the market-place, consumed some sort of a meal (a plate of ham or a mutton-pie) in a local eating-house, and finally, softened with stout and proud of his bargaining prowess and indeed of the few hundred pounds he had added the fortunes of his as yet unwed daughters, he allowed himself to be driven home in triumph.

That day has gone! Today the loudspeaker yap-yap-yap of the mart auctioneer has replaced the centuries-old ritual of fair-day bargaining.

At Kilconnell, seven miles west of Ballinasloe and close to Aughrim, is the picturesque but ruined Franciscan abbey founded by the O'Kellys in which a late seventeenth century epitaph to the memory of Lord Trimliston abuses 'the usurper Cromwell who transported his family into Connaught'.

It is flat uninspiring country all the road via Mount Bellew Bridge and Athleague to Roscommon, capital of the county of the same name; the twin-headed claim of the county town to distinction is based on the ruins of the thirteenth century Dominican friary founded by King Phelim O'Conor of Connaught who lies buried within its walls, and the resolute bulk of the corner-towered hillside castle erected in 1268 by John D'Ufford, Justiciar.

As is to be expected, the patronymic O'Conor occurs frequently in connection with the history of this area; after a short divagation via Fuerty to scan the inscribed stones of its Patrician foundation, I am tempted to return to Athlone on a scenic road that runs along the western shore of Lough Ree, with the prospect of visiting en route the village of Knockroghery (The Hill of the Hangman) which I associate with the manufacture of clay-pipes, articles which as a boy I often dispensed at the wakes of my dead kinsfolk.

However, on rejoining the road from Roscommon to Castlerea I preferred before reaching Ballymore to branch north-west to Ballintober, a place not to be confounded with the famous Mayo abbey of the same name, there to view the immense pile that is the ruined castle of the O'Conor Don which figured variously as fortress and forum in Tudor, Stuart and minor wars. The O'Conor Don family, with seats at Clonalis and Bellanagare, represent one of the most distinguished native royal dynasties left in Ireland.

A square erected on a line joining Roscommon with Castlerea encloses a plain on which lived the early kings of Connacht: the hill of Rathcroghan (*Cruachain*) a few miles north-west of Tulsk marks the site of the palace of these monarchs. Although there is little to indicate its former importance, here it was that King Ailill —he was more correctly, prince consort,—and his wife Queen Maeve, formerly wife to Conor MacNessa of Ulster, had their famous 'pillow argument' as to which of the pair had the more valuable possessions.

When, to her dismay, Maeve found that her husband tipped the scales by the possession of a single bull, she sent a commission to the borders of Ulster to purchase a finer bull, hoping by this acquisition to discomfit her husband. After having amicably arranged the purchase of the bull in what is now the Cooley peninsula south of Carlingford Lough, the messengers outraged the bull's owner by declaring that it was a damn good job he had decided to sell, else Maeve would have taken it from him by force. This incident sparked off a conflict described in the Irish epic tale *Táin Bó Cuailgne* (The Cattle-raid of Cooley).

Places in the vicinity of Rathcroghan have eloquent names such as 'Hillock of the Corpses', 'The Cave of the Cats' and bathetically enough, 'Maeve's Lump'. 'The Cave of the Cats' was believed to offer an entrance to the netherworld and as such figures prominently in the mythology of Ireland.

A few miles north-west of Rathcroghan is Ballanagare, home of the O'Conors Don. At the point of intersection of Castlerea-Boyle and Tulsk-Ballaghadereen roads is Frenchpark where lies buried Douglas Hyde, (pen-name *An Craoibhín Aoibhinn: The Little Pleasant Branch*), author of *Love Songs of Connaught* and one of the founders of the Gaelic League, who after his retirement from the chair of Irish in University College Dublin was astonished to find himself recalled by the unanimous wish of rival parties in Dáil Éireann to become first President of Ireland under the 1937 constitution.

Hyde, a merry, informal walrus-moustached erudite scholar, on hastening to Dublin in answer to the summons of his people, is alleged to have found his ancient automobile in a traffic snarl in mid-city and to have been read a lecture by the large Garda on point duty who commented ironically on 'ould fellahs up from the country upsettin' the whole traffic of the city'. Absolutely without side, Hyde must have enjoyed the position in which he found himself. Even as I write I seem to see his merry eyes before me and to hear him recite his own translation of the Gaelic quatrain, *Ceo Meala, Lá Seaca:*

A honey mist on a day of frost in a dark oak wood
And love for thee in the heart of me, thou bright white and good.
Thy slender form rich and warm, thy red lips apart
Thou hast found me and hast bound me and put grief into my heart.

Still in County Roscommon, Elphin can trace its ecclesiastical descent from St Patrick himself who appointed Assicus as the first bishop of a local foundation. It also claims, not without opposition from transpontine areas, to have been the birthplace of Oliver Goldsmith. Conceded, however, is the fact that the poet was educated at the local diocesan school.

Almost due north of Elphin and in the County Leitrim is Carrick-on-Shannon, a town which is fast becoming an important boating and fishing centre.

To me the emigration-bled county of Leitrim conveys a picture of small mysterious fields, ubiquitous alder bushes and overgrown little roads. Out of its iron countryside came revolutionaries like MacDermott, born Kiltyclogher in January 1883, a man who would not allow a physical handicap to lessen his determination to liberate his land.

I strolled in Drumshanbo and realized that structurally, even in the stones of which it is built, the town mirrors the countryside, especially the coal-bearing area close to Arigna, west of lonely Lough Allen in north Roscommon, and also the tract of land extending to the point where counties Leitrim, Sligo and Roscommon meet. This sense of the uncompromising in configuration and geographical structure extends westward across the Iron mountains into County Cavan where on the southern slope of Cuilcagh mountain, bubbling up from a pool known as Shannon Pot, Ireland's greatest river has its origin.

Heading due south for Carrick-on-Shannon, thence again south eastward to delighful Drumsna, there to view amid old demesne land the Shannon like a snake doubling on itself and enclosing in its loops 'The Dún', a half-mile of earthwork dating from prehistoric times, I noted in passing mountain, wooded peninsula and fertile alluvial land—a countryside that called for a second savouring.

I am tempted sinuously to travel to the south along the shore of Lough Bofin to Dromod of the iron ore and to lovely Rooskey of the swaying boats, but choose instead to travel to Mohill whence I begin the long haul north-eastward to Carrigallen through a countryside that by no possible leap of the imagination could be reckoned touristically magnetic but which offers me personally its own odd type of uniqueness.

By way of contrast one may push on over the County Monaghan border to Clones where on the occasion of an All-Ireland *Fleadh Cheoil* one may royster or strum tambourines or sing traditionally until grey dawn brings surcease.

Monaghan town, a centre of education and agriculture, set in MacMahon country, lies on the northern rim of my current tour: it claims among its more august sons General Don Juan McKenna of Chile (died Buenos Aires 1814) and Charles Gavan Duffy (1816-1903) founder-editor of 'The Nation' newspaper which had such a dramatic impact on the minds of the Irish people. Duffy later became prime minister of Victoria, Australia. Seven miles south-east of the town is Clontibret, where in 1585, the great O'Neill fought the first battle of the Nine Years War and there inflicted a sharp defeat on an English force.

I sped north-west, delaying at most impressive Farnham House, seat of the Maxwells (Lords Farnham), a family hailing originally from Scotland which over the centuries has carved for itself an important niche in the history of the Church of Ireland. Later I move to the edge of Lough Oughter directly across lake water from Killesandra to view the ruins of Clogoughter Castle, an O'Reilly fortress dating from the thirteenth century, built originally on a crannóg, where in 1649, Owen Roe O'Neill, hope of the Irish cause died under such mysterious circumstances.

The name Ballyjamesduff recalls the ditty of the same name written by Percy French, who may well be called a troubadour in the Irish context but whose verses like *Phil the Fluter's Ball* I find rather like meringues when steaks are more to my liking. That the meringue also has its place on the musical menu I would be foolish to deny.

And so pondering I make my way through Oldcastle which is south of Lough Ramor and over the County Meath border; there I look upwards at the hills due south of the town where on almost every summit is a cairn, a tumulus, a ringfort or a passage grave. These moderate-sized eminences also afford fine views over the central lowlands.

Having loitered long in monastic Fore, east of Castlepollard, with its tale of seven wonders, I came to the edge of scenic Lough Derravaragh, some miles to the west, where legend tells that the Children of Lir, as swans, spent the first 300 of their changeling years. Thence hastening north-west I reached Granard and climbed the grassy moat at the south-western end of that quiet Sunday town in County Longford, and called up the spirit of the Norman de Tuit who had the knoll constructed in 1199 as part of a de Lacy attempt to penetrate Brefni. Peaceful Granard below me was, in 1315, sacked and burned by Edward Bruce as a consequence of his having been refused facilities by O'Farrell. In 1798 ('The Year of Liberty') the hillock also witnessed the summary execution of a party of Insurgents.

On the road west to Longford I passed through Ballinalee, burial place of 130 insurgents executed in 1798 by Lord Cornwallis. The village was also the birthplace of General Sean McEoin, a blacksmith who won fame as a brave and chivalrous officer in the fight for Irish Independence. As a boy the mere mention of 'The Blacksmith of Ballinalee' was enough to cause me to whoop with joy.

The spread of land between Meathus Truim, or Edgeworthstown, in County Longford through Ballymahon to Glassan, a few miles north west of Athlone in County Westmeath is literary terrain *par excellence*: the first named town is associated with Maria Edge- worth, novelist and member of a brilliant family, while the last named is contiguous to Lissoy or Auburn, reputed scene of Oliver Goldsmith's poem *Deserted Village*. Oliver who 'wrote like an angel but talked like poor Poll' was born in Pallas, County Longford, a few miles to the east of Ballymahon. Hereabouts there is rare contention and rivalry as prideful villages identify themselves with scenes in Goldsmith's poems and plays.

To traverse this quiet countryside is to find oneself charioted back in time to the middle of the eighteenth century: this is especially palpable if one sits and sips ale in such a pub as *The Three Jolly Pigeons* named for the country pub in the Goldsmith play *She Stoops to Conquer*.

Hearty Mullingar of the beefy cattle, the bronze crosses of its cathedral gleaming in the sunlight, is set in a ring of the Royal Canal. The mayfly lakes of Owel and Ennel are not far away. In Owel in 845 King Malachi of Meath drowned the Norse chieftain Turgesius, having first wrenched a golden collar from his neck. Mullingar's location seemed always to have determined its destiny as a garrison town: its tale is that of a springboard wherefrom the

English leap-frogged to attack Irish forces crouched in the menacing west.

Edenderry in County Offaly is associated with the family of the Marquess of Downshire and stands in the centre of an area where there are ruined castles galore—keeps that once marked the eastern border of the English Pale. On Carrick Hill, a few miles to the north, crumbling masonry reminds the traveller of the fact that there in 1305, King O'Conor of *Uí Fáilghe* and 31 of his chieftains were treacherously assassinated by Sir Pierce Bermingham and Jordon Cumin.

Hereabouts too are heard legends of witches, saints, and sinners. There are even hoofprints to vouch for the veracity of the tale that tells of a mule that ran off with a saint!

Tullamore, the capital of County Offaly, is a typical, thriving, inland town built close to the site of the once famous monastery of Durrow, one of the most important of St Colmcille's foundations. Its fine tenth century cross is still standing.

To close the midland noose I mention that a typical section of Esker Riada runs close to Kilbeggan while Clara, a flour-milling centre, began its days as a Quaker settlement. Moate had its most imposing mound named for young Grace, wife of Ó Maoilsheach-lainn, chief of the district.

Athlone looms up again as lordly as it is strategic. There is the splendid spread of Lough Ree to be investigated and sunny days to spend lolling along its wooded banks.

CHAPTER NINE

The North

'The North began: the North led on ...'

Night! A mile-long spangle of vehicular rear-lights at Carrickcarnon north of Dundalk as drivers about to cross the border queue up at the customs post.

In a small island a border is an odd experience. I am determined that the frustration it engenders—in either direction—shall not distract me from my purpose of recounting with affection something of the six northern counties of Ireland. But wherever there is a border there are misunderstandings: on certain matters, one part of me is so replete with conviction that no amount of simulated bonhomie will gloss over its unyielding nature: I must however concede that others would scarcely view matters in the same light as I do.

One thing I must set down: the sense of the separatism, identity and unity of the Irish island was first formulated, not by my fellow 'papists', but by dissenters, Presbyterians and Protestants of varying kinds hailing in the main from the North. These men moulded principles derived from the French Revolution so as to fit the Irish scene. Names such as Tone, Gray, Russell, McCracken, Monroe, Orr, Sheares, Parnell and Mitchell bear witness to this apparent anomaly.

To strike a more congenial note: a border also connotes smuggling: like water in an enclosed U-tube the economy of a small island, by means overt or covert, tends to find its own financial level. Thus the prevailing prices of bacon, butter, sugar, tea, razor blades, textiles, tobacco and whiskey, to mention but a few items subject to price fluctuation as a result of subsidy or tax on this side or that, beget smuggling, which it must be admitted engenders more hilarity than heat. The Dublin teenage girl who slips up to Belfast for a rigout which offers the illusion of being closer to the latest English model sweats not a little at the prospect of even a mild customs examination at Connolly Station in Dublin at the end of her return journey. No one takes the whole business very seriously except perhaps a sturdy posse of vigilante farmers determined that pig smuggling shall not do damage to rural economy.

Poised on the border, I glanced backward over my right shoulder towards the storied Cooley peninsula in County Louth.

Due south of Warrenpoint in the County Down and across Carlingford Lough is Omeath, whence there is a ferry to Warrenpoint.

Omeath was the last area in the province of Leinster to lose the Irish language as a spoken tongue, thus providing almost to our day a link with the language of the Irish epic associated with the story of the area. This is a miracle, when one considers the breezes of change that have beaten about the village.

Moving south-westward along the southern and comparatively Rhenish edge of the Lough to Carlingford, a town seated at the foot of toothed Slieve Foy, one finds the harbour dominated by the ruins of King John's Castle which was erected in the early thirteenth century, while the Mint, a highly ornamented town house of the fifteenth or sixteenth century, is said to occupy the site of an original mint erected in 1467. Moving still further to the south-west, quite lovely Greenore, once terminus of a thriving sea-route to Holyhead, fights for its economic life. Quickly swinging south-west to low-lying land there is a further turn to the west so as to rejoin the Dundalk-Newry road at the border close to what is traditionally called 'The Gap of the North'.

The name Newry, that of the first town encountered in rich County Down of the hummocky drumlin countryside, is derived from a telescoping of Irish words which signify *The Yew Tree at the Head of the Beach*: the yew tree in question lived on century after century and was believed by the credulous to have been planted by St Patrick himself.

In the sixteenth century the area lying in the strategic hinterland of Newry, with all the bloody litany of history that strategy implies, was in the possession of Nicholas Begenal who built the first Protestant church, as such, in Newry town. Newry made canal history inasmuch as its man-made water link with Lough Neagh and Carlingford Lough was the first major undertaking of this nature in these islands: begun in 1730, and ended in 1741, the same canal today is green and reedy in most of its idle stretches.

Dean Swift's couplet on Newry:

> *High Church; low steeple;*
> *Dirty town, proud people.*

reminds me of a similar scarifying couplet coopered by a poetaster who was scoffed at on his entry to a Kerry village:

Knockanure, both mean and poor, a church without a steeple
Where bitches and whores look over half doors to scoff at dacent
people.

Rambling in this ancient and always handsome town, set between Slieve Gullion to the east and the Newry mountains to the west, I am reminded to look down the long street of Dromalane on the Armagh side of the county border. Here, son of an Unitarian Minister, the patriot-lawyer John Mitchell died in 1875 and was later buried in the graveyard associated with the First Newry Presbyterian church.

And whence do I recall that grisly Newry legend of a young man called Cochran, executed for the part he played as a United Irishman in the '98 Rebellion? His father was allowed to bury the long exposed and spiked head of his son only after he had paraded the filial skull through the streets shouting 'Traitor!' To this significant pair of Newry citizens may be added the name of a third, John Kells Ingram, also a Presbyterian, later Vice-Provost of Trinity College

Dublin, who composed *The Memory of the Dead* or *Who Fears to Speak of '98?* a 'rebelly' ballad which enjoys a virile life to this day.

I now find myself with a pleasant choice of itineraries. I may move south-west to Warrenpoint, thence due east to tropical Rostrevor where an Irish giant lies buried, and more (and less) hugging the shore, with the kingly Mourne mountains above me and to my left hand, travel through Kilkeel, with possibly an amiable detour to Greencastle once capital of the Mourne Kingdom and held as such by the Norman de Burgos, and eventually reach Bloody Bridge, where in 1641, planters were massacred, finally to call a halt at the seaside resort of Newcastle under the mountain of Slieve Donard.

This is a run as pleasant as can be imagined: its upturned arc forms the band of a wheel south of the Mournes, the hub of which lies on Hilltown. A few miles north of Hilltown, in Goward, is an immense dolmen known as Pat Kearney's Big Stone, the granite capstone of which is said to weigh 50 tons: needless to say, such an unusual boulder carries its normal quota of legendary associations with Fionn MacCumhaill.

The spokes that radiate through the hills from Hilltown, each in its own idiom, offers new and delightful prospects of excursion through the Mourne mountains.

Myself, on this occasion, I chose the more direct road out of Newry: that which moved eastward through Rathfriland, Castlewellan to Clough and Downpatrick.

As the probable burial place of St Patrick, all creeds lay claim to Downpatrick, a town that has its later history indicated in the nomenclature of its five quarters, now streets—Irish Quarter, English Quarter, Scotch Quarter, Windmill Quarter and Barracks Quarter.

I stand on Gallows Hill above Downpatrick town and think of Gallows Hill above Cashel where my first son was born. And of

Gallows Hill above Killarney where Pierce Ferriter, nobleman and poet, was hanged, I think also of Gallows Hill in south-east Clare on the road to Quin Abbey.

And how odd are the alleyways of the mind! For out of all the accumulated woes and glories of the macrocosm that is Ireland and the microcosm that is Downpatrick the prime indignation that takes me is not one of sadness for the O'Neill Kingdom of Ulster lost to de Courcey at the Battle of Down in 1260 but the plight of some wild ducks and geese.

In Downpatrick, I had met dignified Robert Browne in the estate office of Lord Dunleath. Tall, straight Robert Browne, now called to the kingdom of everlasting daffodils. What chemical affinity exists between men, that like knows like at once—an attribute the human being shares with terriers above all the animals in creation?

Downpatrician Maurice Hayes, later to be entrusted in important measure with the herculean task of trying to knit the broken northern community together, had already told me of this unusual man. In springtime it was Robert's custom to cast daffodil bulbs on the sward of Downpatrick cathedral which stands on the height of Rathchealtchair—a name that goes back to the first century A.D.— and dibble in the bulbs where haphazardly they came to rest.

When the daffodils 'were blown to golden flame', Robert plucked an armful and, striding past the balanced façade of the Southwell School, now a special care school, past the grim portals of Downpatrick jail, and also past the door of that esoteric club where a laughing oddfellow once told me that one of the chamber pots had a picture of Gladstone on its inside bottom so that those opposed to Home Rule could with impunity micturate on that statesman's features, he bestowed his flower-bounty on those citizens of Downpatrick who, during the previous year, had in Robert's opinion, done something meritorious. During this ceremony the unusual donor said nothing; the accolade was implicit in the expression in his eyes as he bestowed the blooms.

20 Tenth-century cross at Durrow, Co. Offaly

On the occasion of my visit I found Robert Browne, that lover of nature, genuinely troubled.

From time immemorial the marshes of the River Quoile below the cathedral height had been a sanctuary for wild ducks and wild geese.

Each year in October the eyes of the townspeople swept the skies in anticipation of seeing the flock of brent geese darkening the heavens and filling the streets with their cries and with the creak and rustle of their wings.

But that year the local high school had had to seek a playing pitch. And how better find one than by draining the nearby marshes at the river edge? There, Peter Scott, that eminent painter of wild life and distinguished naturalist, had often kept watch upon the wingéd visitors to the Cathedral Marsh.

There is scarcely a town in Ireland with such an exquisite sense of history as Downpatrick. In 432, in a barn at nearby Saul, St Patrick had read the first mass ever offered on Irish soil. The Danes had sacked the original monastery. That Cheshire cat, de Courcey the Anglo-Norman chieftain—I spent a delightful morning in his remarkable motte-and-bailey which stands by the river's edge—by the 'discovery' of relics of Irish saints and by the addition of the suffix—'-patrick' to the original *Dún* (stronghold) had made Downpatrick an ecclesiastical capital. Here on the opposite bank of the river stand the sad-lovely ruins of Inch Abbey built by a de Courcey in 1180 on the ruins of a still older church. Edward Bruce was in Downpatrick in 1316. United Irishman Russell of 1798—'The Man from God Knows Where'—was hanged outside its jail gate for taking part in the Emmet Rebellion—his grave is in mid-town—so how could such a city not wince at the snapping of a vital link with its past?

But the marshes were drained. The playing-fields became a reality. When October came, the wheeling geese filled the streets of Downpatrick with their cries of misunderstanding: the forebears of these geese had cried over Patrick as he sailed up nearby Strangford Lough.

As the geese flew away seeking asylum, the link of the centuries was snapped. I felt sorry for people like Robert Browne.

21 Market Day, Athlone

Unavoidable? Maybe, worse could occur in my native Kerry. 'Wild ducks?' they ask, 'What good are they?' 'Trees?' 'What the hell good are trees?' Unawareness—and I speak as restrainedly as I can —is omnipresent in Ireland.

From my resting place in Denvir's Hotel (cf. D'Anverre—'of Antwerp'—and, Denver, Colorado called for a surveyor member of the Denvir family) in the holy city of Downpatrick I foraged west to Strangford village (Danish Strang-Fjord), where the ebbing tide bustles and jostles through the narrow opening of Strangford Lough.

On the road I stopped at Saul and walked up the side of the green hill. Viewed from directly beneath it, the large-nostrilled statue of St Patrick was powerfully ugly: turning behind the sacrificial slab just below the statue I ran my eyes over the landscape.

Somewhere in the spread of land below me St Patrick lay buried; it is unlikely that he lies under the great stone labelled PATRIC and placed by F. J. Biggar close to the Cathedral in Downpatrick, but this doesn't take a whit from the antiquity of Rathchealtchair Height. In nearby Saul I visited St Patrick's Wells; one for drinking, one for rubbing to sore eyes, one for bathing women, one for bathing men. It is not an article of Catholic faith to believe in blessed 'wells'— some of these indeed are pagan in origin—but Patrick and his followers are believed to have 'sanctified' them and bent older traditions to Christian usage.

At Ardglass at midnight I waited for the trawlers to return from the Irish sea: as reward for my vigil I received a basketful of prawns. To well-kept Drundrum Castle (1230-40) I hied myself; its ten-foot thick walls forcibly reminded me of the de Lacy attempt to establish a Norman kingdom in Ulster – a venture that abruptly ended when King John crossed from England and put an end to such nonsense. Remembering that the castle was for a short time in the possession of the MacCartans, I also recalled that General de Gaulle had a female ancestor of this name who presumably hailed from this area where the name MacCartan is common.

Viewing the Mourne Mountains from the castle battlements I saw a wave cresting and breaking in the Irish Sea: Maurice Hayes jogged my memory to the effect that this was *Tonn Ruairí*—Rory's Wave—one of the three traditional waves of Ireland which are believed to possess the power of lamentation in a time of national disaster.

From Strangford I crossed to Portaferry on a sunny day, the water limpid under my trailing fingers; landing at the bluestone stained pier, I walked in the aromatic fields at the end of the peaceful peninsula of Ards. Here Scotland was but the spit out of my mouth across the water.

A mile to the west of Ballynahinch three trees mark the graves of Betsy Gray, folk hero of the Rebellion of 1798.

In this battle the demesne of Lord Moira and the hills around Montalto were held by the Ards division of the United Irishmen under Henry Munroe while the English forces, under the command of General Nugent, faced the main body of the insurgents drawn up on Windmill Hill. As was the case elsewhere during the revolt, the issue was knit between artillery and pikemen.

The story tells that Betsy Gray, 'a woman of wondrous beauty enriched by a warm heart', awaited the arrival of her lover, Willie Boal, and her brother George, both active in the insurgent ranks.

At Ballycreen, the yeomen caught up with the pair of rebels: when Betsy came on the scene she found her lover dying and her brother in mortal combat with one of the yeomen. As she grasped the yeoman's sword from behind, another of the yeomen shot her between the eyes.

I visited the spot on the Armstrong farm at Ballycreen where the three lie buried in one grave. Their memory lives on in bathetic ballads of which I recall a line:

Down the hill brave Betsy ran, to save her brother and her man.

The tale also tells that a bugle call from the ranks of the yeomanry, which the insurgents interpreted as a signal to advance, was in reality the signal for an English retiral: the insurgents wavered, and the yeomen, quick to seize their opportunity, turned defeat into victory by charging at the right time. We in the south still sing plaintive songs about Henry Joy McCracken and Henry Munroe, hanged later in Lisburn. Folklore describes the informer who betrayed Munroe as being 'shunned by the old and hooted by the young'.

From Inch Abbey it is a short run to Killyleagh on the western shore of Strangford Lough. Killyleagh village is dominated by the imposing and almost teutonic castle of the Hamilton Rowans.

The castle was variously owned and occupied by de Mandevilles, O'Neills, MacCartans and Whytes, with again a first reversion to Shane the Proud O'Neill and a second reversion to the Whyte family who eventually sold the castle to the brilliant, and sometimes nationally wilful, Hamiltons.

Pondering on the fact that Sir Hans Sloane (1666-1753), born in Killyleagh, could fairly be termed founder of the British Museum, I moved along a clinker-surfaced, nettle-acrid laneway by the side of the castle walls and, having crossed an unkempt field, arrived at a spot close to a pseudo-bleeding Sacred Heart on a cemetery headstone beside which stands the original stile mentioned by Lady Dufferin in her ballad *The Irish Emigrant* popularly called *I'm Sitting on the Stile, Mary*. The ballad was inspired by the sight of a man bemoaning his dead wife prior to his leaving for America.

On the road northward through Comber I genuflected to the east to the ruins of Nendrum Monastery, with a further mild obeisance to ruined Grey Abbey on the shore of the Lough (de Courcy is believed to have been buried here) where an old tale tells that its original founder, the 5th century St Mochari had fallen asleep for 150 years as a result of having heard a heavenly bird singing in the forest. A similar legend is told of an abbot of Innisfallen in Killarney.

Newtownards, a town pleasantly proliferating in factories, has a distinct air of openness and friendliness about it. It is marked from afar by the sight of unconventional and fairy-ridden Scrabo Hill, with its 135 feet high tower of folly, from the top of which a fine view may be had over the surrounding countryside. Lying at one time in the centre of O'Neill territory, Newtonards was later granted to the Montgomerys.

Here, apart from a reference to the much restored Market Cross, mention must certainly be made of the site, one mile to the east, of the sixth century abbey of Moville founded by St Finian. Not the least of Moville's litany of greatness was its importance in spreading Christianity in Scotland following Colmcille's exile in Iona.

In Bangor town hall the most obliging town clerk showed me a man trap and a bear trap. Strolling abroad in this major seaside resort with its gardens and beaches, he and I discussed the immense impact of Bangor Abbey which was founded in 559 by St Comghall and later become one of the monastic glories of Ireland. Its continuous graduation of scholars supplied Switzerland, France and Northern Italy with monasteries. The name Columbanus and Gall are inseparable from the glory of Bangor.

Repeated Norsemen attacks set in train events that led to the decay of the Abbey. In 1121 the reforming St Malachy tried to stay the rot but what was considered his new-fangled continental architecture roused the ire of the more chauvinistic of his monks, some of whom in 1127, after an O'Neill attack, sought asylum in quiet Church Island in Lough Currane near Waterville in County Kerry.

From Bangor it is but a short step westward to Belfast, passing through Crawfordsburn on the way: here there is a 1614 inn, in which some years ago by a curious reversal of expectation, I saw my very first television set. Dining most royally at this inn I blessed the name of William Starman Crawford (1781-1861), sprung of land-lord stock in the village, who, in the British Parliament, advocated Home Rule and the emancipation of Catholics. A must in this area is a visit to Helen's Tower erected in memory of Lady Dufferin the poetess.

Holywood (Sanctus Boscus) situated almost on the edge of Belfast city, is a golfing centre, and boasts a permanent maypole as well as a puckish Rosamund Praeger statue of a boy playing an accordion —the statue is affectionately known the length and breadth of Ireland as Johnny the Jig.

Here I also visited Cultra Manor, the Northern Folk Museum, an excursion which made me quite irascible as we in the south have far richer resources for an official establishment of this kind but seem blind to its possibilities. But then the erudite Professor Estyn Evans (a Welshman no less!) has long proclaimed in the north the sturdy virtues of the artifacts of the countryside and has at last had the satisfaction of being listened to with profound attention.

Let me now be forgiven for retracing my steps to Newry town and for mentioning the more direct run north-east through Loughbrickland, Banbridge, Hillsborough and Lisburn to Belfast.

My first stop on this road is at a village called Emdale, four miles south-east of Loughbrickland, where I paused to hear of a remarkable family called Brunty or Prunty, once famous in athletic and prize-fighting circles, the head of which, a man called Hugh and a storyteller to boot, was owner of a cornkiln.

Hugh had aroused fierce local antagonism by marrying a Catholic, as a result of which one of his sons was known as Pat the Papist. This same Pat, because of his addiction to books, attracted the attention of the local Presbyterian clergyman. With this good man's assistance Pat first became a schoolmaster but presently experienced the chagrin of having his school closed because he had kissed one of the older girls.

In 1802 he made his way to Cambridge. On the road he changed the spelling of his name to Brontë as a snobbish genuflection before Lord Nelson who had the title of Duke of Brontë bestowed on him by the King of Naples. Appointed on ordination to the incumbency of Haworth in Yorkshire, Pat had as daughters the famous Brontë sisters.

The part of the Brontë saga I like best is the crossing to England of Hugh the Giant, brother of the Not-now-so-Papist Pat of Haworth, a newly cut shillelagh in his immense paw, bent on presenting himself at John Murray's the publisher's in London, with the object of whacking the daylights out of a reviewer who in the *Quarterly Review*, had dared to say unkind things about *Jane Eyre*, the first novel published by Hugh's niece Emily under the pseudonym of Currer Bell.

Reference in the review to the 'heathenish doctrine of religion' of the author, being interpreted as a revival of the Papist Pat taunt, especially infuriated the Giant. Baffled by a most cordial London reception (including a dinner given in his honour), he returned to Ireland somewhat mystified and with his niece's honour unavenged.

Banbridge I recall as the town of the remarkable sunken street. This was the result of a famine relief scheme in which labourers sliced right through a hill, a herculean undertaking in pre-mechanical digger days. It is also a town where a praiseworthy municipal effort has been made to harmonize the pastel shades of the shop fronts.

Nearby wooded Hillsborough is called for the Hill family who, in plantation times, were granted thousands of acres of confiscated Magennis land. One member of this family, Wills Hill (1817-93), First Marquess of Downshire, was none other than the intransigent Secretary of State for the American Colonies who lost so much by his inability to ride the prevailing winds. Hillsborough is now the residence of the Governor of Northern Ireland. Its impressive wrought-iron gates came originally from Richill Castle in Armagh and are believed to have been the work of two Falmouth blacksmith brothers.

Lisburn, (in Irish the older name, Lisnagarvey, signifies Gambler's Fort), a County Antrim town lying in the deeps of Lagan valley, derives its prosperity from the importation from St Quinton in Picardy of a Huguenot refugee who, with his whitebeam shuttles and looms, introduced the linen industry to Ulster. At Lisburn one has to fight hard not to succumb to the temation to drive due north to Ballinderry Lower, close to spreading Lough Neagh, to visit the splendidly preserved Middle Church built for author and bishop Jeremy Taylor in 1668.

Odd though it may seem, and as a contrast to its present conservatism. Belfast was once the most revolutionary city in Ireland, even going to the extremity of having an annual commemoration of the fall of the Bastille. So much so that while the Northerners expressed radical ideas in terms borrowed directly from the lips of Rousseau (Paine's *Rights of Man* was the Northern Ireland best seller of its day), similar sentiments, with their overtones of an egalitarian independence, were roundly condemned by the Catholic bishops of the south who stressed the desirability of allegiance to England and the maintenance of the *status quo*. Thus, beset by contradictions no matter how valiantly he may essay to do so, it is difficult for a southerner such as I am to set down coherent impressions of this great northern city. Nevertheless the struggle for pattern and coherency can be illuminating.

Belfast on the river Lagan, a town 'at the mouth of the sandbank on the river', a major port carved out of silt, relies heavily on the manufacture of cotton, linen, rayon, tobacco, as well as ship-building. It is a comparatively modern city: there were only ten slated houses in Belfast in 1700, and it still reminds one of a hobbledoby outgrowing his clothes. Virgin countryside is close about it and one of its chief delights is provided by skyline mountains which offer a mental escape that can be quite ennobling.

Retracing one's step a few centuries one finds the singularly honourable but hard-drinking native chieftain O'Neill being 'gypped' out of his vast estate of Clandeboye by the Devonian Chichesters, the Montgomerys and the Hamiltons. Later, the O'Neill castle in the nearby Castlereagh Hills suffered the ironic ignominy of having a protecting wall built out of its decaying castle walls, leaving little of the original castle to be protected.

The appearance in Belfast Lough in 1778 of Paul Jones, the American privateer, set the town of Belfast aflame with excitement. In the view of thousands of Belfastians, Jones won its first major naval engagement for the United States by defeating an English man-of-war off Donaghadee.

As a result of this sea fight the Ulster Volunteers were founded with the object of defending Ireland from foreign invasion. This force, though dominantly Protestant in personnel, was nothing if it was not ecumenical. In the light of recent events it seems incredible that, in 1783, when St Mary's, the first Catholic chapel or mass-house, was opened in Belfast, it was generously supported by Protestant subscription and its initial ceremonies were made the occasion of rejoicing by the Protestants who marched side by side with their Catholic brethren to mass.

A noteworthy Belfast date is 1795, when five men, Tone, McCracken, Russell, Neilson, and Spiers climbed to Macart Fort, otherwise known as Napoleon's Nose, on Cave Hill above the city, and there took an oath never to rest until Ireland was independent. This promise they kept until death. That same year, an unfortunate misunderstanding between a Catholic secret society called 'The Defenders' and a similar Protestant society called 'The Peep-o'-Day-Boys'—both parties after negotiation having previously almost achieved a *modus vivendi*—led to a sharp faction fight which, in its turn, led to the foundation in Loughgall in Co Armagh of the Loyal Orange Association. Thus were battle lines drawn that have held almost to the present day.

In the 60's of the last century the United States again indirectly but vitally influenced the history of this northern corner of Ireland. During the American Civil War the main source of cotton was cut off. Forced back on its own resources, Belfast learned to develop an indigenous linen trade. The modern manufacture of rayon was a natural development born out of the traditional skills employed in the weaving of cotton and linen.

In the Belfast of today, a far cry from the old town of Ballycool-regalgie built on piles screwed into the silt, there are Victorian architectural elegances that have now come into full fashion. There are telephone kiosks like kidneys, quaint lanes or 'entries', and Victorian front parlours. There is also a wide variety of buildings ranging from the Parliament buildings of Stormont to St Malachy's Christian Brothers' School with the memory of Malachy's illustrious novelist son, Brian Moore, who carved out his literary destiny in Canada.

Strolling north out of Donegal Square with the massive City Hall behind me I move along Donegal place and reach the city centre proper at Castle Junction, which marks the site of a Chichester Castle. Before leaving the square I had paused beneath the doorway of the venerable Linenhall Library (love messages were scribbled beside its doorway) to think back to Thomas Russell, its first rebel librarian.

Belfast's writers come to my mind—Robert Lynd, Helen Wadell (that surname keeps recurring in Northern literary circles) and Forrest Reid. Two of Ireland's most promising young poets are connected with this city—Seamus Heaney and John Hewitt, and out of the past I evoke the shade of Louis MacNeice, son of the ecumenical bishop of Down, Conor and Dromore, as I knew him in *The Stag*, a pub near the BBC of a quarter of a century ago. The list of literary artistic people is long—gentle, erudite Dick Hayward, the writer, who was as much at home in the boreens of Kerry as he was in Belfast, playwrights Sam Thompson and Thomas Carnduff, actors like Tomelty and Goldblatt, and ballad collectors like Herbert Hughes. Then there is the industrious spirit of Edward Bunting who rendered outstanding service to the cause of native music in 1792 at the great convocation of Irish harpers.

An exciting day is ended with a short run out of the city to lovely Dunadry Inn, an old mill converted to a modern hotel, wherein presides Paddy Falloon, a conversationalist at home in an astonishing array of subjects.

Have I forgotten the shipyards? If so, how dare I! As children, we southerners firmly believed that the ill-starred Belfast-built Titanic was sunk by a thunderbolt from God because its (alleged) number 390,904, when read from the back through paper held up to light gave a crude impression of the slogan 'No Pope'. Thus, the overpowering feature in the memory of Belfast is that of the huge gantries of the shipyards (The Island) though minor memories endorse whitened doorsteps, pigeon lofts and the wink of polished copper and firelight in an entry pub.

There are the largely owned Catholic pubs, with Catholic bookies for good measure, Royal Ulster Constables dubious as regards my bright tweed coat, the sound of pipers piping Catholic defiance from hidden halls that also carry the promise—or challenge—of a Sunday class in the Irish language. The Museum and Art Gallery in the Botanic Gardens is understandably the city's pride, with its emphasis on portraits of the U.S. presidents of Ulster descent and also on views of old Belfast. There are good bookshops in a fine central shopping district but there is also the inevitable polarization between the Catholic Falls Road and the Protestant Shankill.

Approaching the Twalth o' July when the Battle of the Boyne is commemorated by marches and arches and the rattle of Lambeg drums there are precise gable-end instructions in Sandy Row on what to do with the Pope, and in other areas the no less pungent instructions as to what should be done with the Queen. And finally there are quaintly worded evangelical pleas designed to take the sting out of the rival injunctions.

A traditional bone of academic contention by wall-decorators at this time of year is whether King Billy's horse should be painted black, white, piebald or skewbald. I had noticed a compromise—the front half black, the back half white, finely executed on a wall at a cross-roads. Another point of perennial friction is whether or not children would fracture the Sabbath by using the park swings on the Lord's Day.

I salvage from the medley of Belfast sounds the voices of writer Michael McLaverty on the phone discussing aspects of Daniel Corkery's stories with me; the voices of those extraordinarily dedicated people of the theatre Dr O'Malley and his wife Mary, and the quiet voice of Professor Jack Magee shedding the illumination of his scholarship on forgotten aspects of Irish history.

The great Norman castle at Carrickfergus (shades of Carrickfergus Rock Salt and the hundred million pigs it has cured), built towards the end of the twelfth century, saw more than its share of sieges. King John took the stronghold from de Courcey's successor, de Lacy, who probably had the castle built about 1205, Edward Bruce reduced the intimidating fortress after a year of siege and, later still, the O'Neills of Tyrone almost destroyed it. In 1597, the MacDonnells of the Glens beheaded the castle governor; in 1690, the Jacobites lost the stronghold to the Williamite General Schomberg; that same year King William landed in the shadow of its walls. The French under Thurot took it in 1790; Paul Jones used it as a landmark in 1778; it later degenerated to a bridewell for United Irishmen and finally became a museum.

Turning a little skew-ways at Whitehead and travelling N.N.W. I headed for Larne, north of which begins the picturesque and much lauded Antrim Coast Road. Across Larne Lough is the sickle-shaped massacre-haunted peninsula of Island Magee, once held by a Norman family called Bissett who had previously been expelled from Galloway and who held this Antrim peninsula on the tenure of an annual tribute of goshawks.

As late as 1711, in the last such trial in Ireland, a native of this most individualistic 'island' was pilloried for witchcraft. The Gobbins cliffs of Island Magee are remarkable for the tunnelling and path-laying of an engineering genius.

Apart from the entry on the historical records that Edward Bruce of Scotland landed at Larne in 1315 (300 ships, 6,000 men) it must be recorded that it was at Larne in 1914 the loyal-to-England Ulster Volunteers, a body formed to oppose, by force of arms if necessary, any attempt on the part of England to grant a measure of Home Rule to Ireland, landed arms from Germany. This action resulted in the formation of the opposition Irish National Volunteers with which Roger Casement's attempt to land German arms in Kerry in 1916 was associated.

The railway station at Larne once housed in the person of Amanda McGettrick Ross, the stationmaster's wife, the most eccentric literary genius Ireland has produced. She was born at Ballinahinch in 1860 and had, as she says of herself, 'a dash of German blood pie-balding my veins'.

Amanda was intoxicated with the sound and fury of words: metaphors and similes (even the perplexities of plot) were used with such valour and ferocity that the writer could well be described as a female Laocoon struggling with the coils of language. She revelled in bathos, only she failed to recognize it as such.

Her work was noted with humorous affection by writers of such disparate talents as Mark Twain and Aldous Huxley: in her personal life Amanda was litigious to an unusual degree and until her death in Larne in 1939 she remained suspicious of patronage. Her visiting cards read 'At home always to the honourable'; towards critics she was especially vitriolic and their reviews she stigmatized as 'biting little bits of buggery'.

Barry Pain called her 'the world's worst novelist': this title I would alter to 'the world's best worst novelist', for there is something endearing, enduring and vital about her work as evidenced by her novel *Helen Huddelson* which continues valiantly to tread the years.

One of her books of verse was called *Poems of Puncture*. Here is her quite sincere poetic reaction to a visit to Westminster Abbey.

> *Holy Moses! Have a look*
> *Flesh decayed in every nook,*
> *Some rare bits of brain lie here*
> *Mortal loads of beef and beer.*

Above me on the coast-cliff as I moved north-west out of Larne were the black chimneys of basalt set against a chalk-white background; this superimposition brought into proximate focus the volcanic origins of the area. Beyond Ballygally Head lay a scimitar of beach; in Ballygally itself was a castle turned hotel—complete with dungeon; I preferred to look out on blue misty Scotland over the water. Past Glenarm Bay, a natural for the inevitable ballad, I rode past Waterfoot into Cushendall.

At Cushendun, in this territory of MacDonnells, O'Neills and O'Cahans, I recalled the poetess, Moira O'Neill. And out of a period somewhat more remote in time I summoned Shane The Proud O'Neill who met his death at Castle Carra when seeking abject asylum from his former enemies, the MacDonnells. Shane's head later bleached to bone on a spike over Dublin Castle. The MacDonnells, a Scottish clan, were recruited as mercenary soldiers or gallowglasses by the Irish rulers to help them in their fight against the Normans; presumably of Dalriada Irish descent, the MacDonnells later married (if indeed assimilation were necessary) into the homeland from which their forebears had originally sprung.

A switchbacking road runs north by Runabay Head and Torr Head. Traversing this, the Mull of Kintyre and the Paps of Jura are mauve mysteries on the northern skyline.

Ballycastle, which I reached after a journey as if on horseback, is associated with the two most sad-beautiful legends in Irish mythology: *The Children of Lir* and *The Fate of Déirdre and the Sons of Uisneach*, wonder-tales of love and treachery still capable of bearing their sorrow across the centuries.

Today the ballad-singers of this northern town lay the ghosts of old by singing of the *Old Lammas Fair of Ballycastle-O*, a song in praise of a blithe annual gathering where the visitors munch a tough toffee called Yalla Man and philosophically chew dulse or edible seagrass.

Beautiful and cold on the northern skyline sat Rathlin of the seabirds. Here Robert Bruce had noted the efforts of a resolute spider and had drawn therefrom the inspiration necessary to recover his kingdom. The white cliffs of this chill island saw no less than three blood-curdling massacres, only one of which after so many gory gobbets, I dare to mention.

This, the most appalling, took place in 1597 when the women, children and infirm of the Antrim MacDonnells were slaughtered by the English while the watching MacDonnell menfolk writhed in powerless agony on the mainland. With so much blood-letting in our Irish story, is it any wonder that Mencken, the American sage, called us Irish 'The Crybabies of the Western World'?

Next, a shout of delight that White Park Bay has been preserved by the National Trust; coastal preservation, especially that of sand-dunes, is a long term investment certain to delight the coming generations.

The ruin of Dunseverick castle stands on a rock upon which was erected one of the great buildings of primeval Ireland: the stones of Dunseverick trace their lineage back to the days of the Red Branch Knights and even to the folk-hero, Conall Cearnach, who is alleged to have been present at the crucifixion of Christ. Highly-embroidered Irish tradition credits Conall with having won the raffle for the seamless cloak and, piling Pelion on the Ossa of our credulity, blandly adds that he walked off without taking his prize.

However, it was not my sense of credulity but my courage that was in jeopardy as I passed through Ballintoy on a red-hot summer day and paused to rest a while on the turf above the rope-bridge linking the mainland with the offshore fishing pinnacle of Carrick-a-Rede. Not having a notable head for heights I had difficulty in forcing myself to cross the slender bridge. Below me on the rock the salmon fishermen were unconcernedly casting their nets. The salmon are lured to the base of the cliff foot by fresh water pouring from a cleft above. The link between mainland and rock seemed dismayingly frail and the quite tenuous ropes could have been strands of a spider's web.

In mid-bridge I looked down and almost sweated blood. However, I reached the rock in safety and spent a while talking to the fishermen. But if going out was bad returning was the refinement of terror!

Moving due west on this most lovely coastline, presently I walked down the pathway under a cliff to view that widely-trumpeted phenomenon of nature, The Giants' Causeway, a wonder 'worth seeing but not worth going to see'.

A tiring walk it was. Before long I felt kin to the stout woman seated on a rock, her shoes removed and her mouth opening and closing like that of a carp on grass. As I passed by she laughed wheezingly. A bad omen, I told myself. Labouring on, I eventually arrived at the Causeway. 'Is this all?' I asked myself, as the rising tide swished geometrically among the basalt pillars rather as if it were a sea invading the foundations of a castle.

Gradually, as I appraised the immense proportions of sea, cliff and open sky, my sense of appreciation and perspective returned. The gulls wheeling against the cliff tops provided me with a tolerably adequate scale of reference.

The Causeway itself is a cooled stream of lava about half a mile in width. It shows and hides as it moves downwards along the cliff sides; gradually it steps down under the sea and bobs up again in prismatic revelation at Staffa in the Isle of Skye.

That there was more than one flow of lava may be proved by the slope of the columns, of which, in all, there are about 40,000. Most of these are hexagonal, but there are enough irregular columns having sides from three to nine, to set one counting rather dottily.

The different formations of the three main sections, the Little Causeway, the Honeycomb Causeway and the Grand Causeway, bear fanciful names having to do with giants and gentlewomen.

Returned to the cliff-top I saw rather fatigued tourists who could, I daresay, have done with a swig from a bottle of whiskey from the venerated distillery in nearby Bushmills.

Pleasant Portballintrae, its cove-face open to the north, was detectable on that midsummer day. I had also seen it in midwinter as a gale howled down from the north pole and flung spume and hailstones against the window of the diningroom where we were celebrating at the wedding-breakfast of one of my sons. But though its summer visage now urged me to loiter I pushed westward to the intimidating fortress of Dunluce castle which is perched on a sea-pitted rock halfway between Bushmills and Portrush.

Burkes, MacQuillans (the Irish form of Mandeville), O'Neills and finally MacDonnells had held this castle in turn. In 1584 Lord Deputy Perrott took it from the MacDonnells but Yellow Somhairle MacDonnell later regained it and, through his descendants the Earls of Antrim, held it until at last the building fell into decay.

I took particular note of the Tinker's Window, where in 1639, a tinker squatted on the 'stool' of a kitchen window, presumably mouthing titbits of victuals, in the intervals of which he drained the whiskey dregs from a noisy party given by the Marchioness of

22 The City Hall, Belfast

Buckingham, wife of Randal MacDonnell, second Earl of Antrim.

This tinker was astonishingly preserved from death when, with a mighty rumble and roar, the servants' quarters collapsed into the sea, leaving the travelling man hung on a pinnacle of rock and masonry. That tinker most certainly had the greatest hangover in Irish history.

Portrush, on the basalt peninsula of Ramore Head, and nearby Portstewart, where Charles Lever, the great Irish humorist and novelist once practised as a physician, are a pair of seaside resorts readily bracketted together in the Irish mind. Having loitered in one or th'other for some pleasant hours I headed for Coleraine, site of a brand-new university and once a town of the O'Cahans, the streets of which I found festooned with red-white-and-blue bunting of 'The Twalth!'

As I left the car in midtown an enormous man emerging from a public house uttered a roar and extended a gigantic paw in my direction. 'You're a blue!' he shouted, 'a royal loyal blue! I can tell it by the set of your jib.'

He was so hugely bear-friendly (with the hug of a bear, too, I daresay) that I relapsed into a discreet republican silence and, nodding smilingly up into his face, gently disengaged myself. As I rode off, I began, for very little reason that I can discover, to chuckle at the recalled story of the taciturn northern man who stopped his car at a petrol pump and was questioned by the proprietor.

'Is she using a great deal o' petrol?' 'No!' 'Is she using a lot o' oil?' 'She would, the bitch, if she got it!'

Maurice drove right across the north to greet myself and the city of Derry.

I had no idea that Derry was so beautiful. Its sandstone walls reminded me of St Malo in Brittany. An asphalt roadway runs along the top of the walls which, speckled with white chippings, gives one

23 Whitepark Bay, Co. Antrim

the impression of a woodland pathway on which the hawthorn petals of autumn are forever falling.

Looking down from the walls, one sees the cemetery where the Catholic dead fill the sloping riverside fields above the Foyle; nearer one's point of vantage is the Bogside, the story of which would fill many tomes and superficial comment on which would constitute an impertinence.

And yet despite its many superficial contradictions this lovely old city conveys a sense of Irishness as valid as that of Dunquin in Kerry or Cashel in Tipperary.

Latter-day gates pierce old walls as if to mimic Quebec and the Heights of Abraham. Here cannon mouths appear to gape across the centuries while below the walls the Foyle flows seaward to join the exiles' 'bowl of tears' so that one hums a line of an old ballad: *As down the Foyle, the waters boil, an' our ship stands out from the land.'*

In Derry the women are the breadwinners: linen and shirt-making are responsible for this domestic inversion with its resultant social repercussions. In Derry, too, the dirtiest word one can utter is 'Hong Kong', as cheap shirts from that city sorely harrass the city's economy.

Founded by St Colmcille and loved intensely by that holy man even in his exile of Iona, Derry was primarily a monastic foundation. Its location close to the northern sea track resulted in its being recurrently attacked by the Danes. Later it attracted the unwelcome attentions of the Normans. The medieval city was accidently blown up and subsequently fire-destroyed. After the suppression of an O'Doherty rebellion it was granted in 1613 by James I, together with an enormous tract of land, to the citizens of London who planted the area and enwalled the town.

The highest point of its history was the siege of 1688-89. Attacked by Jacobite forces, the citizens, spearheaded by the city's apprentice boys banged out the week-kneed governor Lundy and, inspired by the Reverend George Walker, held out until, after 7,000 citizens had died, three relieving ships sailed up the Foyle to sever the boom of floating beams which had blocked the river. Thus was raised an epic siege.

Southward then to Strabane where the pleasant Foyle winked with a silver eye. As we rode through the town we recalled a man called Dunlap, printer of the Declaration of American Independence, who hailed from this locality. We were bound for Fermanagh of the lakes, a county laid north-west by south-east, which at Belleek barely fails to reach the sea at Ballyshannon.

Fermanagh has made the most ambitious plans to develop its lakeland district. At St Angelo airport beside Enniskillen, a seaplane base during the Second World War, if current plans mature, coarse anglers from Britain will drop from the clouds to game-fish and coarse-fish to their hearts' content. All this has been plotted with professional care and every possible natural phenomenon appraised.

As we walked the pleasant streets of Enniskillen of the Maguires, a town set in the hour-glass waist of great lakes, we recalled the name of Nobel award-winner, Samuel Beckett, as well as that of Oscar Wilde, both of whom had attended the famous Enniskillen Portora Royal School which was founded by James I in 1628.

North-east now through Fivemiletown to County Tyrone and into Ben Kiely country where no diversion however attractive could prevent us from following in the footsteps of that unique novelist, William Carleton, born in 1794 in Prolusk near Clogher.

Standing before Carleton's cottage, now marked with a plaque, we seemed close to the spirit of him who, by his *Traits and Stories of the Irish Peasantry*, had opened from the inside a window on to the teeming, fecund, sprawling, brawling, Bueghel-worthy, poteen-drenched, contradictory, roaring life as it was lived by the Irish before the famines of 1846-7.

While others of his hour saw the cabin from a distance, Carleton looked out from the rowdy interior and, impishly inviting the passers-by to enter, interpreted, not without prejudice, of course, the prides, aspirations, fears, hopes, and loves of a vital peasantry.

Despite his many contradictions, his moralizings, and his prolixity, Carleton the writer, begotten of the confluence of classical, Irish and English cultures and, with seemingly, no lawful literary progenitor, was as sturdy a literary workman as the mule, and proved also, in terms of literary progeny, to be equally as barren.

As a Ribbonman in his youth, Carleton had flayed the Protestant landlords. Afterwards as a 'spoiled priest', and under the influence of that strange Protestant clergyman, Caesar Otway, he had scarified what he called 'Romish superstition'. A violent, complicated, powerful writer Carleton certainly was; in the peaceful countryside where we loitered there remained no vestiges to indicate that the life he had portrayed had ever existed. Long since the fallen mud-cabins of his tales had merged with their brother clay. On all sides were trim farm-houses with rooks raucously calling. A girl carrying a brand new tennis racquet came cycling by on a gleaming bicycle.

I had a special reason for visiting Dungannon. When I was in the United States I met an Indian poet by the name of Gangpadha at a mid-Western university. When he heard that I was Irish he asked me if I had ever heard of a woman called Margaret Elizabeth Noble. 'Her name is cherished in my native land where she was known as Sister *Nivedita*, "The Dedicated One". She was a native of Dungannon and became a disciple of the famous Swami Vivekanada. She advocated the use of force as a means of freeing India and in 1907 she supplied materials for bombs from the college laboratories to which she had access.' He asked me to find out some of the facts of her early life in Ireland as there existed only a rather sentimental biography written by a Frenchwoman.

Recalling this conversation, and fired by the recollection of such a pursuit as *The Quest for Corvo*, Maurice and I hied ourselves to Dungannon, a place popularly associated with the 'ould Orange Flute' of ballad memory. The Protestant owner of this instrument had changed his religion, subsequent to which the loyal flute was alleged to have played 'The Protestant Boys' as it was burned at the stake as a heretic.

On the lawn in front of Dungannon Royal School stands a Delhirejected statue of John Nicolson of the Indian Mutiny. In the finely-tilted Square we met a man wearing a *fáinne* on his jacket. I asked him in Irish to enumerate the scholars of Dungannon and he immediately mentioned W. K. Hutchinson, author of *Tyrone Precint*, an authoritative book on local history.

We found Mr Hutchinson mowing under his apple trees; a barley scarer was banging somewhere in the background while beside us a dachshund was nosing for an improbably early windfall. W. K. Hutchinson was a scholar of the first water but he had not heard of Margaret Noble. As, in the distance, the barley scarer continued to bang out its anthem of physical force, I began to doubt the existence of the woman or her connection with Dungannon—or Tyrone.

We said goodbye to Mr Hutchinson and set out for the house of Major Dickson. His was the oldest dwelling in Dungannon; wreathed in Virginia creeper with its iron balcony poised above a green sloping lawn it was also probably the loveliest.

Major Dickson—his father and grandfather had been liberal M.P.'s at Westminster—had anecdotes about T. M. Kettle the poet, and Tim Healy, the politician (wasn't it Tim who referred to Tom as M. T. Kettle?). Presently we were caught up in an exciting world of copper pans, blunderbusses, election broadsheets and No Rent manifestoes. But as regards Margaret Noble there was not a whisper of local folklore to indicate that she had ever lived in Dungannon town. Perhaps I had dreamed up the woman?

Much later, as a result of a further return to the United States and a further search through library stacks I was able to fill in some of the missing details.

Descended from the Nobles of Rostrevor, a liberal Wesleyan family, her father, Samuel Noble had married Mary Hamilton, and, having first set up a cloth shop in Dungannon where his daughter Margaret was born on 28th October, 1867, he later went to England to become a Wesleyan minister like his grandfather John Noble.

The family moved first to Oldham and later to Great Torrington in Devon. When Swami Vivekanada visited England, Margaret Noble became his disciple; she later travelled to India where she studied Hindu philosophy and allied herself with the Indian underground,

Sri Aurobindo. She then joined the famous Ramakrisna Missions.

Henceforward her life was governed by two passions—India and Ireland. In September 1908, she visited Ireland, ostensibly to see her brother; on her arrival in Ireland she 'kissed the Irish earth and ran it through her fingers'. She died in India on 13th October, 1911, 36 years before India was granted freedom.

Margaret Elizabeth Noble, as well as an Irish poet called James H. Cousins, later of Mandanapalla, South India, who had also succumbed to the mysticism of India, deserve far more than this passing mention.

Dungannon, a town with a name like a hammer blow, was one of the seats of the O'Neills; town and castle were burned by the Irish after the disaster at Kinsale.

Previous to this, the Great Hugh O'Neill had for long deceived Elizabeth I by pleading that he needed lead to roof his Dungannon house: the metal he had industriously used to make rebel bullets. In a later age Liberal Dungannon saw Protestant Volunteers claim parliamentary independence for Ireland; these same volunteers sincerely rejoiced at the easing of the Penal Laws on their Catholic brethren. North of Dungannon and immediately to the west of Lough Neagh are the Sperrin mountains and moors, with their wealth of prehistoric remains.

At Moygashel, beside Dungannon, I thought fondly on my linen jacket and on the tablecloths that are the pride of Ireland. At Moy a bugler in stone seemed to hurry us on; presently we found ourselves in the brick-red priory of Benburb, eight miles south of Dungannon hearing plans designed to establish the priory as a religious, social, and cultural centre in the north. The talk turned on the recent launching of a magazine called *Aurora* as the first step in this direction.

We continued to chat with the editor, Father Farrell, while a fine modern painting by a brilliant young artist called Vallely looked down on us from the wall; then a priest-poet from Armagh appeared—Father Réamonn Murray his name—and we talked of poetry, history and literature, while dusk thickened in the fields outside the windows where once walked Shane the Proud and where

too, above the sluggish Blackwater river, Eoghan Rua O'Neill, professional soldier from Spain, his war cry *Sancta Maria*! had, with the
aid of pits dug in front of his lines, won in 1646 a memorable Irish
victory over a mighty Scots-English army under General Monroe.

For the ending of a journey round and through Ireland I do not
think anywhere could be more fitting than Armagh, Ireland's
primatial city and once the home of Ireland's prehistoric Red
Branch Knights.

Presumably because of its considerable associations with Queen
Macha, St Patrick, *circa* 445, chose Armagh as the site of his principal
church; despite alternating fortune which included a sacking by the
Danes and subsequent disagreement regarding abbatial and episcopal
offices, Armagh has held its position of Irish ecclesiastical preemin-
ence until the present day.

It was once the site of what for the early Christian centuries
constituted a university, of which Prince Alfred, afterwards King of
Northumbria, was a distinguished alumnus. From the fourteenth
century onward the English saw to it that the primatial office was
held only by those with English affiliations; in those times, however,
control by the primates was nominal and was exercised from
Termonfeckin in County Louth. This state of affairs lasted until the
power of the Northern O'Neills was broken in the sixteenth
century.

In Armagh lie buried King Brian Ború, benefactor of Armagh, and
his son Murrough—the reputed grave of both lies outside the north
transept of the Church of Ireland cathedral, a building which sits
on the hilltop whereon St Patrick built his first church.

The Catholic cathedral stands on another hilltop site on the crest
of a soaring flight of steps, with *Ara Coeli*, the residence of the
Cardinal Archbishop, close beside it. A few miles north of the town
on the River Callan is *Áth Buí*, The Yellow Ford, scene of a battle
in 1598 in which the Great Hugh O'Neill defeated an English army
led by Sir Henry Bagenal.

Armagh city today is peaceful, even somnolent, characteristics underscored by its Georgian-Regency houses. In Portadown and Lurgan there are much wilder memories of O'Hanlon the highwayman, a member of a Tanderagee clan.

Eamhain Macha itself, two miles west of Armagh, or as it is known in English, Navan Fort, has a low cairn and a ring fort to mark a place known to Ptolemy as Isamnium. Here, if mythology speaks the truth, lived the great Conor Mac Neasa, King of Eamhain; hither, too, came young Setanta, afterwards known as Cúchulainn, with his spear, his hurley and his ball of silver to amaze assemblies with his boyhood feats. Here the heroes of the Red Branch drank ale, dined, sang songs, recited genealogies, wore enamel, declaimed poetry, fought, loved, and died. In Tray may be seen the countersunken remains of the King's stables.

The whole area is powerfully evocative with layer after layer of history most clearly in evidence.

First there is the prehistoric Celtic world of Eamhain Macha, then the coloured and incense-scented world of Christianity, next the violent Danish world, which in its turn is followed by the clangorous Norman world. The mere Irish world follows with again the several layers laid down by English settlers and finally the plantation stratum added by the Scots-Irish.

One could grow sentimental and nostalgic in such a place as Armagh, but there are qualifications implicit in the vapour trails in the sky. For these remind us that the Ireland of today, like many another island, is marching out of its history into what will prove a fuller—or a falser—destiny.

Index

From necessities of space, natural features (rivers, lakes, hills and mountains, and islands except where otherwise significant) are omitted.

Index

Index

Index

Index

Index

Index

West, Rebecca 35
Westmeath, *county* 201–3
Westminster Abbey 221; Hall, roof 127
Westport, *Co. Mayo* 150, 164
Wexford, *county* 43–7; *town* 43, 45
Whaley, Buck 20, 21
Whelan, Leo, *artist* 76
White, John Davis 122
White Abbey: *see under* Adare
Whitepark Bay, *Co. Antrim* pl. 23 opp. p. 225
Wicklow (name) 20; *county* 42
William II (*of Orange*), *King of England* 26, 30, 36, 114, 220

Wolfe, Thomas 166
Wood, *Mrs* Henry 59
Wyatt, James, *architect* 164

Yale university, U.S. 29
Yeats, William 13, 18, 21, 137, 139–40, 174, 176, 178, 182
Youghal, *Co. Cork* 53–4
Young Ireland movement 59, 127
Ypres, *Belgium* 157

'Zozimus', [Michael Moran], *singer* 21

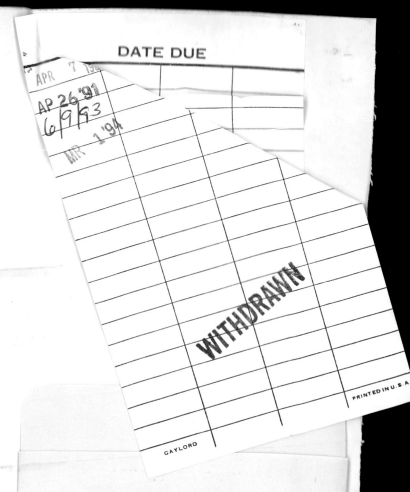

Macmahon, Bryan
Here's Ireland